A WONDERFUL LIFE
The Films and Career of James Stewart

Books by Tony Thomas

The Films of Errol Flynn (with Rudy Behlmer and Cliff McCarty)
The Busby Berkeley Book
Ustinov in Focus
Music for the Movies
Cads and Cavaliers
The Films of Kirk Douglas
Song and Dance: The Films of Gene Kelly
The Films of Marlon Brando
The Films of the Forties
The Great Adventure Films
Hollywood's Hollywood (with Rudy Behlmer)
Burt Lancaster
Gregory Peck
Sam Wood: Hollywood Professional
From a Life of Adventure
Film Score
Harry Warren and the Hollywood Musical
Ronald Reagan: The Hollywood Years
The Films of 20th Century-Fox (with Aubrey Solomon)
Hollywood and the American Image
The Films of Olivia de Havilland
Queen Mary and the Spruce Goose
The Films of Henry Fonda
That's Dancing
Howard Hughes in Hollywood
The Cinema of the Sea

A WONDERFUL LIFE

The Films and Career of
James Stewart

By Tony Thomas

A Citadel Press Book
Published by Carol Communications

For Betty

Acknowledgments

A book of this kind can only be done with a lot of help. As on many past occasions I am grateful to Linda Mehr and her staff at the library of the Academy of Motion Picture Arts and Sciences in Los Angeles. In Toronto I had access to the files of the Ontario Film Institute, thanks to director Gerald Pratley, and in Provo, Utah, I was able to see the James Stewart memorabilia in the Arts and Communications Archives of Brigham Young University, through the kindness of curator James D'Arc, who also allowed me the use of their Stewart photographs.

I am grateful to Jean Firstenberg, the director of the American Film Institute, and to George Paris, the Vice President of Syndication and Special Projects at MGM-UA; also to Ernst Korngold, Packy Smith, Aubrey Solomon, Douglass M. Stewart, Jr., Eddie Brandt and the Collectors Bookshop, Hollywood. Lastly, and most importantly, I am grateful to the gentleman who is the subject of this book. To write about a man like James Stewart was a pleasure and to receive his help was an honor.

Tony Thomas

Copyright © 1988 by Tony Thomas

A Citadel Press Book
Published by Carol Communications

Editorial Offices
600 Madison Avenue
New York, NY 10022

Sales & Distribution Offices
120 Enterprise Avenue
Secaucus, NJ 07094

In Canada: Musson Book Company
A division of General Publishing Co. Limited
Don Mills, Ontario

Queries regarding rights and permissions should be addressed to: Carol Communications, 600 Madison Avenue, New York, NY 10022

Manufactured in the United States of America

15 14 13 12 11 10 9 8 7 6 5 4 3 2

Library of Congress Cataloging-in-Publication Data

Thomas, Tony, 1927-
    A wonderful life : the films of James Stewart / by Tony Thomas.
       p.   cm.
    ISBN 0-8065-1081-1 : $15.95
    1. Stewart, James, 1908-   —Criticism and interpretation.
I. Title.
PN2287.S68T47   1988
791.43'028'0924—dc19   87-37493
                                                                   CIP

Designed by *Paul Chevannes*

CONTENTS

James Stewart at four, with mother.

James Stewart - Little Pieces of Time

"In Europe an elderly couple came up to me. The husband said, 'We didn't want to pass you without speaking to you. If it means anything to you, we want to tell you that over the years you have given us a lot of pleasure and entertainment.' I told them that what they had just said meant *everything* to me. That's what I've tried to make my life all about, and if they write 'He gave people a lot of pleasure' on my epitaph I shall be very pleased. I've had many people tell me that they remember certain little things I did in pictures. I think it's wonderful to have been able to give people little pieces of time they can remember."

James Stewart is not the only man to have referred to motion pictures as "little pieces of time" but no one has a better right to use the term. Two-thirds of his working life is preserved on film, and for those of us who began going to the movies in the mid-1930's, or at any point thereafter, Stewart is a part of our lives. We have grown up with him. Even for those who have never met him he is like a close relative. He has evolved from young man to middle-ager to senior citizen to revered elder right before our eyes. And perhaps more than any other Hollywood figure he seems to have personified America in the best of ways. An American Everyman—who also happens to be one of the most accomplished actors in the history of film.

It was the veteran MGM director W. S. Van Dyke who tried to explain the appeal of Stewart by calling him "unusually usual." If nothing else it is a start in explaining the success of a man who is probably the most complete actor-personality Hollywood has ever produced. He seems to have always been playing himself, but that, like the art of acting itself, is deceptive. He has cultivated an aura of easygoing, affable folksiness and he has charmed several generations with his drawling, hesitant, almost-stammering manner of speaking, all of which have made him a favorite of impressionists, but Stewart is a tougher and shrewder man than the unsophisticated image would suggest. He is a Princeton graduate, a decorated wartime Air Force officer and afterwards a brigadier general in the reserve, and an actor who has largely charted his own course with an intelligence that is not usual among actors.

He is an actor of world stature and yet he neither started out to be an actor nor had any training to be one. Until the age of twenty-four it had not even occurred to him to be an actor, and it would not have happened had it not been for the pushing and encouragement of friends, who saw in him something that he could not see in himself. And unlike most actors, he did not have to struggle terribly hard to become successful. His friend Henry Fonda, whom he met in 1932, often told the story of his amazement, in the first two years of their knowing each other, in watching parts come Stewart's way with ease while Fonda was out beating the bushes trying to find work. Fonda always said that Stewart was an instinctual actor and that he brought qualities to his work that could not be taught. Years later Frank Capra enlarged upon that view: "There is bad acting and good acting, fine performances and occasionally great performances, but there is a higher level than great performances in acting. A level where there is only a real, live person on the screen. A person audiences care about immediately. There are only a few actors, very few, capable of achieving this highest level of the actor's art and Jimmy Stewart is one of them."

Stewart, with characteristic modesty, has little to say about being successful as an actor beyond the fact that he sees his work as basically requiring him to play himself but with deference to the character being performed. "If you can get through a film and not have the acting show then you have believability on your side, and if you can get the audience believing in what they're seeing on the screen, then you're in pretty good shape." Again it requires somebody else to make the point more precise. George Stevens, who directed Stewart in *Vivacious Lady* in 1938, afterwards said, "To overcome disbelief is the most difficult thing to do in films. And Jimmy, with this extraordinary earnestness that he has, just walks in and extinguishes disbelief."

Stewart quickly brushes off any discussion of acting as an intellectual art with a matter-of-factness that is also characteristic: "Look, the most important thing about acting is to appreciate it as a craft and not some mysterious type of religion. You don't have to meditate to be an actor." It is a no-nonsense point of view that is rare among theatre and movie people, but Stewart is himself rare in the community of which he has been a part for more than fifty years. His wife, Gloria, claims, "My husband is much too normal to be an actor." There is no reason to doubt the claim. He is a man who has never been a high society reveller, preferring to spend most of his time at home, and his one home since his marriage in 1949 to his only wife has been a house on Roxbury Drive in Beverly Hills. Apart from the comfort and security

Age eight, with sister Mary.

assured by his vast income over the years, Stewart's lifestyle is not greatly different from that of the small town, family environment into which he was born—and not even the most prying reporter has ever been able to come up with any hint of scandal in his life. In the midst of an industry and a social community blighted by chaotic changes and uneasy, unreliable and sometimes neurotic relationships, James Stewart has managed to sail through with apparent tranquility. Obviously, W. S. Van Dyke knew what he was talking about in saying this most durable of movie stars is "unusually usual."

Quite apart from the talent and the success, Stewart is remarkable for being quintessentially American, almost as if he had been an invention of painter Norman Rockwell. Very rarely has he played anyone other than an American, and ideally he has exemplified Americans more clearly than any other Hollywood star. Kim Novak, who played opposite Stewart in *Vertigo* and *Bell, Book and Candle*, says,

In 1923, age fifteen, graduating from the Model School.

"He was what I wanted my America to represent—pride, dignity and honor in a place where people were incapable of deception. You couldn't take your eyes off the screen when Jimmy Stewart started stammering, you didn't believe he was acting for a moment. He might have been the guy down the block, or at least the fellow you saw occasionally at the market, but he was the sexiest man who played opposite me in thirty years. It was that boyish charm, that enchanting innocence."

Stewart has not only not "gone Hollywood" in all the years he has been a part of the town-industry, but the term seems to make little sense to him. "I am a Presbyterian. I support the Salvation Army and the Boy Scouts. They are considered quaint in some quarters but I admire their work. I've become known as a Republican. I have always been a conservative and I come from a conservative background." That background began on May 20, 1908, in the county-seat town of Indiana, a town in the foothills of the Allegheny Mountains of Pennsylvania, about a one-hour drive east of Pittsburgh. It was then a community of about six thousand and its merchants catered to the surrounding rural area. Among its most prominent merchants was Alexander Stewart, who named his son James Maitland Stewart after his father, who set up a hardware store, J. M. Stewart and Company, in 1853. Of Scots-Irish stock, grandfather Stewart served with the Union Army in the Civil War and his son Alexander joined up to fight in both the Spanish-American War of 1898 and the First World War. After graduating from Princeton, Alexander married Elizabeth Jackson, the daughter of General S. M. Jackson, and they settled in Indiana in order to run the family business. James was their first child and only son, followed by Mary in 1912 and Virginia in 1914.

The values of small town, middle-class family life are rooted in James Stewart. His parents were churchgoers, his father was a member of the volunteer fire brigade and his mother busied herself with church activities. James was a bright and lively boy, who liked to build model airplanes and radio crystal sets, who enjoyed playing with chemistry sets, took pride in being a Boy Scout, dabbled in magic games in the parlor and, most of all, admired his somewhat gruff but full-of-life father. When Stewart was ten he announced he intended to go to Africa on a safari at the end of school term. Others scoffed but his father helped him prepare for the trip, although extending the preparations to the point where young enthusiasm started to wane. But whatever the boy wanted to do he could always rely on the interest of his father.

Not unnaturally, Stewart looks back on his early years with strong attachment. "When I was eight we moved to Vinegar Hill, to a rambling house of no particular architecture but with a large front porch loaded with wicker furniture. The living room, high ceilinged and trimmed with dark woodwork, held a grand piano, around which we gathered for family sings. My sister Virginia played the piano, my other sister, Mary, played the violin, and I played the accordion—after a fashion. During these sessions, Dad sang very softly—compared to the bellowing he did in church—so as not to cover up Mother's clear sweet voice. Her name was Elizabeth, and he called her Bessie and adored her. Though small and gentle and not given to contention, she frequently had her way over his because she possessed patience and endurance."

When President Harding died in 1923, his body was returned to his home, with the funeral train scheduled to pass through a town twenty miles from

Home from Princeton in the summer of 1930, age twenty-two, outside the family store with father Alexander (left) and his grandfather, who founded the store in 1853. Inset above are photos of two of the grandfather's brothers.

Stewart's first work as a film actor: a bit in a Vitaphone short made in New York, in 1934, Art Trouble, *with Shemp Howard, Harry Gribbon and Eddie Quillan. Several months later Stewart did a bit in another Vitaphone short,* Important News.

Indiana. "I wanted desperately to go and see this train, but Mother pointed out that it passed at 3:30 in the morning of a school day. And that ended the discussion. At 2:30 that morning, however, I was awakened by Dad's hand on my shoulder. He said, in a voice near to a whisper as his nature would allow, 'Jim, boy, get up. It's time to go and see the funeral train.' We drove through the night without talking much, but bound together by the comradeship of disobedience." Years later his mother would say, "The best compliment you could pay Jimmy was to say that he was just like his Dad."

With America's entry into the war in 1917, Alexander Stewart returned to the Army, with the rank of captain in the Ordnance Corps and a posting at Camp Dodge in Iowa. His nine-year-old son elected himself head-of-household and performed his father's nightly job of locking all the doors in the store and the house. He also buoyed the patriotic spirit of the town by writing plays with titles like *The Slacker* and *To Hell with the Kaiser,* and staged them

in the basement of the Stewart home. Says his sister Virginia, "Jim was terribly intense about his plays, just as he is about everything he gets interested in. There are no halfway measures with Jim." However, with his father's return in 1919, James's ventures into showmanship ebbed and disappeared—until they were resurrected at Princeton nine years later.

The interests of schoolboy James Stewart were normal ones, abetted by part-time jobs on the weekends and in the summer months. In the fall of 1923 he entered Mercersburg Academy and stayed there until he matriculated at Princeton five years later. At Mercersburg he took part in sports, notably track events, sang with the glee club and worked on the school's yearbooks due to his proficiency in art. After leaving Mercersburg he tinkered with the idea of entering the United States Naval Academy at Annapolis, but after discussions with his single-minded father, who knew exactly where he wanted his son to tackle higher learning, Stewart enrolled at Princeton.

At Princeton Stewart first studied political science and engineering, but he was advised to switch to architecture. His academic achievements were above average, but his years in this bastion of the Ivy League are mostly of importance to his later life because of his activities in the Princeton Triangle Club. Because he had admitted to having acted as a

11

child and because of his interest in singing and playing the accordion, Stewart became a member of this reputable amateur performing society. One of its primary leaders was Joshua Logan, who was also involved in a summer stock company at West Falmouth, Massachusetts, called the University Players. Stewart achieved his Bachelor of Science degree in architecture in the Spring of 1932 and on graduation day, standing on the campus, he was persuaded by Logan to spend the summer with his players—not as an actor but as an accordionist.

It was the time of the Great Depression and with no prospects for work in architecture, Stewart proceeded to West Falmouth, there to be assigned to playing in the Old Silver Beach Tearoom, which adjoined the theatre. "I guess my luckiest break came from my father's insisting that I learn to play the accordion. So I played in the tea room, until one day the company's director came up and told me I could have a small part in a play if I'd just put away my accordion. He said my playing spoiled his appetite— and that's how I got my first job as an actor."

Giving his acceptance speech after winning the Oscar for The Philadelphia Story. *The ceremony was held at the Biltmore Hotel, Los Angeles, on the evening of February 21, 1941.*

The University Players of 1932 deserve a footnote in the annals of the American Theatre. It could boast not only of Logan but of Henry Fonda— although he was working in New York for most of that summer—Margaret Sullavan, Mildred Natwick, Myron McCormick and director Bretaigne Windust. Stewart was first given a walk-on in a play titled *Magnolia*, a bit in *It's a Wise Child* and then a small part as a chauffeur in *Goodbye Again*. Audiences seemed to take to the gangling young man and he was next given the role of Officer Gano in *Carrie Nation*, which play would result in his becoming a professional actor. Stewart had planned either to return to Indiana to work for his father or to continue with graduate studies, but a New York producer, Arthur Beckhard, called for Stewart to repeat his role as Gano when the play opened at the Biltmore Theatre in New York on October 29, 1932. Stewart moved in with Fonda, Logan and McCormick in their small apartment on West 64th Street. When the play closed after a few weeks he intended to leave town, still having no ambition to make a career as an actor.

Arthur Beckhard next decided to stage *Goodbye Again* and asked Stewart to once more play the chauffeur. It opened at the Masque Theatre on December 28, and ran for more than two hundred

Private James Maitland Stewart, U.S. Army, March, 1941.

performances. With that run, plus a good notice in the press, he thought he would at least give the acting business a try. He could always go back to the family store. *Goodbye Again* starred Osgood Perkins (the father of Anthony), and Stewart admits that this is the actor who most impressed him and whose style most affected him. In the spring of 1933 Stewart was hired by Jane Cowl, not as an actor but as her stage manager for *Camille*, followed by another job as a stage manager for Blanche Yurka in *Spring In Autumn*, which also allowed him a small role. After it closed Stewart again thought of returning to the hardware business, but he was offered a part in *All Good Americans*, which led to his first important role in the New York theatre, that of the idealistic Sergeant O'Hara in Sidney Howard's *Yellow Jack*, which opened at the Martin Beck Theatre on March 6, 1934, and ran for several months. By the following October, Stewart had a substantial role in *Divided by Three*, starring Judith Anderson.

Henry Fonda often talked about going back-stage to see Stewart while he was doing *Divided by Three*. "He was playing the son of Judith Anderson, a formidable actress. But he was standing up there eye-to-eye with her and he was just marvelous. In his dressing room I looked at him and sat there shaking my head, wondering, 'Where did this come from?

How the hell did he get to be so good?' I guess by this time it dawned upon Jim himself that he was pretty good at what he was doing, so he decided to stay in the business and go on from there. But it ruffled my feathers a little. Here I was busting my shoe leather trying to make it in the theatre and this lackadaisical fellow Stewart just stumbled into it."

Divided by Three ran for only thirty performances at the Ethel Barrymore Theatre, but one of the other players, Hedda Hopper, brought Stewart to the attention of Al Altman of MGM's New York office—or so she always claimed. While appearing in his following play *Page Miss Glory*, which opened at the Mansfield Theatre on November 27, Stewart was tested by MGM, who after a long deliberation decided to offer him a three months' contract. By the time the contract was signed Stewart had committed himself to another play, *A Journey by Night*, which ran for only seven performances at the Shubert Theatre in April of 1935. The failure of the play was fortunate for Stewart because it released him to go to California. It also brought him his only bad notice so far in New York. He played a Viennese named Carl, and one critic said he was about as Viennese as hamburger. The slap was too late to do him much damage—he was already signed for delivery to MGM.

His contract, giving him a starting wage of $350 per week, was renewable for whatever periods MGM decided and extendable over a period of seven years. In Stewart's case the contract never ran its course due to his being drafted for military service in 1941.

Stewart's career as an actor in New York had not been spectacular but it had been respectable, and for a fledgling actor a remarkably lucky one. He had been asked by Joshua Logan to join the University Players on Cape Cod and he had been offered roles both there and in New York. It had involved little effort on his part and had required none of the aggression that usually marks a young actor's fight to get into the business. In three years in New York he had appeared in eight plays and had drawn good critical comment, and he had had a career virtually handed to him—an actor in spite of himself and somewhat to his astonishment. Within a year of his arrival in Hollywood he would find himself a successful film actor, and again somewhat to his astonishment.

The man Stewart thanks for getting his movie career going was Billy Grady, then an MGM talent scout and director of tests, and later a casting director at the studio: "It was really his faith in me

13

that got me started." On his arrival in Los Angeles, Stewart was met by Henry Fonda, who had just started his own movie career, starring in *The Farmer Takes a Wife* for Fox. Fonda invited him to share his apartment, and helped ease him into the vastly different lifestyle of Los Angeles and the film community. Looking back, Stewart says, "When I arrived in Hollywood it was just as exciting as one hears. The big studios were much more than the huge factories they are today. They were big families of contract players and technicians where actors could learn their business in the best possible way—by experience."

As soon as he reported to the MGM studios in Culver City, Stewart was assigned a small role in a film already in production, *The Murder Man*, Spencer Tracy's first film under his new contract with MGM. After this first rushed assignment he was dismayed to find himself waiting some three months before his next role, that of Jeanette MacDonald's young, criminal brother in *Rose Marie*. He found, however, that it was not a case of being idle. Contract players were usable commodities, assigned to do screen tests with actors and actresses being tried out, sent out on publicity promotions, given all kinds of lessons and training in acting, singing, dancing, sports and, particularly in Stewart's case, put through courses in the studio's gymnasium. At a height of six feet, three inches and a weight of 138 pounds he was considered a bit too slender for filming.

Many of the actors with whom he had been friends in New York were now in Hollywood, among them Margaret Sullavan, who by this time had married and divorced Henry Fonda, which fact had no bearing upon her affection and professional regard for Fonda's roommate. She asked Universal to borrow him from MGM to co-star with her in *Next Time We Love*, a generosity that was a boon to his standing in the business, this being only his third film. From then onwards Stewart was one of the busiest young actors in Hollywood. He was seen in eight films in 1936, giving him an enormous range of experience and exposure. Stewart was seen in pictures with Clark Gable, Jean Harlow, Joan Crawford, Myrna Loy, William Powell and Eleanor Powell. As was the custom in these Golden Years of Hollywood, Stewart was available for loan-outs to other studios—and it was some of these loan-outs that brought him his most important early successes, particularly so in the case of the Frank Capra films for Columbia, *You Can't Take it With You* and *Mr. Smith Goes to Washington*, and the Marlene Dietrich

Corporal Stewart, participating in an NBC radio broadcast, Salute to the Champions, *on September 22, 1941.*

comedy-western, *Destry Rides Again* at Universal.

The private life of James Stewart has never been one to yield much grist for the gossip columnists, not even in his first years in Hollywood. On his arrival in the film colony he was advised by his father to find a wife and settle down, but Stewart was probably having too much fun to accept the advice. In fact, it would be 1949 before Stewart senior would have a daughter-in-law. Stewart the young movie star dated a fair spectrum of ladies, most of them being in the same line of work and some of whom were MGM set-ups for publicity purposes. It was said of Stewart that he had a tendency to fall in love with all his leading ladies and that it took him a long time to divest himself of the habit of being star-struck in the company of legendary actresses.

Stewart has nothing but fond recollections of MGM in its prime and he is grateful to have been a part of that pre-war era. "The executives were not power-drunk tyrants. Producers and directors and writers had freedom and were treated very well. And actors were treated so well. You worked all the time, 52 weeks a year. And they took you under their wing.

14

Lieutenant Stewart gives advice to Rookie Charlie
McCarthy, along with Edgar Bergen, at a camp show
in early 1942.

With his parents.

With fellow officers of the Second Air Division of the Eighth Air Command in England, 1944.

They protected you if you got into a scrape. They fixed your teeth and gave you voice lessons and got you new clothes and took care of your publicity."

By the late thirties Hollywood was not only America's film capital but it was the center of network radio programming, giving the film community yet another outlet for its talent. It was an important outlet, using actors, writers, directors, musicians in a vast variety of productions. In early 1937 Stewart began his own radio career as a host on the *Good News* show, jointly sponsored by MGM and Maxwell House Coffee, an hour of talk, interviews and music. He also appeared on the Sunday afternoon series *The Silver Theatre*, and on June 14, 1937, he appeared with Ann Harding in *Madame X* on *The Lux Radio Theatre*, Hollywood's most prestigious drama series, hosted by Cecil B. DeMille. From then until the demise of radio production brought about by the rise of television, Stewart appeared on more radio shows than he can remember. He regards radio performance as an impor-

tant adjunct to that of visual acting and regrets that so little of it is available to actors today.

No actor could have asked for more luck than Stewart in those Hollywood pre-war years, with a constant variety of movies, averaging four a year. His twentieth film, *Mr. Smith Goes to Washington*, registered him as more than an appealing actor of light comedies but one with some emotional substance. It resulted in his being nominated by the Academy of Motion Picture Arts and Sciences for the 1939 Best Actor Oscar. He lost to Robert Donat in *Goodbye Mr. Chips* but he won the following year for his performance as the cynical but vulnerable newspaperman in *The Philadelphia Story*. Stewart believes, as do many others in the film business, that his Oscar was something of a compensation for not having won for *Mr. Smith*. He also believes, as do others, that the 1940 Best Actor Oscar should have gone to Henry Fonda for *The Grapes of Wrath*. He also maintains that his own vote went to Fonda. On February 27, 1941, at the Biltmore Hotel in Los Angeles, Stewart accepted the award from Alfred Lunt, thanking him and adding that the honor was made the moreso "by receiving it from you."

On active duty.

The fascination with aviation that Stewart had shown as a child grew with time and as a film actor with a solid income he indulged himself in 1938 by buying an airplane, a two-seat Stinson 105. With the outbreak of the Second World War in September of 1939 he believed America would eventually be involved and he clocked up as many hours of flying time as he could in order to eventually qualify as a military pilot. He was drafted in January 1941, although underweight for a man of his height. But, by the day of his induction, March 22, 1941, he managed to meet the requirements by a matter of ounces. No actor of any fame at that time more eagerly tried to get into the armed forces than this one. He stills recalls his draft number—308—and his pride in becoming a soldier. His salary dropped from $12,000 to $21 per month, and at the end of the first month of service he sent his agent Leland Hayward a check for $2.10 as his commission. Hayward, long a close friend, kept it as a souvenir.

After basic training Stewart was sent to the Army Air Corps training base at Moffet Field, California. By the end of 1941 he had been commissioned a lieutenant and it was in his uniform that Hollywood got its first glimpse of him since he had left town. On February 26, 1942, he appeared at the Academy Awards to hand Gary Cooper his Oscar for *Sergeant York*. His only other Hollywood assignment was the reprising of his role in the radio version of *The Philadelphia Story* on July 20, 1942, broadcast on The Lux Radio Theatre, when Stewart again appeared in uniform, in the company of Katharine Hepburn and Cary Grant, with the show used as a victory promotion for bonds. In early 1942 Stewart also narrated two short government films—*Fellow Americans* and *Winning Your Wings*. However, for the next four years Stewart's services were entirely of a military nature.

Stewart was mostly involved in the training of bomber pilots until November of 1943, when, now a captain, he proceeded to England as part of the Second Air Division of the Eighth Air Command. He was based at a station near the village of Tibenham in Norfolk and from there he flew in some twenty major bombing raids over Germany. He was a major by the time he was awarded the Distinguished Flying

Cross for his leadership in the February 20, 1944, raid on Brunswick. Stewart had previously won the Air Medal, with Oak Leaf Cluster, and at the end of the war he was given the Croix de Guerre by the French government for his war services. As a squadron commander with several hundred planes in his group, Stewart led eleven missions and in July of 1944, with the rank of lieutenant colonel, he was made Chief of Staff of the Second Combat Wing of the Eighth Army Air Corps. By the time of his discharge from service in September of 1945 he had been promoted to full colonel, making him one of the highest ranking and most combat-involved celebrities to have served in the war.

With many thousands of other demobilized servicemen Stewart returned to the United States aboard the ocean liner-troopship *Queen Mary* and his first stop was his hometown of Indiana, Pennsylvania. His hopes of a quiet return were dashed with a major magazine coverage by *Life,* whose editors found, as did other reporters, that Stewart would not discuss his war experiences. He might say, "I had some close calls—the whole war was a close call," but that was about the extent of it. Sensing that the war might become a promotional gimmick for him in Hollywood, he had a clause written into all his contracts that no mention could be made of his war service in connection with the publicity on any film for which he was hired. The same stipulation extended to Stewart's continued service in the US Air Force Reserve.

It was not until years after the war that he talked about his experiences as a bomber pilot, and then only on rare occasions. Asked about fear, Stewart said that his chief fear was one of making a mistake while seated at the controls during an operation, fear of making a wrong decision, and that "Fear of a mistake was stronger than my fear of personal safety." He admits to having felt fear many times during those bombing raids but he tried to remember the advice given him by his father. "I asked him if he had been afraid during his war services. He said, 'Every man is, son, but just remember you can't handle fear all by yourself. Give it to God. He'll carry it for you.' I re-read the 91st Psalm that my father had given me when I left and I felt comforted, felt I had done all I could."

Fear also played a part in Stewart's return to Hollywood. He had been out of the business for more than four long years, years in which the world had changed, as he had himself. He still had a house in Brentwood, a residential community to the west of Beverly Hills and he still had a year and a half to go

Receiving the Air Medal.

on his MGM contract. It had lapsed during the time he had been away but Louis B. Mayer told Stewart that he would be happy to offer him the remainder of the contract as a token of his appreciation to a distinguished ex-serviceman. But Mayer and the MGM high command were surprised to have the offer rejected. Stewart was not at all sure of what he wanted to do, except that he did not want to be tied to a studio system as he had previously been. He would free-lance. It was a radical decision. Clark Gable and Robert Taylor, both returning from war service, were happy to be welcomed back by MGM. Most actors were happy to return to any kind of offer. Not Stewart. He wanted to think it over, but with the passing of the months he began to wonder if he was an unemployed actor as well as an unemployed flier.

Stewart's postwar dilemma was solved by Frank Capra, who called him and said he had an idea for a film. The two of them got together and Stewart listened as Capra unfolded a tale of a family man in a small town and how his business fails to the point where he wants to kill himself, until a guardian angel named Clarence appears...and so on, with Capra becoming confused and embarrassed by what sounded like a ridiculous picture. He thought he had lost Stewart. Instead the actor simply said, "I'll do it."

Home from the war. With his parents and sisters Mary and Virginia, in the family home in Indiana, Pennsylvania.

Wedding Day, August 9, 1949. The bridegroom and the former Gloria Hatrick McLean pose with best man Billy Grady, the MGM talent scout who brought Stewart to the studio, and Mrs. Gregg Draddy, sister of the bride.

With Gloria and their twin daughters, Kelly and Judy, in late 1951.

Colonel Stewart on duty with the Air Force Reserve.

The result, *It's a Wonderful Life,* emerged at Christmastime, 1946, and met with modest reaction, even though it brought Stewart his third Oscar nomination for Best Actor of 1946. With time the film has been accepted as a classic piece of Americana and a film to study for technique, construction and spirit.

During the course of production Stewart several times talked about possibly retiring from the business and getting into something else. Clark Gable had let it be known that after serving in the war the whole idea of acting and making movies seemed less vital than it used to be. Stewart felt somewhat the same, until Lionel Barrymore took him aside for a talk. Barrymore, who played the Scrooge-like villain in *Wonderful Life,* had known Stewart all through the MGM years. He said, in regard to the actor wrapping up his film career, "Forget about this, Jim. Forget about being away for five years. Don't you realize you're moving millions of people, shaping their lives? What other profession has that kind of power? Acting, young fella, is a noble profession. Now just do what you're doing. You're doing fine.

Now keep up and don't go moping around here. I don't like that." The advice was heeded.

Stewart's next film, *Magic Town,* was also Americana but one that caused its star to reassess his movie image. A number of critics pointed out that his folksiness had become passé and one went so far as to say he was bored by "this drawling stringbean" and wondered how much longer he was going to have to put up with him. Again Stewart heeded advice, and started to look for tougher projects. *Call Northside 777* was a step in the right direction and Hitchcock's *Rope* gave him something more intellectual than he had tackled before, but it was not until *The Stratton Story* in 1949 that he could claim his first postwar box office hit.

In 1950 Stewart became one of the first major stars to enter into the business aspect of picture making. He signed with Universal to make two films for modest up-front money but with a guarantee of a percentage of the profits, a decision that proved wise and which gradually became a norm in the industry. It was a gamble, but so was his decision to make *Winchester '73.* The script had been lying around the studio for years and no actor seemed interested in taking on this tale about two brothers who hate each

In his many radio jobs, the one Stewart most enjoyed was the one-season series The Six Shooter, *which began on September 20, 1953; it presented Stewart as a drifter named Britt Ponset, who was subject to a variety of western adventures.*

other and compete for a prized rifle. With the encouragement of his agent, Lew Wasserman, who later became the head of Universal, Stewart opted in favor of *Winchester '73*, in conjunction with the second film, *Harvey*. Both would turn out to be among his most important successes, with the western starting his long association with director Anthony Mann. Together they would make eight films, five of them westerns and all five of which are now regarded as classics in the genre. *Winchester '73* is of particular interest in Stewart's career because it marked a turning point, one in which he presented a harder and more complex screen image and one that was accepted by the public. "I had to toughen up and I found that in westerns I could do it and still retain what I was."

The fifties became the major decade in the career of James Stewart. He entered into a new phase of success and popularity. He had by 1950 been a movie star for fifteen years, a period during which most stars enjoy most of their success and then move into decline. This was not the case with Stewart. With the fifties he for the first time entered the ranks of the Top Ten at the box office. It was the decade in which he made twenty-three films, including all of his films with Anthony Mann, three of Hitchcock's major successes—*Rear Window, The Man Who Knew*

Too Much and *Vertigo*— and Otto Preminger's *Anatomy of a Murder,* which contains what many people regard as his best performance. Had Stewart retired at the end of the fifties he would still be regarded as one of the most successful of all film actors. Fortunately he chose to continue into the sixties, the seventies and the eighties.

In 1949 Stewart ended his long bachelorhood. On August 9 he married Gloria Hatrick McLean, who had two young sons from her previous marriage, Ronald and Michael. His bride was, in Hollywood terms, a non-professional, which seemed a logical choice for a man who preferred as normal a home life as possible amid the emotional chaos of the movie community. On May 7, 1951, they became the parents of twin girls, Kelly and Judy. The Stewarts have lived a low-profile life in Beverly Hills, with every indication that they have enjoyed a very successful marriage in a business not noted for them. The consensus is that the bright, humorous and strong-minded Mrs. Stewart has been "just right for Jimmy." The only tragedy in their marriage has been the loss of Ronald, who was killed as a Marine lieutenant in Vietnam in June of 1971. Stewart's only comment on the loss of his son is that he was proud of him and believed he died doing his duty for his country.

Stewart takes pride in his military career, in the twenty-seven years in which he was associated with the Air Force. In 1957 he was nominated for promotion to the rank of brigadier general and found himself the center of a small controversy when Senator Margaret Chase Smith of Maine opposed the promotion. She claimed it was because of his public stature as an actor, an opinion not shared by his fellow officers, who succeeded in overcoming the objection. He served in the reserve until 1968, when his age (60) required him to retire. Upon retiring he toured air force bases and addressed the men on duty. To add to his previous decorations he was awarded the Distinguished Service Medal, accompanied by a commendation for his services. Stewart says that it was a sad point in his life and caused him to reflect for the first time that age was creeping up on him. To bolster his spirits he bought himself a small airplane, which he thereafter attempted to fly at least on the weekends. But again age crept up and in 1981 he decided that his days of flying had reached their end. "I gave up my beloved little Piper Super Cub because my hearing was failing. I miss it. But I had forty-five years of flying and I guess that's long enough. I had a good run."

Aside from his feature films Stewart has hosted

At the ANTA Theatre in New York, in March of 1970, with daughters Kelly and Judy, then nineteen, who had just seen their father's performance in Harvey *and went backstage to kiss Elwood P. Dowd's invisible friend.*

With William Windom in Hawkins—A Life for a Life (1973), the fourth of the eight telefilms in the series Hawkins, *generally considered Stewart's best work in television.*

Outside his old stomping grounds, the MGM studios, in 1974, as one of the hosts of the Golden Age compilation That's Entertainment.

or narrated a variety of short documentaries for the government or for charities, among them *Thunderbolt* (1947), *Ambassadors with Wings* (1958) and *Sentimental Journey* (1979), all of which deal with aviation. He was part of Peter Bogdanovich's two films about John Ford in 1971, and he narrated *Pat Nixon: Portrait of a First Lady* (1972). In 1974 Stewart was one of the hosts used in the MGM production *That's Entertainment,* in which certain stars associated with the glory days at Metro conducted tours of the old lot and revelled in nostalgia. In Stewart's case he seemed to take delight in poking fun at his song-and-dance performance in *Born to Dance.*

Stewart's first work in television was an episode of the General Electric Theatre in 1955, *The Windmill,* in which he co-starred with Barbara Hale. He did two half-hour dramas in 1957; in February he appeared in *A Town With a Past,* in which he was introduced by his friend Ronald Reagan, and in December he both starred in and directed *The Trail to Christmas.* Two years went by before his next television drama, *Cindy's Fella,* an episode of Ford

Startime, but by now he and his wife had begun making occasional appearances on *The Jack Benny Show.* He also showed up in the variety programs of Dean Martin and Johnny Carson, and on one occasion he took one of his biggest fans, Carol Burnett, by surprise by coming on her show without her knowledge and doing his party piece, "Ragtime Cowboy Joe." Of his dramatic television roles the most impressive is *Flashing Spikes* (1962), an hour directed by a man who hardly had anything to do with TV—John Ford.

Stewart has been involved in two television series. The first was *The Jimmy Stewart Show* in 1971, a weekly half-hour situation comedy which ran for twenty-four episodes and was then cancelled. The critical consensus was that it failed because it used the old, genial, bumbling Stewart image and not the more incisive, dramatic one. It gave him the role of Professor James K. Howard, the more-often-than-not confused father of a somewhat crazy family and came off like a pale version of *Father Knows Best.* Anyone who had seen him in *Mr. Hobbs Takes a Vacation* (1962), *Take Her, She's Mine* (1963) and *Dear Brigitte* (1965) had no need to see *The Jimmy Stewart Show.* There was, however, every reason to see him as a small town lawyer named Billy Joe Hawkins, a role somewhat inspired by the character he played in *Anatomy of a Murder.* There were eight episodes, each ninety minutes in length. The first, *Hawkins on Murder,* appeared on CBS in March of 1973, followed by *Hawkins—Murder in Movieland* (October, 1973), *Hawkins—Die, Darling, Die* (October, 1973), *Hawkins—A Life for a Life* (November, 1973), *Hawkins—Blood Feud* (December, 1973), *Hawkins—Murder in the Slave Trade* (January, 1974), *Hawkins—Murder on the 13th Floor* (February, 1974), and *Hawkins—Candidate for Murder* (March, 1974).

His work as Billy Joe Hawkins brought Stewart the Golden Globe Award for Best TV Actor in a dramatic series and a great deal of praise, but it was hard work for a man in his mid-sixties. He claims that learning dialogue has never been easy for him and that in television he has never been able to use cue cards because he cannot see them. *Hawkins,* with its long courtroom scenes, called for a large amount of dialogue. He says, "The reason I hem and haw and take such a long time to deliver lines is that I'm trying to remember them," which may or may not be true. The eight *Hawkins* telefilms were filmed at MGM, but a different MGM than the one he had enjoyed before the war. There was no longer a spirit of fun about making pictures, they were shot faster, and stars were no longer given chauffeurs to get them to locations—they were simply handed instructions on how to get there.

In between *The Jimmy Stewart Show* and the *Hawkins* series, Stewart reprised *Harvey* for television. It became a Hallmark Hall of Fame presentation on NBC on March 22, 1972, directed by Fielder Cook and with Helen Hayes playing the role of sister Veta. The critical and public receptions were excellent and Stewart feels he gave a better interpretation than he had in the 1951 movie, that he was able to bring more shading and subtlety to this version of Elwood P. Dowd. By now almost everyone had forgotten that Frank Fay was the actor who had originated the role on Broadway and made his mark with *Harvey;* now the mantle of the play's keeper appeared to have passed to Stewart—and it will be interesting to see if it ever passes to any other actor, such is his identity with it. "Wherever I go I'm always asked about Harvey, about how he is and where he is. At first I thought it was a joke but then I could see people were serious. So I just say that he's home with a cold and that I'll pass along the regards. Harvey's had a big effect on my life."

As the lonely janitor in Mr. Krueger's Christmas *(1980), in which he played a man living out his fantasy as a conductor of the Morman Tabernacle Choir.*

Stewart's first contact with *Harvey* came in 1947 when he was hired as Frank Fay's summer replacement, Fay having played the role since its opening in 1944. It took Stewart back to Broadway for the first time since his work there in 1935. His reviews were not good but when Universal filmed *Harvey* in 1951 there was no talk of anyone other than Stewart getting the part. Twenty years later he returned to Broadway to again play *Harvey,* with Helen Hayes as Veta, and won excellent notices and good business. *The New York Times* said, "This production of *Harvey* restores James Stewart and a sense of innocence to the American theater. As Elwood his garrulous, gentle, genial presence is a delight." The *New York Daily News* let it be known that "He is offering a master class in acting with each performance." When asked why he had left the comfort of Beverly Hills to drag himself back to these chilly months of early 1972 in New York he replied that things were rather dull in Hollywood. Besides, he had never been really satisfied with his movie version and he wanted to have another crack at the material, now that he was of a more appropriate age for Elwood.

The 1972 television version was an outcome of Stewart's Broadway success, and three years later he took yet another crack at it. On April 9, 1975, Stewart and *Harvey* made their British bows in London's Prince of Wales Theatre, with Mona Washbourne as Veta and Anthony Quayle as its director. It

As the southern lawyer, a cameo role in the 1986 ABC mini-series North and South, Book 2.

zoo conditions are of particular interest to the Stewarts.

Most of Stewart's film work in the eighties has been for television. In 1980 he starred in the well-received *Mr. Krueger's Christmas,* which told a dramatic story and also involved the Mormon Tabernacle Choir. Directed by Kieth Merrill, it was sponsored by the Mormon Church, a pleasant association for the actor, which later resulted in his decision to donate his memorabilia to the Arts and Communications Archives of Brigham Young University in Provo, Utah. His most important film for television is *Right of Way,* co-starring Bette Davis and directed by George Schaefer. It was the first film made expressly for cable television and shown on HBO. With both Stewart and Davis playing several years beyond their own ages—in actual fact Davis is about a month and a half older than Stewart—this is the story of a couple deciding to end their lives in suicide. The telefilm was first seen at the Montreal Film Festival on August 23, 1983, the critical concensus being that it was more admirable than enjoyable.

As a cinematic elder statesman Stewart has been the subject of numerous tributes, among the most important being his winning of the American Film Institute's Life Achievement Award in 1980 and as one of the 1983 honorees at *The Kennedy Center Honors* in Washington, the others being Katherine Dunham, Elia Kazan, Virgil Thomson and Frank Sinatra. He has also been honored with more film retrospectives than he can recall. An honor of particular satisfaction was the celebration given him in his hometown, Indiana, Pennsylvania, on the occasion of his seventy-fifth birthday, May 20, 1983, which included the unveiling of a statue. Not long after that he flew to England to join a number of Second Air Division colleagues in a sentimental visit to the places they had known during their years of war service.

Stewart has never been one to pontificate about acting. It has simply been his business and one at which he was prepared to work. He told *Los Angeles Times* columnist Joyce Haber, "As an actor you have to develop a style that suits you and pursue it, not just develop a bag of tricks. The stage teaches you all sorts of basic things. But the movies is a different ball game. On Broadway you have to sustain a mood for twenty minutes—in movies for twenty seconds. Back in my early Broadway days, you didn't act by religion or method. There was no cult. You were just told to learn your craft and you did." As for the difference in acting for the stage and for the camera, "It's much

was a triumph at least the equal of the last Broadway venture, with standing ovations from the Londoners for a movie star they had long loved. Even the usually caustic critics were mellow, one of them suggesting that Stewart had raised relaxation to a new art form. London's *Variety* reviewer said, "Stewart is superb as Elwood P. Dowd, and his reading of the second act finale is one for the textbooks." The *London Times* noted, "It is a tribute to Mr. Stewart's timing that even the most predictable lines exert a comic shock." He could hardly have hoped for a better reception for Harvey and himself than this warm get-together in London.

Since the triumph of *Harvey* in London in 1975 Stewart has lived a life of semi-retirement, with no need to work other than when the spirit has moved him to do so. He gladly accepted a cameo role in John Wayne's final film, *The Shootist* (1976), and another one in *Airport '77.* To date, the last feature film in which he has been seen is *The Magic of Lassie* (1981), although there has been one other, *The Green Horizon,* a Japanese film made in Kenya in 1981, which has never been released theatrically in the United States or the British Commonwealth and probably never will be. It is doubtlessly the least successful film in which he has ever appeared. It came about only because Stewart and his wife were in Kenya at the time, visiting a wildlife preserve, which they had visited several times before. Animal preservation and more difficult to maintain a consistent performance in a movie than in a play, although the theater is a tougher racket."

Among other things James Stewart is Hollywood's Grand Survivor, although it is an honor upon which he prefers not to dwell. Of the major male stars of the Golden Years of the Thirties and Forties he is the only one left—Spencer Tracy, Gary Cooper, John Wayne, Clark Gable, James Cagney, Fred Astaire, Henry Fonda, Robert Taylor, Humphrey Bogart, Errol Flynn, Tyrone Power, Cary Grant, William Holden—all gone.

As for the caliber, the quality and the spirit of contemporary film, they are also something on which Stewart does not care to dwell at length. The violence, the vulgarity and the image of America contained in most modern movies is deplorable. Nothing Stewart has ever done has called for a restricted rating: "I've done some pretty rough scenes and been involved in some pretty torrid romances but mostly, I believe, they were comparatively decent. I didn't select them for that reason, but I suppose the Stewart image has gravitated toward the kind of roles I've played. If I had attempted to play a thief, a hoodlum or a killer, people would just laugh and say, 'What's that man trying to do?' But what bothers me most today is the lack of variety. You get porno, sex, violence. The pictures are all alike. It's a medium with a tremendous capacity for showing all sorts of things but we're not getting a variety. The films today are cynical and it's hard to tell the good guys from the bad guys."

All men are of their time, and James Stewart is grateful to have been a film actor during the years in which he flourished. To him it has been a life of extraordinary luck and good fortune. When he was given the award by the American Film Institute, he took it in his hands, looked at the audience and said, "It's kind of like tying a happy ribbon around a wonderful lifetime that has blessed me by letting me get paid doing work I loved to do." On the PBS documentary, *James Stewart—A Wonderful Life*, host Johnny Carson asked him how he would like to be remembered. "I'd like to be remembered as a man who believed in hard work and decent values, as one who believed in love of country, love of family, love of community, love of God."

On the occasion of the tribute by the American Film Institute, Stewart was lauded by many from whom warm words were naturally expected, from old friends like Henry Fonda and Frank Capra. Somewhat surprisingly the most touching words came from an actor with whom he had never worked or even met—Dustin Hoffman. "Mr. Stewart, you made my parents happy. You've made me happy. I'm making sure you make my children happy. And if this world has any kind of luck, you're going to make my grandchildren happy."

But of all the words of praise and gratitude given him during his half century of success, perhaps none have been more simple or more to the point than these made by Prince Philip in London. Said the Prince, "Thank you for being Jimmy Stewart."

With Henry Fonda and Grace Kelly at the American Films Institute's presentation of its Life Achievement

Award to Stewart on the evening of February 28, 1980, held at the Beverly Hilton Hotel, Beverly Hills.

The Films of James Stewart

At far right, Spencer Tracy is looking at Stewart.

Robert Warwick and Harvey Stephens. The blurred figure in the upper left-hand corner is Stewart.

MURDER MAN

MGM, 1935

Produced by Harry Rapf; *Directed* by Tim Whelan; *Written* by Tim Whelan and John C. Higgins, based on a story by Whelan and Guy Bolton; *Photographed* by Lester White; *Music* by William Axt; *70 minutes.*

CAST:

Steve Gray, Spencer Tracy; *Mary Shannon,* Virginia Bruce; *Captain Cole,* Lionel Atwill; *Henry Mander,* Harvey Stephens; *Robins,* Robert Barrat; *Shorty,* James Stewart; *Pop Gray,* William Collier, Sr.; *Carey Booth,* Bobby Watson; *Red Maquire,* William Demarest.

Spencer Tracy first appeared in an MGM picture in 1934, *The Show Off,* at a time when he was under contract to Fox Pictures. Irving Thalberg, the head of production at MGM, decided Tracy was MGM star material and the following year Tracy signed a contract with Metro that would stretch through most of the rest of his life. His first film under the new contract was to have been *Riff Raff,* opposite Jean Harlow, but production was delayed and Tracy was shunted into a modest programmer titled *The Murder Man,* a film of little interest other than that it started the film career of James Stewart.

Stewart found himself put to work as soon as he arrived on the lot. *The Murder Man* was already in production but the role of the newspaperman known as Shorty had not been cast. Producer Harry Rapf first rejected the skinny, elongated Stewart when it was suggested he play Shorty, but after a while the humor of the situation appealed to him. And so Stewart made his movie debut as a gangling, enthusiastic young newshound with the inappropriate nickname. The title applies to Steve Gray (Tracy), a hot-shot reporter who specializes in murder stories but otherwise lives a slap-happy kind of existence. Another reporter, Mary Shannon (Virginia Bruce), tries to straighten him out. His life takes a dramatic turn when his father's wife commits suicide, following the father's having been wiped out by a business fraud. In revenge Gray kills one of the two men responsible and pins the blame on the other, Henry Mander (Harvey Stephens). It is a perfect crime and Gray cleverly reports it as such. Mander is sentenced to death but he is saved by Gray, whose sense of decency causes him to admit the scheme.

The Murder Man was a passing product of its time, the kind of story that would now be an episode of a police TV series. Stewart played his few scenes with perhaps a little too much boyishness, and he was shocked at his image when he first saw it on screen: "I was all arms and legs." Few reviewers made note of his small role as the reporter eagerly after a story, but the critic of the *New York Herald Tribune* remembered having seen his work in the theatre: "That admirable stage juvenile, James Stewart, who was so fine in *Yellow Jack,* is wasted in a bit that he handles with characteristically engaging skill."

Stewart was a little concerned about his movie debut and began to wonder if it would lead to a career, especially when several months slipped by before being assigned to another film. But *The Murder Man* had one real boon—it began a friendship with Tracy, whose own roots were on Broadway and who favored actors with stage training. He liked Stewart's earnestness about acting and his eagerness to learn. Said Tracy, "I told him to forget the camera was there. That was all he needed. In his very first scene he showed he had all the good things."

ROSE MARIE

MGM, 1936

Produced by Hunt Stromberg; *Directed* by W. S. Van Dyke; *Written* by Frances Goodrich, Albert Hackett and Alice Duer Miller, based on the musical play by Otto Harbach and Oscar Hammerstein, 2nd; *Photographed* by William Daniels; *Music* by Rudolf Friml and Herbert Stothart; *Musical direction* by Herbert Stothart; 110 minutes.

CAST:

Marie de Flor, Jeanette MacDonald; *Sergeant Bruce,* Nelson Eddy; *Meyerson,* Reginald Owen; *Anna,* Una O'Connor; *Boniface,* George Regas; *John Flower,*

With Jeanette MacDonald and Nelson Eddy.

Stewart photographed for a sequence not used in the film.

James Stewart; *Romeo,* Allan Jones; *Bella,* Gilda Gray; *Cafe Manager,* Robert Greig; *Storekeeper,* Lucien Littlefield; *Premier,* Alan Mowbray; *Teddy,* David Niven; *Mr. Daniels,* Herman Bing; *Mr. Gordon,* Halliwell Hobbs; *Commandant,* Russell Hicks.

A Trivial Pursuit question might be this one: In which MGM musical do two future Academy Award winning stars play bit parts, one at the start of the picture and the other at the end? Answer: the 1936 version of *Rose Marie,* which has David Niven as a dressing room visitor-admirer of the opera star heroine, and James Stewart as her criminal brother, who is finally nabbed by the Royal Canadian Mounted Policeman hero.

    Rose Marie began its life on Broadway in 1924 and remains one of the few operettas of that period to continue to have a life. MGM first filmed it in 1928 as a silent with a recorded orchestral accompaniment. In that version Joan Crawford played the heroine as a French Canadian wildcat, which characterization bears no relationship to the one concocted in 1936 for Jeanette MacDonald. In her second pairing with Nelson Eddy, following the great success of *Naughty Marietta,* the emphasis was on

music, with several portions of genuine opera. The film opens in Montreal, where Marie de Flor (MacDonald) learns that her young brother John Flower (Stewart) has killed a policeman and fled to the woods of Northwest Canada. She goes there in order to find him and comes into contact with Sergeant Bruce (Eddy), who is also trying to find him. Marie is robbed and dumped by the guide she has hired, so she attempts to make some money by singing in a saloon. The sergeant comes to her rescue and helps her find her way through the wilds, knowing full well she is on her way to see her brother. Marie and the sergeant fall in love but that does not stop him from doing his duty. Shortly after she finds John, the sergeant appears and takes him into custody. Marie is disgusted with the policeman. She returns to the world of opera but suffers a nervous breakdown. While convalescing, Sergeant Bruce comes to see her and, presumably, they are reunited by love.

    Rose Marie proved to be an even bigger hit than *Naughty Marietta* and made further MacDonald-Eddy romances inevitable. It also did a good deal for James Stewart, whose short role was commented upon by reviewers, who found him appealing as the wayward brother, saddened and contrite in his crime and humbled by the devotion of his sister. If Stewart had doubts about his future because of the silly role in *Murder Man,* he now had reason to be optimistic. In fact, he was about to make the quantum leap from bit player to co-star.

NEXT TIME WE LOVE

UNIVERSAL, 1936

Produced by Paul Kohner; *Directed* by Edward H. Griffith; *Written* by Melville Baker, based on the story *Say Goodbye Again* by Ursala Parrott; *Photographed* by Joseph Valentine; *Music* by Franz Waxman; *87 minutes.*

CAST:

Cicily, Margaret Sullavan; *Christopher,* James Stewart; *Tommy,* Ray Milland; *Madame Donato,* Anna Demetrio; *Jennings,* Grant Mitchell; *Cartaret,*

Robert McWade; *Desk Clerk*, Harry C. Bradley; *Conductor*, Broderick O'Farrell; *Porter*, Buddy Williams; *Hanna*, Hattie MacDaniel.

Margaret Sullavan made only sixteen films and four of them co-starred her with James Stewart, whom she had known since her marriage to Henry Fonda broke up in 1932. Fonda thereafter roomed with Stewart in New York and Stewart became a friend of Sullavan. She began her film career in 1933 at the age of twenty-two and quickly gained favor with her warm, sexy manner and slightly husky speaking voice. There was also an appealing quirkiness about her, a quirkiness that would tragically enlarge into neurosis and her eventual suicide in 1960 at forty-nine. In 1936, after making only four films, Sullavan was successful enough to tell Universal whom she wanted as her co-star for *Next Time We Love*. She wanted Stewart, and MGM did not hesitate in loaning him out. If another studio wanted to gamble on a new bit-player in a leading role, it was fine with them.

Next Time We Love turned out to be what was once condescendingly known as a "woman's picture," a rather soggy and sad tale of young love,

misunderstandings and the death of the husband at an early age. He, Christopher (Stewart), is an ambitious young newspaperman, who marries Cicily (Sullavan) while she is still in college. Their best friend, Tommy (Ray Milland), helps their financial situation by introducing her to a theatrical manager, who gives her a role in a play. She does well and refuses to go with Christopher when he is posted to Rome, feeling she would not be of any help to him at this stage in his career. He resents this but proceeds to Italy, where some months later he learns, by way of Cicily's landlady, that he is a father. He deserts his post to be with her and their child, which causes him to be demoted and assigned to local reporting. Seeing how unhappy this makes him, she pleads with his editor to give him more important work. This results in his being sent to Europe and a gradual estrangement, as she becomes a celebrated actress on Broadway and he builds his reputation as a correspondent.

Cicily's life becomes more complicated when Tommy confesses his long-held love for her and asks her to divorce Christopher. She goes to Europe to see him but finds that he is a dying man, having contracted a disease while on duty in China. He tells her

With Billy Gratton and Margaret Sullavan.

With Grant Mitchell and Margaret Sullavan.

there is little time left and she responds by letting him know she will stay with him until the end and that "next time we love, maybe we'll have time for each other."

Next Time We Love was an old-fashioned soap opera even by 1936 standards and its success was due to the appealing performances of Sullavan and Stewart. Sullavan, with her refined kind of sensuality, could illuminate material as flimsy as this and the critics said so in a variety of ways. But they also had nice comments on this new leading man. *The New York Times* referred to him as a welcome addition to the ranks of young movie actors and *Time* called him

"natural, spontaneous and altogether excellent." It also praised him for presenting a decent portrait of a newspaperman, rather than the usual Hollywood version of harsh and loud flippancy, a man devoted to hard work and craftsmanship, not drunkenness and lechery. In short, *Next Time We Love* was a definite step in the right direction for an actor appearing in only his third film. It would not, however, guarantee him leading roles when he reported back to MGM. Mighty Metro was in no hurry to rush him into stardom. They felt, and probably wisely, that Stewart needed a little more development in a variety of projects.

33

WIFE VERSUS SECRETARY

MGM, 1936

Produced by Hunt Stromberg; *Directed* by Clarence Brown; *Written* by Norman Krasna, Alice Duer Miller and John Lee Mahin, based on the story by Faith Baldwin; *Photographed* by Ray June; *Music* by Herbert Stothart; *85 minutes.*

With Jean Harlow and Tom Mahoney.

CAST:

Van Stanhope, Clark Gable; *Helen "Whitey" Wilson,* Jean Harlow; *Linda Stanhope,* Myrna Loy; *Mimi,* May Robson; *Joe,* Hobart Cavanaugh; *Dave,* James Stewart; *Underwood,* George Barbier; *Simpson,* Gilbert Emery; *Edna Wilson,* Margaret Irving; *Tom Wilson,* William Newell; *Eve Merritt,* Marjorie Gateson; *Taggart,* Leonard Carey; *Hal Harrington,* Charles Trowbridge; *Mr. Jenkins,* John Qualen; *Mary Connors,* Hilda Howe; *Ellen,* Mary MacGregor; *Joan Carstairs,* Gloria Holden; *Finney,* Tommy Dugan; *Howard,* Jack Mulhall; *Mr. Barker,* Frank Elliott.

Clark Gable and Jean Harlow made six films together and in the fifth, *Wife Versus Secretary,* James Stewart could hardly expect to be more than a supporting player, especially since the cast also included Myrna Loy. The Gable-Harlow packaging had been a gold mine and it would doubtlessly have gone beyond their sixth picture, *Saratoga,* had she

not died during its making. Stewart claims that simply being in a film with them was an education and that he learned that movie acting was something beyond the mere ability to act, that it had much to do with the projecting of personality. Gable and Harlow may not have been gifted actors, but for the screen they were able to register a presence that does not necessarily come with an education in acting.

In this marital comedy, the wife is Linda (Loy), the secretary is Whitey (Harlow) and the husband is Van Stanhope (Gable), an enterprising young publisher. Whitey is engaged to a nice young man called Dave (Stewart). Linda has no reason to be jealous until people point out to her that Whitey remains a secretary even though her talents qualify her for more important work. Why? When Stanhope leaves for Havana on a business venture, Whitey follows him to give him vital information, but to Linda it appears to be something more personal. Her suspicions are heightened when she telephones her husband at night and finds the call answered by Whitey, who is working late. Linda decides on a separation and books passage on an ocean liner to Europe. On the day of the departure Whitey comes to the ship and explains to Linda that she has no cause to doubt her husband and that she would be a fool to leave him. Besides, says Whitey, she has a man of her own—the ever-faithful Dave. Poor Dave has had his nose put out of joint by Whitey's devotion to her boss, but Whitey now sees that work isn't everything. Being devoted to a husband of her own might be much better.

Wife Versus Secretary is a typical glitter product of its time, its plotlines no more important than those of a Metro musical. In the midst of Gable, Harlow and Loy, James Stewart might well have been expected to fade from memory, and it is a tribute to his own natural sense of presence that he did not. Indeed, the reviewer for the London *Observer* commented, "What I liked best about the picture was the performance of Mr. James Stewart as the secretary's fiancé. He acts Gable and Harlow off the screen. He is one of those young moderns of whom you feel, with a start of surprise, that good actors don't stop with your own generation—they keep right along coming." It was warm encouragement for a role that might in other hands have made little impression.

Apparently Jean Harlow made quite an impression on Stewart, who remembers her as every bit as sexy as legend would have it. MGM's famed costume designer Adrian crafted gowns for Harlow, who seemed to have been poured into them. Stewart recalls her as being "all woman. When she kissed, she really kissed. Some actresses fake it. Not Jean. I did quite a love scene with her—long before it became the thing to do on screen. I remember it to this day— we did it six times. And that dress. Yes, she was braless and she didn't seem to wear anything under the dress. Well, I forgot my lines. That's what I did."

SMALL TOWN GIRL

MGM, 1936

Produced by Hunt Stromberg; *Directed* by William A. Wellman; *Written* by John Lee Mahin, based on the novel by Ben Ames Williams; *Photograghed* by Charles Rosher; *Music* by Herbert Stothart; 90 minutes.

CAST:

Kay, Janet Gaynor; *Bob*, Robert Taylor; *Priscilla*, Binnie Barnes; *Elmer*, James Stewart; *Dr. Dakin*, Lewis Stone; *Ma Brannan*, Elizabeth Patterson; *Pa Brannan*, Frank Craven; *George*, Andy Devine; *Emily*, Isabel Jewell; *Dr. Fabre*, Charley Grapewin; *Catherine*, Agnes Ayres; *Mrs. Dakin*, Nella Walker; *Childers*, Robert Greig; *Captain Mack*, Edgar Kennedy; *Mrs. Hyde*, Mary Forbes; *So So*, Willie Fong; *Pat*, John Harron; *Cissie*, Nora Lane; *Jim*, Walter Johnson; *Felicia*, Drue Leyton.

Having co-starred with Margaret Sullavan in *Next Time We Love*, James Stewart was possibly puzzled to find himself relegated to a bit part in MGM's *Small Town Girl*. On the other hand, he was kept so busy in 1936 he had little time to ponder the matter. The young Metro man getting the build-up at that time was handsome Robert Taylor and for *Small Town Girl* they matched him with, and gave him second billing to, Janet Gaynor, here making her first film away from Fox after nine years with that studio. Gaynor had been the ace Fox player until Shirley Temple came along, and she would make only four more films before retiring in 1938 at the age of thirty-two.

Since Gaynor specialized in poignant romance, *Small Town Girl* was tailored to her style. Here she is

With Janet Gaynor.

Kay Brannan, a girl bored with living in the small town of Carvel, Massachusetts. One day Dr. Bob Dakin (Taylor) stops by to ask directions and becomes so enchanted with Kay he asks her to go along with him and point the way to the spot he is trying to find. The dashing doctor is a lot more exciting than her boyfriend, Elmer (Stewart), who is earnest but unsophisticated and whose clumsy ways exasperate her.

Kay and Bob have a fine time together and drink a lot, and wake up the next morning to find that they are married. This is especially worrisome for Bob because he is engaged to marry socialite Priscilla (Binnie Barnes). His parents suggest that due to his social position and his career, he and Kay should keep up a pretense of marriage for at least half a year before applying for divorce. As part of the pretense they keep an apartment and also take a yacht cruise together, all of which kindles the growing love she has for him and the confusion he feels about her. When it gets too much for her she returns to Carvel and the open arms of the dumb but loving Elmer. Eventually Bob decides which of the two women in his life he wants and poor Elmer gets shoved aside.

Small Town Girl pleased the fans of Janet Gaynor and helped Robert Taylor with his rapidly developing popularity. It did little for Stewart, other than prove to his employers that he could play just about anything they handed him. Perhaps as a reward for playing Gaynor's ungainly visitor, they next gave him a picture in which he could have his name at the top of the cast list.

SPEED

MGM, 1936

Produced by Lucien Hubbard; *Directed* by Edwin L. Marin; *Written* by Michael Fessier, based on a story by Milton Krims and Larry Bachman; *Photographed* by Lester White; *Music* by Edward Ward; 65 minutes.

With Wendy Barrie.

CAST:

Terry Martin, James Stewart; *Jane Mitchell*, Wendy Barrie; *Gadget*, Ted Healy; *Josephine Sanderson*, Una Merkel; *Frank Lawson*, Weldon Heyburne; *Fanny Lane*, Patricia Wilder; *Mr. Dean*, Ralph Morgan; *George Saunders*, Robert Livingstone; *Doctor*, Charles Trowbridge; *Doctor*, William Tannen; *Uncle*, Walter Kingsford.

It was now time for MGM to try James Stewart as a lead player, albeit in a programmer designed for the bottom half of a double bill. Such pictures usually centered on crime or sporting activity, with the focus

With player, Ted Healy, Wendy Barrie and Weldon Heyburn.

on action. *Speed* is almost a textbook example. Here Stewart is busting-at-the-seams with confidence as a race car mechanic and test driver, who just knows he can come up with a new kind of high-speed carburetor that will put the Emory Automobile Company ahead of the competition.

Terry Martin (Stewart) also has an eye for a pretty girl, especially June Mitchell (Wendy Barrie), who has just joined the company's public relations department and who also just happens to be the niece of the company boss. She is on her toes to show that her job depends on her ability and not on nepotism. She admires the cocky Terry but she also receives plenty of attention from engineer Frank Lawson (Weldon Heyburn) which bothers Terry, especially when Lawson offers valuable suggestions on the perfection of the carburetor. June advises Terry to accept Lawson's help and the machinery is tested on the Indianapolis Speedway. The car spins out of control and crashes. Terry and his driver, Gadget

(Ted Healy), are overcome by the fumes when the car bursts into flames and it is Lawson who comes to their rescue. Terry is humbled by the failure and is ready to quit, until June tells him it is he she loves and not Lawson and that he must go on with the experiment and make it work. He does and it does.

Like many another B picture of its day, *Speed* was shot quickly on a small budget, with plenty of stock footage. In this case it was simpler than usual, since MGM had access to all kinds of Indianapolis Speedway material, added to which they padded the 65-minute picture with a tour of a Detroit automobile factory. *Speed* was well titled—it zipped along at a good clip and strained the mind of no one, and certainly did burgeoning star Stewart no harm.

Today just about all Stewart can remember about *Speed* is that it featured the veteran character actor Ted Healy and that Healy gave him a piece of advice he has never forgotten. "He told me to think of the audience not simply as watchers but as collaborators, as sort of partners in the project. He was right, and that helped me in my attitude toward the business."

THE GORGEOUS HUSSY

MGM, 1936

Produced by Joseph L Mankiewicz; *Directed* by Clarence Brown; *Written* by Ainsworth Morgan and Stephen Morehouse Avery based on a story by Samuel Hopkins Adams; *Photographed* by George Folsey; *Music* by Herbert Stothart; 102 minutes.

CAST:

Peggy O'Neal Eaton, Joan Crawford; *Bow Timberlake,* Robert Taylor; *Andrew Jackson,* Lionel Barrymore; *John Randolph,* Melvin Douglas; *Roderick "Rowdy" Dow,* James Stewart; *John Eaton,* Franchot

With Melville Cooper.

Tone; *Sunderland,* Louis Calhern; *Mrs. Beall,* Alison Skipworth; *Rachel Jackson,* Beulah Bondi; *Cuthbert,* Melville Cooper; *Lady Vaughn,* Edith Atwater; *Daniel Webster,* Sidney Toler; *Major O'Neal,* Gene Lockhart; *Emily Donaldson,* Phoebe Foster; *Louisa Abbott,* Clara Blandick; *John C. Calhoun,* Frank Conroy; *Maybelle,* Nydia Westman; *Aunt Sukey,* Louise Beavers; *Martin Van Buren,* Charles Trowbridge; *Secretary Ingram,* Willard Robertson. Peggy O'Neal, an innkeeper's daughter, was something of a courtesan in Washington during the presidency of Andrew Jackson. She was said to have had many lovers and her friendship with Jackson put the President in the line of gossip. That she was an advocate of women's suffrage made her even more controversial. In 1936 Samuel Hopkins Adams's novel about O'Neal was filmed with Joan Crawford in the flamboyant role, but unhappily devoid of true flamboyance. *The Gorgeous Hussy* might better be made today, allowing the greater candor, but the somewhat antiseptic 1936 version left audiences wondering just what it was about O'Neal that qualified her as a hussy. The gorgeousness applied more to the costumes created for Crawford by Adrian than to Crawford herself, who was always too modern to be credible in costume pictures. The same

With Joan Crawford.

With Leyland Hodgson, Willard Robertson, Frank
Conroy and Charles Trowbridge.

might be said of young James Stewart, who received sixth billing as one of the lovers and simply faked his way through the silly role.

The story centers on O'Neal's love affairs with several prominent politicians, particularly Senator John Randolph (Melvyn Douglas), who rejects her. On the rebound, she marries a handsome naval lieutenant (Robert Taylor), but he is soon killed in action and then she takes up with cabinet minister John Eaton (Franchot Tone). They marry and Peggy rises through the ranks of Washington society, despised by some and admired by others. Among the admirers is a dashing young blade known as "Rowdy" Dow (Stewart). She likes him but allows him only limited access. She has other problems, especially when it is whispered that her friendship with the President is more than a friendship. Her liberal ideas cause the gossip to become bitter and she is made the subject of political intrigue. To put an end to it Jackson orders an official inquiry into the charges, resulting in Peggy's exoneration and the dismissal of a number of cabinet members. Then, in order not to further embarrass the President, she leaves Washington, to be fondly remembered by her admirers, including "Rowdy" Dow.

The most that can be said for Stewart in *The Gorgeous Hussy* is that he did his best with an impossible part. As an ambling aristocrat, with elegant tailoring, waved hair and long sideburns, Stewart might have thought he was back at Princeton doing a play for the Triangle Club. However, he barely had time to ponder this costumed folly. *Hussy* was but one of eight movies in which he appeared in 1936 and a much bigger and more rewarding role was in preparation even as he pulled off the fake sideburns.

BORN TO DANCE

MGM, 1936

Produced by Jack Cummings; *Directed* by Roy Del Ruth; *Written* by Jack McGowan, Sid Silvers and B. G. De Sylva; *Photographed* by Ray June; *Songs* by Cole Porter; *Music Director*: Alfred Newman; 108 minutes.

CAST:

Nora Paige, Eleanor Powell; *Ted Barker*, James Stewart; *Lucy James*, Virginia Bruce; *Jenny Saks*, Una Merkel; *Gunny Saks*, Sid Silvers; *Peppy Turner*, Frances Langford; *Capt. Percival Dingby*, Raymond Walburn; *James McKay*, Alan Dinehart; *Mush Tracy*, Buddy Ebsen; *Sally Saks*, Juanita Quigley; *George and Jalna*, Themselves; *Policeman*, Reginald Gardiner.

MGM followed up the success of Eleanor Powell's *The Broadway Melody of 1936* with *Born to Dance*, which title seemed about as neat a comment on the fabulous tapper as could be made. For the leading man they assigned James Stewart, giving him the distinction of being the man who introduced the Cole Porter classic, "Easy to Love," which he pleasantly croak-crooned to Powell. The fact that Stewart was given the role was due to none other than Porter himself, who helped set up the film at MGM. In his diary entry for April 24, 1936, Porter noted his notion of Stewart as leading man and getting MGM approval, provided the actor could sing: "The next day Stewart came over to the house and I heard him sing. He sings far from well, although he has some nice notes in his voice, but he could play the part perfectly." The part was that of US Navy petty officer Ted Barker.

Like all movie musicals of the period, the plot of *Born to Dance* is paper thin. The film begins with

With Raymond Walburn.

With Eleanor Powell.

With Frances Langford, Buddy Ebsen, Eleanor Powell, Una Merkel and Sid Silvers.

a submarine arriving in New York harbor and the crew, Barker included, singing "Rollin' Home." Ted and his chums Gunny (Sid Silvers) and Mush (Buddy Ebsen) proceed to the Lonely Hearts Club, where newly arrived Nora Paige (Powell) impresses everyone wth her "Rap Tap on Wood" number. Ted is immediately smitten with Nora and they are soon dancing and singing "Hey, Babe, Hey," a waltz clog, in which everybody joins in. Complications develop for the lovers when Broadway star Lucy James (Virginia Bruce) pays a visit to the submarine for publicity purposes, with her manager (Alan Dinehart) concocting a romance between her and Ted. Nora is hired as Lucy's understudy for the Broadway musical in preparation, but Lucy takes a dislike to the dancer when she realizes how good she is. Lucy objects to her manager's publicity romance and walks out when she sees a newspaper headline announcing her engagement to Ted—a trick engineered by Ted himself, so that Nora can take over Lucy's role and be a smash hit. The finale is the epic battleship-setting "Swingin' the Jinx Away," after which the lovers fall into each other's arms.

Born to Dance is an Eleanor Powell vehicle all the way, a lighthearted and heady piece of entertainment for Depression-emerging audiences. Stewart made a charming leading man for Powell, joining her in a few dance steps and doing quite well. His big number, "Easy to Love," was crooned to her in a park. It was at first dubbed by a professional singer but the result was unconvincing and MGM decided, with Cole Porter's encouragement, to let Stewart sing the song himself. It was a wise choice because his delivery of the song is appealing. Stewart has always been somewhat self-deprecating about his vocalizing in *Born to Dance*, but he has no need to be. There has been a lot worse singing in the movies than this.

AFTER THE THIN MAN

MGM, 1936

Produced by Hunt Stromberg; *Directed* by W. S. Van Dyke; *Written* by Frances Goodrich and Albert Hackett, based on a story by Dashiell Hammett; *Photographed* by Oliver T. Marsh; *Music* by Herbert Stothart; 110 minutes.

CAST:

Nora Charles, Myrna Loy; *Nick Charles*, William Powell; *David Graham*, James Stewart; *Dancer*, Joseph Calleia; *Selma Landis*, Elissa Landi; *Aunt Katherine*, Jessie Ralph; *Robert Landis*, Alan Marshall; *Lt. Abrams*, Sam Levene; *Polly Byrnes*, Dorothy McNulty (later Penny Singleton); *Charlotte*, Dorothy Vaughn; *Helen*, Maude Turner Gordon; *Floyd Casper*, Teddy Hart; *Lum Kee*, William Law; *General*, William Burress; *William*, Thomas Pogue; *Dr. Adolph Kammer*, George Zucco; *Henry*, Tom Ricketts; *Phil Byrnes*, Paul Fix.

William Powell and Myrna Loy appeared together in fourteen films, but it is the six in which they played Nick and Nora Charles in the *Thin Man* stories of Dashiell Hammett that give them their enduring identity as a film team. In 1934 MGM scored a hit with *The Thin Man* but they waited two years before doing a sequel, which turned out to be even more popular than the original. *After the Thin Man* was given increased production values, allowing the dapper Powell and elegantly feisty Loy to be even more at ease as the diletante detectives, solving crimes while enjoying life among the elite society. It occurred to MGM that giving James Stewart third billing in this adventure of Nick and Nora would help build his image and growing popularity. It was a dubious decision and a film that Stewart looks back on with mixed feelings.

The film begins with Nick and Nora arriving back in San Francisco after a trip to New York, vowing not to be involved with detection for a while and yet being immediately drawn into a family investigation. Nora's cousin Selma Landis (Elissa Landi) begs them for help in locating her missing husband Robert (Alan Marshall). Nick finds this irresponsible playboy in a night club, where he has been having an affair with a singer, Polly Byrnes (Penny Singleton, then using the name Dorothy McNulty). David Graham (Stewart), a young gentleman of the social set, gives Robert $25,000 to get out of town because David himself is in love with Selma and wishes to marry her. As Robert is about to take the offer and leave, he is shot and killed. This confuses Selma, since she would like to kill Robert herself. She is further confused when she learns how many other people had the same thing in mind,

With William Powell, Myrna Loy, Elissa Landi and
Sam Levene.

With Sam Levene and Dick Rush

With Robert E. O'Connor.

With George Zucco (wearing glasses) and (at right)
Sam Levene and Joseph Calleia.

including Polly and the owner of the night club, Dancer (Joseph Calleia), who was set to blackmail Robert and then kill him. In the course of tracking the killer three other people lose their lives. Finally Nick gathers all the suspects together and unravels the puzzle, pointing the finger at the murderer: David. The seemingly affable David is really off his rocker, having been driven to this state by his bitterness at being rejected by Selma and by a desire to take revenge, first killing Robert and then the others to confuse the issue and protect himself.

Any mention of *After the Thin Man* has Stewart shaking his head. It was wonderful, of course, to be involved with Powell and Loy in such a popular picture, but the role was beyond him at this point in his career. Even at this junction his image had been set as a nice young fellow, especially after *Born to Dance,* and to suddenly crop up as a deranged killer...no, it was a mistake. The final scene, in which Stewart is fingered as the villain and then pulls a gun before being overpowered, is one that causes Stewart to shudder. "I was ludicrous, I think people must have burst out laughing."

SEVENTH HEAVEN

20TH CENTURY-FOX, 1937

Produced by Darryl F. Zanuck; *Directed* by Henry King; *Written* by Melville Baker, based on the play by Austin Strong; *Photographed* by Merritt Gerstad; *Music* by Louis Silvers; 102 minutes.

CAST:

Diane, Simone Simon; *Chico,* James Stewart; *Nana,* Gale Sondergaard; *Boul,* Gregory Ratoff; *Father Chevillon,* Jean Hersholt; *Aristide,* J. Edward Bromberg; *Gobin,* Victor Kilian; *Sewer Rat,* John Qualen; *Marie,* Mady Christians; *Brissac,* Thomas Beck; *Durand,* Sig Rumann; *Madame Frisson,* Rafaela Ottiano; *Sergeant Gendarme,* Georges Renavent.

With Simone Simon.

With John Qualen.

With John Qualen, Jean Hersholt and player.

With Simone Simon and player.

Nineteen thirty-six had been an incredible year for James Stewart. He had appeared in eight films, in a variety of parts with many of the top players of the time. It was the kind of apprenticeship every actor craves for but rarely gets, certainly not in the Hollywood of today. Now, after just two years in the picture business, his was a respected and reliable name. He had played some small, supporting roles, but from here on it would be star billing for Stewart, and if other studios wanted him for leading roles, MGM would be willing to negotiate. In late 1936, 20th Century-Fox asked MGM for Stewart for their re-make of *Seventh Heaven*. It might have been better had Stewart's home studio declined.

In 1927 Fox had scored a smash hit with the teaming of Janet Gaynor and Charles Farrell in their filming of the 1922 play *Seventh Heaven*. It was a silent film, except for the music score and its theme song, "Diane," which became one of the most popular pieces of music written for the silent screen. Had the Gaynor-Farrell version been a talkie, it is doubtful if it would have been as successful because it is a love story of the most fanciful kind. If audiences had heard banal dialogue and the American voice of Farrell they might well have been put off. This became the problem with the re-make. No matter

how much sincerity Stewart put into the role of Chico, a Parisian sewer worker, he could not be credible. It was even hard for his deliciously French co-star Simone Simon to be believable as Diane, the prostitute waif he takes off the street and into his garret.

The story is set in Paris before the First World War. Chico has been disillusioned in love and he is also an atheist. Diane is thrown out of a brothel and is destitute until she meets Chico. He takes her out of compassion, and despite his rejection of love he finds himself gradually drawn to the sweet, loving nature of the girl. With the help of kindly Father Chevillon (Jean Hersholt), the two are persuaded to marry. But war breaks out and Chico joins up before a ceremony can be set. The lovers swear their loyalty to each other and Chico goes off to battle. Diane waits for four years, and, even though she is told Chico has been killed, she never gives up hope. He comes back, but he is blind, which makes little difference to the adoring Diane in the garret they call their seventh heaven.

This *Seventh Heaven* failed to please either critics or public. Fine sets, an interesting range of character actors and film direction by the veteran Henry King could do little to disguise the problem—the story was absurdly dated and unplayable, especially for an actor as essentially American as James Stewart.

48

THE LAST GANGSTER

MGM, 1937

Produced by J. J. Cohn; *Directed* by Edward Lustig; *Written* by John Lee Mahin, based on a story by William A. Wellman and Robert Carson; *Photographed* by William Daniels; *Music* by Edward Ward; 81 minutes.

With Rose Stradner.

CAST:

Joe Krozak, Edward G. Robinson; *Paul North, Sr.*, James Stewart; *Talya Krozak*, Rose Stradner; *Curly*, Lionel Stander; *Paul North, Jr.*, Douglas Scott; *Casper*, John Carradine; *Editor*, Sydney Blackmer; *Fats Garvey*, Edward Brophy; *Acey Kile*, Alan Baxter; *Warden*, Grant Mitchell; *Corman*, Frank Conroy; *Shea*, Morini Olsen; *Wilson*, Iavn Miller; *Borderick*, Willard Robertson; *Gloria*, Louise Beavers; *Billy Ernst*, Donald Barry; *Bottles Bailey*, Ben Welden; *Limpy*, Horace McMahon; *Brockett*, Edward Pawley.

It is ironic that Edward G. Robinson gained so much film identity for his playing of gangsters. In person he was among Hollywood's most cultured gentlemen

With Rose Stradner and Sidney Blackmer.

With Edward G. Robinson, Douglas Scott and Rose Stradner.

and one of its leading art collectors. He disarmed his critics by claiming that he needed to support his "habit." This was surely his reason for accepting an offer from MGM to play a vicious hood in *The Last Gangster*, causing him to take time off from his cinematic law breaking at the Warner Bros. studios in Burbank. Since the screenplay also called for the secondary role of an upright newspaperman, MGM needed no great wisdom to decide to hand the script to James Stewart.

The plot: Joe Krozac (Robinson) is a crook of slavic background who returns to his native land with the purpose of getting a wife. He picks Talya (Rose Stradner) and takes her back to the States. At about the time their son is born, Krozac runs afoul of the law and, on a charge of evading income tax, he is sent to Alcatraz. Once he is behind bars his former associates let his naive wife know what a thug he is— she has had no knowledge of his business—and when she visits him in jail he confirms the information. He married her only to get a son, whom he hopes will grow up to be a racketeer like him. She decides to desert him, change her name and seek some obscure place to live. Part of the decision is due to the trick of a brash young San Francisco newspaperman, Paul North (Stewart), who has printed a photo of her baby with a gun in its lap.

North becomes sympathetic when he gets to know Talya and learns her story. He falls in love with her and, once she gets a divorce, marries her and moves to Boston, there accepting a job as a newspaper editor. After ten years Krozac is released and he heads east to reclaim his son. His former colleagues want to know the whereabouts of the treasure Krozac stashed away before he went to jail. He refuses to tell them, so they kidnap his son (Douglas Scott) and beat the boy in front of him. This causes Krozac to change his mind about his son and the future he had planned. He realizes it is better that he consider North his father and grow up in the good and normal life North and Talya can offer him. Having made that decision Krozac now tackles his vengeful rivals and dies in battle with them, making sure to kill the one who could reveal the identity of his son.

While far from his triumph as *Little Caesar*, Robinson's Joe Krozac is a convincing portrayal of a vicious hood with a modicum of residual decency. Viennese actress Rose Stradner was brought to America for the film but despite a solid performance it did not result in an American film career for her. For Stewart it was one more opportunity to play a good-hearted citizen, although playing it with a false

moustache that did not suit him in the least. It would be thirty-four years before he again wore one on the screen—a real one in *Fools' Parade*.

NAVY BLUE AND GOLD

MGM, 1937

Produced by Sam Zimbalist; *Directed* by Sam Wood; *Written* by George Bruce, based on his novel; *Photographed* by John Seitz; *Music* by Edward Ward; 94 minutes.

CAST:

Roger Ash, Robert Young; *Truck Cross*, James Stewart; *Captain "Skinny" Dawes*, Lionel Barrymore; *Patricia Gates*, Florence Rice; *Mrs. Gates*, Billie Burke; *Richard Gates, Jr.*, Tom Brown; *Richard Gates, Sr.*, Samuel S. Hinds; *Tommy Milton*, Paul Kelly; *Weeks*, Frank Albertson; *Graves*, Barnett Parker; *Lt. Milburn*, Minor Watson; *Superintendent*, Robert Middlemass; *Kelly*, Philip Terry; *Commander Carter*, Charles Waldron.

One of the side benefits of being a film actor is the opportunity to live out fantasies. As a boy James Stewart thought about attending the United States Naval Academy at Annapolis but decided instead on Princeton. However, in 1937 he did become a naval cadet at the academy—in MGM's *Navy Blue and Gold*, and on the very best of terms. As an actor he could be part of the glory for just a few weeks and then go on to something else.

In 1937 movies about the armed forces, especially those about West Point and Annapolis, stressed patriotism pure and simple. This one certainly does. It tells the tale of three midshipmen, all of them crack football players. Richard Gates, Jr. (Tom Brown) is a New York socialite, Roger Ash (Robert Young) is an ambitious, calculating cadet, and Truck Gross (Stewart) is a former enlisted man, whose father was once a top football-playing Annapolis man until he was dishonorably discharged. Truck himself runs afoul of the Academy when, during a lecture in which he hears his father malign-

During a break with Florence Rice and Robert Young.

With Robert Young.   *With Florence Rice.*

ed, he breaks out in anger and claims that it is all lies. He is suspended at the time of the big Army-Navy game but because of the honesty of his confession of family background Truck is reinstated and helps Annapolis win the game. One of the big reasons for the middies to win the game is to pay honor to the Academy's beloved patriarch Captain Skinny Dawes (Lionel Barrymore), and since Truck was the one who scored the winning point he is allowed to ring the victory bell.

Navy Blue and Gold was a well-aimed picture and almost defied criticism, being both a tribute to the Naval Academy and a football epic. Romance was supplied in the form of Florence Rice as the sister of the socialite cadet, romanced by cadet Ash, who is turned into a better man because of the romance, and Barrymore was on hand to represent tradition. Veteran director Sam Wood milked the Army-Navy game for all it was worth, although the most interesting part of the film is the opening sequence, in which the three new cadets are introduced to academy life and the viewer gets to see how the venerable institution functions.

The film was a winner for Stewart, who played an upstanding young fellow who overcomes a difficult background and proves himself fully qualified to be an officer and a gentleman. The New York *Herald Tribune*, seemingly always ready to root for the actor, claimed it was an engaging performance. "If *Navy Blue and Gold* is not the most beguiling service-college picture yet filmed, it is not Mr. Stewart's fault." It went on to say it was the kind of work that should be seen more often on the screen. "Although he has been denied Robert Young's beauty and has been endowed with none of the strong, silent intensity of Gary Cooper, he breathes life into his character to hold a formulized theme to a strict pattern. It is due to his expert rendition of a rather preposterous part that a rather preposterous show becomes generally exciting."

With Florence Rice.

54

OF HUMAN HEARTS

MGM, 1938

Produced by John W. Considine, Jr.; *Directed* by Clarence Brown; *Written* by Bradbury Foote, based on the story "Benefits Forgot," by Honore Morrow; *Photographed* by Clyde Devinna; *Music* by Herbert Stothart; 100 minutes.

CAST:

Ethan Wilkins, Walter Huston; *Jason Wilkins,* James Stewart; *Mary Wilkins,* Beulah Bondi; *George Ames,*

With *Charles Coburn, Beulah Bondi and Ann Rutherford.*

Guy Kibbee; *Dr. Charles Shingle,* Charles Coburn; *President Lincoln,* John Carradine; *Annie Hawks,* Ann Rutherford; *Mr. Meeker,* Charley Grapewin; *Quid,* Gene Lockhart; *Sister Clarke,* Leona Roberts; *Mr. Inchpin,* Arthur Aylesworth; *Elder Massey,* Clem Bevans; *Jason at 12,* Gene Reynolds; *Annie at 10,* Leatrice Joy Gilbert.

Of Human Hearts was James Stewart's first major piece of Americana, his first serious foray into the nature of the American spirit. This story of frontier life in a village on the banks of the Ohio River in the days preceding and during the Civil War was a pet project of director Clarence Brown. He had long admired Honore Morrow's book *Benefits Forgot,* published twenty years previously, but MGM had resisted the story because it dealt with the Civil War, which had never been a commercially viable movie subject. Once the screenplay was approved, Brown conducted a radio contest to come up with a film title and a prize of $5000 was awarded to a high

With Walter Huston.

With John Carradine.

With Beulah Bondi.

school student in South Carolina, Ray Harris, for *Of Human Hearts*. Since this was a story about a mother's sacrifices for an ungrateful son, MGM thought they now had something with which to work. Stewart was given the part of the son and Beulah Bondi, who would play his mother in several more films, drew the role of the tender-hearted lady. Top billing went to Walter Huston as the father, a stern, uncomprimising and not very kindly minister.

Ethan Wilkins (Huston) arrives in a village of bigots and narrow-minded people with his wife, Mary (Bondi) and his 12-year-old son, Jason (Gene Reynolds). He finds his salary is less than promised and that his family is begrudgingly given food and cast-off clothing. The minister and his long-suffering wife accept all this as part of the humility they practice, but the son rebels against the meanness and the petty tyranny of the community, and despises his father's willingness to tolerate it. The father and the son are at loggerheads, with the boy constantly being whipped by his father.

When Jason becomes a young man (Stewart) he continues the conflict, and the relationship with the father becomes a feud. With the help of his mother, who sells whatever possessions she has in order to finance him, Jason leaves for Baltimore to study medicine. In time he becomes a surgeon and with the outbreak of the war he joins the Union Army in that capacity, eventually rising to be the head of medical staff in an army corps. He does not, however, communicate with his mother, and therefore does not know of the death of his father. The mother writes to President Abraham Lincoln (John Carradine) to find out whether her son is alive or not. After finding out that he is indeed alive, the President calls Jason into his office and lectures him about his filial ingratitude. Jason realizes the truth of what Lincoln has told him and he goes to see his mother.

Although somewhat too slowly paced, *Of Human Hearts* stands up as a good evocation of period, with remarkable performances by Huston as the zealous preacher and Bondi as his gentle soul of a wife. The film also did a great deal for Stewart. This was his first crack at a fully developed dramatic characterization, and its success made it obvious that he was an actor with a definite future.

With Ginger Rogers.

VIVACIOUS LADY

RKO, 1938

Produced and *directed* by George Stevens; *Written* by P. J. Wolfson and Ernest Pagano, based on the story by I. A. R. Wylie; *Photographed* by Robert de Grasse; *Music* by Roy Webb; 92 minutes.

CAST:

Francey Brent, Ginger Rogers; *Peter Morgan,* James Stewart, *Keith Morgan,* James Ellison; *Martha Morgan,* Beulah Bondi; *Peter Morgan, Sr.,* Charles Coburn; *Helen,* Frances Mercer; *Jenny,* Phyllis Kennedy; *Apartment Manager,* Franklin Pangborn; *Culpepper,* Grady Sutton; *Charlie,* Jack Carson; *Joseph,* Alec Craig; *Miss Barton,* June Johnson; *Porter,* Willie Best.

With Alan Curtis, James Ellison and Ginger Rogers.

By the time she made *Vivacious Lady* at RKO in early 1938, Ginger Rogers had already appeared in six films with Fred Astaire, an enviable success but one which left her with a desire to prove herself as an actress rather than as a dancer. *Vivacious Lady* proved that she was an actress with a gift for light comedy and that the actor RKO had borrowed from MGM to play opposite her also was similarly gifted. In fact, *The New York Times* referred to James Stewart's work in this film as a "priceless bit of casting." His role is that of a shy associate professor of botany, dominated by a shrewd mother—Beulah Bondi once again but vastly different from the mother in *Of Human Hearts*. This is a mother who feigns a weak heart, mostly as a device to get her way. Since her husband (Charles Coburn) is the president of the college at which their son is employed, this mother has a lot of sway.

Peter Morgan (Stewart) goes to New York to try to persuade his brother Keith (James Ellison) to give up his playboyish ways, many which seem to center around a night club. At the club Peter meets an entertainer, Francey (Rogers), and the two immediately fall in love. After a whirlwind courtship they get married. Everything is wonderful until Peter gives thought to how he will break the news to his stuffy parents in the world of academe. It is assumed that Peter will himself one day be the president of the college—but will he be, with a vivacious, blonde show girl as his wife?

Brother Keith assumes responsibility for Francey when it becomes apparent that Peter hasn't the heart to tell the truth to his peremptory father and snobbish mother. This creates a problem for the newlyweds in trying to spend time together, especially since his parents assume that their son is engaged to Helen (Frances Mercer). Another problem is the excitement stirred up by the glamorous Francey among the male students. After a goodly number of comic complications, Peter finds the courage to tell his parents that Francey is not only his wife but a lady who will be a credit to him in his academic life.

A great deal of the success of the film is due to the sly humor of George Stevens' direction. He was a master of inuendo. He had been responsible for one of the best Astaire-Rogers musicals, *Swing Time,* and he clearly knew how to use Rogers' comic ability. With *Vivacious Lady* he also had a pair of brilliant players in Charles Coburn and Beulah Bondi, with Bondi being unwittingly hilarious in trying to dance the Big Apple. With Stewart, Stevens also had someone with a blossoming sense of comedy. Here he is expert as the repressed, diffident pedagogue who finally summons up the courage to break loose from his constraints. Stewart's own life in academe no doubt helped him shape the character, and like any good actor he mined his own persona. The critic for the *New Republic* made a good point: "I've liked James Stewart's face since the first time I saw it; it wears well and gets better, and probably because he has in himself the true qualities he must describe."

THE SHOPWORN ANGEL

MGM, 1938

Produced by Joseph L. Mankiewicz; *Directed* by H. C. Potter; *Written* by Waldo Salt, based on the story "Private Pettigrew's Girl," by Dana Burnett; *Photographed* by Joseph Ruttenberg; *Music* by Edward Ward; 85 minutes.

With Margaret Sullavan.

CAST:

Daisy Heath, Margaret Sullavan; *Bill Pettigrew*, James Stewart; *Sam Bailey*, Walter Pidgeon; *Dice*, Net Pendleton; *Thin Lips*, Alan Curtis; *Leer*, Sam Levene; *Martha*, Hattie McDaniel; *Wilson*, Charley Grapewin; *Mr. Gonigle*, Charles D. Brown; *Elevator Boy*, Jimmy Butler; *Sally*, Eleanor Lynn; *Minister*, William Stack; *Jack*, Hudson Shotwell; *Speaker*, John Merton; *Bellboy*, Wesley Giraud; *Eddy*, Harry Tyler.

For his second film with Margaret Sullavan, James Stewart had no need to be loaned to another studio. Her agent husband, Leland Hayward, had negotiated a contract with MGM, which would result in her making six films at that studio, the first of which was *Three Comrades*, released in early 1938. Immediately afterwards Stewart was assigned as her co-star in *The Shopworn Angel*, which Paramount had filmed in

With Margaret Sullavan and Walter Pidgeon.

With Walter Pidgeon, Margaret Sullavan and William Stack.

On the set with Sullavan.

she is indeed his girl. She also finds it impossible to turn down his proposal, and shortly before he sails overseas they are married.

Daisy marries Bill with the rationale that it will help him get through his service in Europe and that she will dissolve the relationship when he returns. But she finds the correspondence with him a source of strength and an affirmation of human values that have not previously been much a part of her thinking. Bailey, himself showing some sense of understanding, allows the marriage on the grounds that it will end with Bill's return. However, fate makes the decision easy for both Daisy and Bailey with the news that Bill has been killed in action. Bailey comforts her as he realizes that the young soldier has taught him something about love.

The sentimental nature of Dana Burnett's story, "Private Pettigrew's Girl," needed a lot of shoring up for 1938 audiences. The veteran scenarist Waldo Salt was able to give it some substance, although it remains, especially today, highly sentimental stuff. It is doubtful if the film would have been a success had it not been for the playing of Sullavan and Stewart. There was a chemistry between them that is hard to explain. Perhaps it was the result of their own friendship and their understanding of each other. Sullavan had a wistful and appealing aura and the ability to show the feminine side of a woman like Daisy, whom life has made a little hard. Vulnerability was Sullavan's forte. And Stewart, after only two years in the movies, had already mastered the art of appearing to be natural and ordinary. In fact it was with *The Shopworn Angel* that the image of folksy Jimmy Stewart solidified. His Bill Pettigrew is the all-American innocent, slightly fumbling of manner and drawling of speech. It is difficult not to refer to the performance in terms of apple pie because one of the most effective scenes in the film centers around apple pie. At a trip to Coney Island, Bill tells Daisy that she is exactly the kind of girl he wants, her and no other. He can only explain it in terms of the kind of pie his mother used to make. It was the best, and if pie isn't just like his mother's, he doesn't want it. Same with Daisy, it's her or no one.

In his review for the New York *Herald-Tribune*, Howard Barnes pointed out that it was the authority of the two performances that made the film bearable. He felt that Sullavan invested her scenes with an eloquence of expression and that Stewart made the characterization solid, even though the script was not really much to work with. "Unless I am mistaken, *The Shopworn Angel* boasts two of the finest actors appearing on the screen today," he concluded.

1928 with Gary Cooper and Nancy Carroll. Like *Next Time We Love*, this Sullavan-Stewart picture would also be a weepy kind of sad romance, and once again Stewart would have to die.

The setting is New York in 1917 just after America's entry into the World War, when a rather glib actress, Daisy Heath (Sullavan), almost knocks over a young soldier, Bill Pettigrew (Stewart). She finds this young farmer from Texas refreshingly different from any man she has ever known. He is wide-eyed with wonder at her being an actress and he is decency personified. He soon falls deeply in love with her, but she fails to tell him that she is the mistress of a producer, Sam Bailey (Walter Pidgeon). Bill wants to marry Daisy and, so as not to embarrass him in front of his soldier buddies, she allows that

YOU CAN'T TAKE IT WITH YOU

COLUMBIA, 1938

Produced and *Directed* by Frank Capra; *Written* by Robert Riskin, based on the play by George S. Kaufman and Moss Hart; *Photographed* by Joseph Walker; *Music* by Dimitri Tiomkin; 127 minutes.

CAST:

Alice Sycamore, Jean Arthur; *Martin Vanderhoff*, Lionel Barrymore; *Tony Kirby*, James Stewart; *Anthony P. Kirby*, Edward Arnold; *Kolenkhov*, Mischa Auer; *Essie Carmichael*, Ann Miller; *Penny Syc-*

With Jean Arthur.

amore, Spring Byington; *Paul Sycamore*, Samuel S. Hinds; *Poppins*, Donald Meek; *Ramsey*, H. B. Warner; *DePinna*, Halliwell Hobbs; *Ed Carmichael*, Dub Taylor; *Mrs. Anthony Kirby*, Mary Forbes; *Rheba*, Lillian Yarbo; *Donald*, Eddie Anderson; *John Blakeley*, Clarence Wilson; *Professor*, Joseph Swickard; *Maggie O'Neill*, Ann Doran; *Schmidt*, Christian Rub; *Mrs. Schmidt*, Bodil Rosing; *Henderson*, Charles Lane; *Judge*, Harry Davenport.

In casting *You Can't Take It With You* Frank Capra needed a particular kind of leading man, one who fitted his concept of an idealized America. He says, "I had seen Jimmy Stewart play a sensitive, heart-grabbing role in MGM's *Navy Blue and Gold*. I sensed the character and rock-ribbed honesty of a Gary Cooper, plus the breeding and intelligence of an ivy league idealist." It was an astute judgment and one that would lead Stewart to two of his most acclaimed films—*Mr. Smith Goes to Washington* and *It's a Wonderful Life*, both of them Capra master-pieces. In projecting images of ideal male Americana, Capra never found two more perfect specimens than Stewart and Gary Cooper.

With Russell Hicks, Eddie Cane, Pierre Watkin, Byron Foulger, Edward Arnold and Ian Wolfe.

With Ann Miller, Jean Arthur and Mischa Auer.

With Edward Arnold and Lionel Barrymore.

Capra persuaded the frugal chieftain of Columbia Pictures, Harry Cohn, to pay $200,000 for the film rights to the Pulitzer-winning play by George S. Kaufman and Moss Hart and to borrow Stewart from MGM, convincing Cohn that no other actor was right for the part. Once again MGM allowed another studio to help develop the career of one of their players, although never paying him any more than his regular MGM salary. MGM, on the other hand, made a profit on the deal, as did all studios in this kind of negotiating. Stewart also profited, by exposure in a hit movie and one which helped mould his image as a charmingly bumbling, slightly awkward, diffident but unquestionably decent young American. And as Capra suspected, he was perfect as a rich man's son in love with the daughter of a lovable eccentric.

The setting of the film is the home of the wacky Vanderhof family, presided over by Grandpa (Lionel Barrymore), a cheerful, retired businessman who decided long ago that money is something that can't be taken with you when you go, so spend it and enjoy life to the fullest. For Grandpa this involves having his house packed with friends, no matter how daffy they might be. The immediate family includes his daughter Penny (Spring Byington), who writes plays, her husband Paul (Samuel S. Hinds), who makes fireworks in the basement, and Penny's daughter Essie (Ann Miller), who floats around the house doing ballet, under the guidance of resident Russian choreographer Kolenkhov (Mischa Auer). Essie's sister Alice (Jean Arthur), falls in love with Tony (Stewart), the son of a business tycoon, Anthony P. Kirby (Edward Arnold). Alice invites the snobbish Kirby parents to dinner and they are horrified by the antics and the strange characters.

After the chaotic dinner the Kirbys make to leave the house but as they do so a pair of federal agents arrive to investigate the complaints about explosions in the cellar. The confusion is so overwhelming that the agents decide to arrest everyone and haul them off to jail, including the stunned

Kirbys. A sympathetic judge allows them all to leave without punishment but not without a lecture on public behavior. Alice, embarrassed by her crazy family, decides to leave home and a slightly subdued Grandpa agrees to sell his home to Kirby, who has wanted it all along as part of a large real estate concept. Kirby offers Tony the presidency of one of his firms but Tony, much in love with Alice and understanding of her affectionate family, turns against his father and refuses the job. He favors eccentricity rather than ruthlessness. The decision helps Kirby see things in a new light and he decides to let the Vanderhofs keep their home, resulting in Alice's returning and accepting Tony's proposal. All's well that ends well, and as the family, with the Kirbys, sit down for another dinner, Grandpa speaks directly to God: "Well, Sir, here we go again."

You Can't Take It With You, either as film or play, is a much-dated piece of Americana, a product of the thirties with no relationship to contemporary life. It is enjoyable only with that realization. Capra's work was well rewarded, being selected for an Oscar as Best Film of 1938, with another one going to Capra as Best Director. Robert Riskin's screenplay is basically the same as the stage play but with slightly more emphasis on the uninhibited, carefree nature of the Vanderhofs and on Grandpa's edict that the only thing you can take with you is the love of your friends. Capra and Riskin decided to add a character to the original, that of Mr. Poppins, played by an actor who seldom seemed anything less than eccentric, Donald Meek. As a maker of ingenious toys, Mr. Poppins seems well at ease among the Vanderhofs.

James Stewart could hardly have failed to benefit from exposure in such a successful and affable movie, particularly since the role of Tony Kirby was that of a young man showing some moral spine. As Capra says, "One might believe that young Stewart could reject his father's patrimony—a kingdom on Wall Street." It is, of course, this believability that is the basis for Stewart's success as an actor. And in this, his sixteenth movie, the image was well on the way to being fully formed. The critic for the *New Statesman* commented on another obvious facet of Stewart's presence on the screen, the ability to appear natural: "No actor on the screen today manages to appear more unconscious of script, camera and director than Mr. Stewart." No thirty-year-old actor could ask for higher praise than that.

With Carole Lombard

MADE FOR EACH OTHER

UNITED ARTISTS, 1939

Produced by David O. Selznick; *Directed* by John Cromwell; *Written* by Jo Swerling; *Photographed* by Leon Shamroy; *Music* by Lou Forbes; 90 minutes.

CAST:

Jane Mason, Carole Lombard; *Johnny Mason,* James Stewart; *Judge Joseph Doolittle,* Charles Coburn; *Mrs. Mason,* Lucile Watson; *Dr. Healy,* Harry Davenport; *Eunice Doolittle,* Ruth Weston; *Carter,* Donald Briggs; *Conway,* Eddie Quillan; *Annie,* Esther Dale; *Hilda,* Rene Orsell; *Lily,* Louise Beavers; *Sister Agnes,* Alma Kruger; *Doolittle's Brother,* Fred Fuller; *Messerschmidt,* Edwin Maxwell; *Hutch,* Harry Depp.

With Lucille Watson and Carole Lombard.

With Charles Coburn.

Carole Lombard was that rarest of actresses—a beautiful woman who was also funny. By 1939 she had established a reputation as something of a comedienne and it had begun to bother her. Films like *My Man Godfrey, Nothing Sacred* and *Twentieth Century* had shown how amusing and appealing she could be, but she felt the need to prove her dramatic abilities. David O. Selznick agreed with her and commissioned Jo Swerling to write an original screenplay about the problems of a young married couple. Both Selznick and Lombard felt that the perfect actor to play the husband would be James Stewart, which required another loan-out from MGM. The home studio had no objection to other

producers building up the career of one of their players.

Made for Each Other is the story of a young New York lawyer John Mason and his bride Jane. Their happiness is somewhat marred by two people. One is John's haughty widowed mother (Lucille Watson), who lives with John and who will live with the couple in their new apartment, and John's hard-of-hearing boss, Judge Doolittle (Charles Coburn), who shows little sign of emotion and almost no reaction to the news of the marriage. Just as the newlyweds are about to embark for Europe, an associate, Carter (Donald Briggs), arrives to tell John that he is urgently needed at the office to take on a case. The honeymoon trip will have to be cancelled. The obsequious Carter clearly takes some pleasure from this. Besides, with John married to Jane, he can now court the boss's daughter Eunice, which results in marriage and a posting as a partner, a position John had been expecting to fill. John works hard but luck does not seem to come his way. He is delighted when Jane gives birth to their son, but with time he finds his salary not equal to the costs of being a family man. He is shy and easygoing by nature, and Jane urges him to be more demanding. He summons up the courage to ask for a raise, but finds himself taking a cut in wages because, as the boss explains, times are difficult.

They get more difficult when their baby son falls ill and develops pneumonia. However, it is this sad turn that brings out the better characteristics of both the mother and the boss. The mother stands by Jane in her distress and asks for understanding ("I wasn't always a bitter old woman"), and the boss lends support when John explains that he must have some money in order to buy the serum necessary to save his son's life. The hospital has none of the required serum but it learns of some in a distant city. It is now the dead of winter and it is only because of the compassion of a pilot, Conway (Eddie Quillan), who is willing to fly through a snowstorm, that the child's life is saved.

With the survival of his son and the change in his employer and mother, John's life begins to change. He becomes more assertive and he lectures the boss and the partners on the need to change their methods, which results in his being made a partner. Thus, *Made for Each Other* draws to its happy, albeit highly contrived ending. Seen today it is very much a film of the Hollywood past, and without the pleasing performances of Lombard and Stewart it would have little to recommend it. Lombard's humor shines through, even though the part does not call for comedy, and by now Stewart has a firm hold on his guise as the shy but sunny, diffident but optimistic all-American that would be the bedrock of his screen persona.

The film was a modest success but not the winner Selznick had hoped for. At the initial screenings he found the audience reaction somewhat mild, due in his estimation to a lack of dramatic tension. He then shot new material of the effort to get the serum to the ailing child, making it a drawn-out sequence of aerial travail, including the pilot becoming lost in a snowstorm, parachuting with the serum tucked in his flight suit and crawling to a farmhouse, where the farmer then telephones the hospital. The sequence barely passed muster in 1939, but now it borders on the ludicrous.

THE ICE FOLLIES OF 1939

MGM, 1939

Produced by Harry Rapf; *Directed* by Reinhold Schunzel; *Written* by Leonard Praskins and Florence Ryerson; *Photographed* by Joseph Ruttenberg and Oliver T. Marsh; *Music Director:* Roger Edens; 83 minutes.

CAST:

Mary McKay, Joan Crawford; *Larry Hall*, James Stewart; *Eddie Burgess*, Lew Ayres; *Douglas Tolliver*, Lewis Stone; *Mort Hodges*, Lionel Stander; *Paul Rodney*, Truman Bradley; *Effie Lane*, Marie Blake; *Kitty Sherman*, Bess Ehrhardt; *Max Norton*, Charles Williams; *Hal Gibbs*, Eddie Conrad; *Director*, Arthur Loft; *Lady Hilda*, Mary Forbes; *Barney*, Charles Brown.

The Ice Follies of 1939 was well named. As an MGM musical it hovers around the bottom of the list. The critic for the New York *Herald Tribune* noted, "Since some kind of story was needed to lead up to the film debut of 'The International Ice Follies,' and top-flight players to give it necessary publicity gloss, Joan Crawford, James Stewart and Lew Ayres were given the unenviable job of trying to make it digestible." How digestible they made it is open to question. Crawford was not happy about the assignment and it seems apparent, and the sight of Stewart and the dignified Lew Ayres floating around on ice skates is only slightly less than risible.

The story: Mary McKay (Crawford) is an ambitious actress in love with a skater, Larry Hall (Stewart), who is himself ambitious. He wants to be a producer-director of ice shows. He, Eddie Burgess (Ayres) and Mary do an act together, but without much success. Still, Mary and Larry get married, which union goes awry when Mary gets an offer from Hollywood and Larry doesn't. She becomes a star while Larry tries to promote his idea for an Ice Follies show. Things become strained between the couple, until Mary comes to her senses and realizes she is likely to lose her husband. She asks the head of

With Joan Crawford and Lew Ayres.

her studio, Douglas Tolliver (Lewis Stone), to release her from her contract. But Tolliver is no fool. He not only doesn't want to lose his star but he has seen some of Larry's production concepts. Happy solution—Larry is hired as the director of Tolliver's movie about the Ice Follies, starring Mary.

The best thing about *The Ice Follies of 1939* is the spectacular ending, with the film suddenly turn-ing into Technicolor and revealing the artistry of such luminaries as Bess Ehrhardt, Roy Shipstad, Oscar Johnson and squads of graceful skaters performing fancy ice dances and gymnastics. But despite all that, the film did not do well at the box office amd caused Crawford to demand better treatment from MGM. She was given *The Women*, taking second billing to Norma Shearer, which helped her recover somewhat from *Ice Follies*, amd Stewart geared up to do a pleasant comedy with Claudette Colbert.

IT'S A WONDERFUL WORLD

MGM, 1939

Produced by Frank Davis; *Directed* by W. S. Van Dyke; *Written* by Ben Hecht and Herman J. Mankiewicz; *Photographed* by Oliver T. Marsh; *Music* by Edward Ward; 86 minutes.

With Ernest Truex.

CAST:

Edwina Corday, Claudette Colbert; *Guy Johnson*, James Stewart; *Captain Streeter*, Guy Kibbee; *Sergeant Koretz*, Nat Pendleton; *Vivian Tarbel*, Frances Drake; *Lieutenant Meller*, Edgar Kennedy; *Willie Heyward*, Ernest Truex; *Major Willoughby*, Richard Carle; *Dolores Gonzales*, Cecilia Callejo; *Al Mallon*, Sidney Blackmer; *Gimpy*, Andy Clyde; *Captain Haggerty*, Cliff Clark; *Madame Chambers*, Cecil Cunningham; *Herman Plotka*, Leonard Kibrick; *Stage Manager*, Hans Conried; *Bupton Peabody*, Grady Sutton.

The listing of *It's a Wonderful World* among James Stewart's films is often regarded as a mistake. Surely the reference must be to *It's a Wonderful Life*? No, *It's a Wonderful World* is an MGM comedy made in early 1939 and co-starring Stewart with Claudette Colbert. However, even without the similarity of

With Claudette Colbert.

With Edgar Kennedy, Claudette Colbert and Nat Pendleton.

title, this one seems to have slipped between the cracks. It came toward the end of Hollywood's cycle of so-called screwball comedies, a breed of picture making marked by lighthearted lunacy among the middle-to-upper classes, with characters describable in outdated terms as delightfully daffy. In movies of this kind it was acceptable for the actors and the stories to be silly. This one was. It allowed Stewart his first chance to be something of a cad, as a novice detective with shady principles and a markedly disdainful regard for women.

Guy Johnson (Stewart) decides to be a private detective and his first client is much-married, millionaire playboy Willie Heyward (Ernest Truex), whose fifth wife Vivian (Frances Drake), is up to no good. One night Guy finds Willie standing over the dead body of an ex-girlfriend, drunk and with a gun in his hand. Guy suspects Willie has been framed and hustles him away, only to be nabbed by the police. For conspiracy Guy is sentenced to a year in Sing Sing but en route he jumps from the train and makes his escape. Witness to all this is poetess Edwina Corday (Colbert), whose car Guy requisitions, along with the poetess, who is assumed to be kidnapped.

With Edwina in tow, Guy's predicaments be-come ever more involved. She falls in love with him despite his cavalier manner. Boy Scouts are among those sent out to find the missing poetess. Guy captures one of the leaders and appropriates his clothing and dark glasses, and then pretends to be an Englishman Edwina has married. To further escape detection Guy gets caught up with a theatrical company and plays a Southerner in a show. During the performance an actor is murdered but it turns out he is a substitute for an actor being held at an auto camp, an actor who knows how Willie was framed. Edwina invents a wild story that leads the police to the auto camp, and the case is solved. Guy decides to give up being a sleuth and with his $100,000 fee from Willie he sets out for a life, probably wacky, with the unpredictable poetess.

With such a plot *It's a Wonderful World* can only be regarded as Hollywood hokum, circa 1939, and it is a fair assumption that MGM made a fair profit. Briskly paced by old reliable W. S. Van Dyke, the picture skims along with its improbable gags. It pleased Colbert fans, who expected this kind of thing from the delightful actress, but Stewart fans may have been a little disturbed to find him playing a woman hater, who at one point socks Colbert on the jaw. But any misgivings on their part were soon to be swept away by the upcoming classic film and classic Stewart performance.

MR. SMITH GOES TO WASHINGTON

COLUMBIA, 1939

Produced and *Directed* by Frank Capra; *Written* by Sidney Buchman, based on the story by Lewis R. Foster; *Photographed* by Joseph Walker; *Music* by Dimitri Tiomkin; 125 minutes

CAST:

Clarissa Saunders, Jean Arthur; *Jefferson Smith*, James Stewart; *Senator Joseph Paine*, Claude Rains; *Jim Taylor*, Edward Arnold; *Governor Hubert Hopper*, Guy Kibbee; *Siz Moore*, Thomas Mitchell; *Chick McGann*, Eugene Pallette; *Ma Smith*, Beulah Bondi; *Senator Agnew*, H. B. Warner; *Senate President*, Harry Carey; *Susan Paine*, Astrid Allwyn; *Emma Hopper*, Ruth Donnelly; *Senator McPherson*, Grant Mitchell; *Senator Monroe*, Porter Hall; *Senator Barnes*, Pierre Watkins; *Nosey*, Charles Lane; *Bill Griffith*, William Demarest; *Carl Cook*, Dick Elliott.

With Jean Arthur.

The bone-tired young senator croaks and staggers after hours of filibustering on the floor of the Senate, "You think I'm licked. You all think I'm licked. Well, I'm not licked and I'm going to stay right here and fight for this lost cause even if this room gets filled with lies like these, and the Taylors and all their armies come marching into this place. Somebody'll listen to me. Some..." And then he collapses.

It is, of course, James Stewart as the earnest idealistic, rather naive Jefferson Smith, who went to Washington. And it is a role as identified with Stewart as Rhett Butler is with Clark Gable and Robin Hood is with Errol Flynn. That he was cast in the role was entirely due to Frank Capra. When *Mr. Smith Goes to Washington* was being prepared for production the assumption in the film industry was that Gary Cooper, who had excelled in Capra's *Mr. Deeds Goes to Town* (1936), would be cast as Jefferson Smith. Capra thought otherwise. Smith was a Boy Scout leader, an idealistic innocent. For Capra the image was Stewart, not Cooper. Capra needed someone who could convincingly gawk in wonder at the historical monuments of Washington and recoil with disgust at political corruption, while having enough strength to stand up for his ideals in the face of tough, cynical opposition. It is to the credit of both Capra and Stewart that the film has lost none of its impact.

Jefferson Smith is the leader of a chain of boys' clubs known as the Boy Rangers and as such he appears to Governor Hopper (Guy Kibbee) and party

With Harry Carey and Claude Rains.   With Jean Arthur.

On the set with Jean Arthur and director Frank Capra.

boss Jim Taylor (Edward Arnold) as a perfect cover for their political dealings. With their backing he wins appointment as the state's junior senator, with expectations that he will be docile and move according to their guidance. The senior senator is Joseph Paine (Claude Rains), who in Smith's eyes is a pillar of virtue. He is not. Smith's expressed patriotism and his political idealism invite the ridicule of the Washington press and veteran members of the government. However, he has two allies. One is his feisty secretary Clarissa Saunders (Jean Arthur) and the other is her reporter friend Diz Moore (Thomas Mitchell). They support him when he wavers in disillusionment and the thought that he should resign.

Things become tough for Smith when he realizes the corruption of the men who are responsible for his appointment. Senator Paine tries to advise him to be less of an idealist: "You have to check your ideals outside the door, like you do your rubbers. I've had to compromise. I've had to play ball." Smith is of no mind to compromise, but when he talks of resigning, Paine and the others convince him that he should stay and fight for his pet project, a national boys' camp. The project happens to be a front for their own plans to appropriate funds, and when it appears their corruption might be exposed they shift the blame to Smith, causing him to be the subject of a Senate expulsion inquiry. Smith takes the floor and talks non-stop for twenty-three hours, trying to gain time while the results of his own investigation into corruption can reach him. Bushels of telegrams from his constituents arrive to give him support and members of the bored press and the gallery start to pay attention. Smith faints with exhaustion but Paine comes onto the floor to confirm that the charges are true. He cries, "I am not fit for office." Smith is completely exonerated and the Senate breaks into wild cheering and applause.

Just about the only people who objected to *Mr. Smith Goes to Washington* when it was released in October of 1939 were a few politicians, who felt it showed the government in a dim light, especially at a time when war had broken out in Europe and America might be needed for leadership. The effect was the opposite; both at home and abroad the film was accepted as decent criticism and a safeguard against corruption. It was a triumph for Capra, who was again nominated for Best Director, Best Picture and in several other categories. But it was the year of

With Eugene Pallette, Edward Arnold, Allan Cavan,
Maurice Costello and Lloyd Whitlock.   With Claude Rains.

Gone With the Wind and Capra's film ended up with only one Oscar, to Lewis R. Foster for his Original Story, a vote made somewhat odd by the failure of the Academy to award another Oscar to Sidney Buchman for his *Smith* screenplay. That particular Oscar went to Sidney Howard for his screenplay of *Gone With the Wind*.

James Stewart was nominated for an Oscar as Best Actor of 1939 but lost to Robert Donat for *Goodbye Mr. Chips*. He was somewhat compensated by having the New York Film Critics Award for Best Actor come his way, plus a raft of fine notices, all of them commending him for his splendid performance as a one-man crusader against political corruption. The consensus was that he had given Capra's film its appeal and its emotional punch almost single-handedly. The critic for the *Nation* stated that the performance placed Stewart in first place among Hollywood actors: "Now he is mature and gives a difficult part, with many nuances, moments of tragi-comic impact. And he is able to do more than play isolated scenes effectively. He shows the strength of a character through experience. In the end he is so forceful that his victory is thoroughly credible. One can only hope that after this success Mr. Stewart in Hollywood will remain as uncorrupted as Mr. Smith in Washington." This critic in 1939 was unwittingly pointing to the basis of James Stewart's great esteem in the film community and with an international public over more than half a century—that he is indeed a decent and uncorrupted man, with not a shred of evidence to the contrary.

DESTRY RIDES AGAIN

UNIVERSAL, 1939

Produced by Joseph Pasternak; *Directed* by George Marshall; *Written* by Felix Jackson, Gertrude Purcell and Henry Myers, based on the novel by Max Brand; *Photographed* by Hal Mohr; *Music* by Frank Skinner; *Songs* by Frederick Hollander and Frank Loesser; 94 minutes.

CAST:

Frenchy, Marlene Dietrich; *Tom Destry*, James Stewart; *Boris Callahan*, Mischa Auer; *Wash Dimsdale*, Charles Winninger; *Kent*, Brian Donlevy; *Gyp Watson*, Allen Jenkins; *Bugs Watson*, Warren Hymer; *Janice Tyndall*, Irene Hervey; *Lily Belle Callahan*, Una Merkel; *Lem Claggett*, Tom Fadden; *Judge Hiram Slade*, Samuel S. Hinds; *Clara*, Lillian Yarbo; *Rockwell*, Edmund MacDonald; *Bartender*, Billy Gilbert; *Sophie Claggett*, Virginia Brissac; *Claggett Girl*, Ann Todd; *Eli Claggett*, Dickie Jones; *Jack Tyndall*, Jack Carson; *Sheriff Keogh*, Joe King.

James Stewart's first western remains among the least typical westerns ever made and still a delightfully rowdy spoof of the genre. By 1939 a little spoofing was in order. Westerns had become rigid formula, the arteries hardened with cliches. *Destry Rides Again* arrived like a comic torpedo, while at the same time giving western lovers lots of the spirit and action contained in the conventional species. It was also a boon, virtually a re-birth, to the career of Marlene Dietrich, who had been off the screen for two years, following a string of heavy-hearted film romances that had caused her popularity to sink. *Destry* allowed her to show a comic flair and an almost Mae West-like sexuality. And for Stewart, coming only two months after the release of *Mr. Smith Goes to Washington*, it was a career galvanizer.

The Max Brand story had first been filmed by Universal in 1932 as one of the last vehicles of the legendary cowboy star Tom Mix, but the 1939 screenplay uses the Brand original more as an inspiration than a basis. In this version the action takes place in the wide-open town of Bottle Neck somewhere in the neighborhood of 1870 and mostly in the Last Chance saloon, owned by a slick rogue named Kent (Brian Donlevy) whose ace attraction is singer-hostess Frenchy (Dietrich). Kent virtually runs the town and instructs the venal mayor (Samuel S. Hinds) to appoint a sheriff, for appearances' sake. They pick the town drunk, Wash Dimsdale (Charles Winninger), who causes great concern by sobering up and taking the job seriously. He also sends for Tom Destry (Stewart), who is the son of the famous marshall for whom Wash was once a deputy.

The fears of the Bottle Neck establishment abate with the arrival of Tom, who turns out to be a pleasant young man who does not carry firearms because, as he explains to Kent after being challenged, "You see, if I had carried a gun, one of us might have got hurt—and it might have been me."

With Marlene Dietrich. *With Dietrich and Brian Donlevy.*

With Jack Carson.

With Marlene Dietrich.

With Allen Jenkins and Charles Winninger.

The barroom crowd bursts into laughter and Frenchy hands Tom a broom, with the comment that for the cleaning up he is likely to do in Bottle Neck this is the only equipment he will need. Destry, it seems, is a pacifist, at least until push comes to shove.

Less pacifistic is Lilybelle Callahan (Una Merkel), who storms into the saloon and demands back her husband's pants, taken from him by Frenchy in a card game. A brawl ensues (the most celebrated female brawl in the history of film) and Tom breaks it up by dumping a pail of water on the two entwined women. The furious Frenchy goes after Tom with a vengeance and he escapes the saloon. But it is the dawning of respect for him, and her affections gradually switch from Kent to Tom when she sees his efforts in cleaning up the town. Lilybelle's husband Boris (Mischa Auer) is sworned in as deputy and Tom manages to accumulate more and more evidence to reveal Kent's crimes.

Things take a dramatic turn when Wash Dimsdale is killed by Kent's men. Tom now becomes militant and straps on his guns, with which he is an expert shot. He leads the good people of the town in a raid on the saloon, and Frenchy, now completely on Tom's side, leads all the women of the town in a march down the main street to protect their men from getting shot. In the saloon Tom goes after Kent and kills him, but not before Frenchy steps into the line of fire to block the bullet meant for Tom. She

dies in his arms, after letting him know she loves him.

Destry Rides Again was a winner on all counts—at the box office and as a milestone in the careers of Marlene Dietrich and James Stewart. The film is comedy, drama, farce, a good western, and a musical to boot. Dietrich was given three songs and one of them, "The Boys in the Back Room," became one of her most celebrated numbers. Casting Stewart opposite her was a master stroke. In the opinion of the late movie critic Bosley Crother, "It was a masterpiece of underplaying in a deliberately sardonic vein—the freshest, most offbeat characterization that this popular actor ever played. It was, in my mind, even better than the rampant young senator in *Mr. Smith Goes to Washington*."

Stewart's Tom Destry is indeed a droll piece of work. He is an incongruously amiable man in a very wild west, a strangely misplaced pacifist, who is first spotted by the townspeople as he steps out of a stagecoach holding a parasol and a birdcage. He happens to be holding them for the young lady who next steps out of the coach, but it is a bizarre introduction to the new deputy sheriff, made the more so when he tells his new boss that he doesn't carry guns because he doesn't believe in them. When asked what he believes in he replies, "Law and order." And therein lies the strength of the man. The sheriff, the villians and the townspeople have to learn this is no wimp. As subtly played by Stewart he is both appealing and persuasive—a well-carved notch in a steadily advancing career.

80

THE SHOP AROUND THE CORNER

MGM, 1939

Produced and *Directed* by Ernst Lubitsch; *Written* by Samuel Raphaelson, *based on the play* Parfumerie by Nicholaus Kaszlo; *Photographed* by William Daniels; *Music* by Werner Heyman; 97 minutes.

With Margaret Sullavan and Frank Morgan.

CAST:

Alfred Kralik, James Stewart; *Klara Novak*, Margaret Sullavan; *Matuschek*, Frank Morgan; *Ferencz Vadas*, Joseph Schildkraut; *Flora*, Sara Haden; *Perovitch*, Felix Bressart; *Pepi Katena*, William Tracy; *Ilona*, Inez Courtney; *Detective*, Charles Halton; *Rudy*, Charles Smith

All four of the Margaret Sullavan-James Stewart films are love stories but only one has a happy ending; the others all end in the death of either Sullavan or Stewart. That *The Shop Around the Corner* should end merrily is not surprising in view of its being the work of that master of amorous whimsy, Ernst Lubitsch. His famous "touch" lent an atmosphere of sexiness to scenes which otherwise might have seemed devoid of it. Lubitsch was suggestive, in a nice and often humorous way. Most of his best comedies involved the amorous antics of the upper classes. With *The Shop Around the Corner* he was dealing with the working class, and the formula

With Joseph Schildkraut and Felix Bressart.

With Margaret Sullavan.

With Margaret Sullavan.

82

With director Ernst Lubitsch and Margaret Sullavan.

was not quite as effective. He was also attempting to tell an Hungarian story with American actors, and in the case of Stewart it was like a man wearing a suit a size too big or too small for him.

Here Stewart is Alfred Kralik, the head clerk in a leather and gift shop owned by Matuschek (Frank Morgan). He is a bachelor yearning for a mate and begins a correspondence with a girl who has advertised in the press for a pen pal. Their letters, signed only as "friend," are rewarding for both of them. During the Christmas rush Matuschek hires Klara Novak (Sullavan), who is the girl in correspondence with Alfred, although neither are aware of this. They do not get along at all well. They argue and irritate each other. As correspondents they are eager to meet, but when Alfred turns up at the rendezvous in a restaurant he is dumbfounded to find his pen-pal is Klara. He does not reveal his identity and Klara becomes annoyed that he is bothering her. She explains she is waiting for someone.

Alfred loses his job when Matuschek assumes him to be his wife's lover. The real culprit is Ferencz Vadas (Joseph Schildkraut), a fellow clerk in the store, and when Matuschek learns the truth he apologizes to Alfred and re-hires him, this time as general manager. In his shame Matuschek attempts to shoot himself but his messenger boy prevents it. While Matuschek goes to the hospital for a rest cure, Alfred runs the store efficiently and also finds it hard to be anything but gentle and considerate toward

Klara. In this new atmosphere she warms to him, and when he reveals his identity as her lover/correspondent they realize that their hopes have come true.

The Shop Around the Corner is a nice picture, but it fell short of being a box office winner. Perhaps the material was too delicate, especially under Lubitsch's subtle direction, to appeal to an American audience. The critical reaction to Stewart was generally favorable but most reviewers pointed out that the actor could hardly pass for an Hungarian, that his manner was uniquely American. It might have been better for him had the story been switched to small town America, particularly since as the son of a small town store owner Stewart would have been thoroughly familiar with the milieu. In 1949 MGM did this with their musical version, *In the Good Old Summer Time*, starring Judy Garland and Van Johnson as the lovers. The story also turned up in another musical version on Broadway in 1963, titled *She Loves Me*.

Perhaps because he was not fullly at ease with the characterization, Stewart appeared somewhat overly earnest as the shy clerk in search of love. This caused him to almost lapse into self-caricature, and the critic for *Time* commented on his performance as walking through "the amiable business of being James Stewart." After four years in the movies Stewart had at least established a distinct persona. The problem of going against his American grain was not one he would often have to face, but it was about to crop up again immediately, and once more with Margaret Sullavan.

83

THE MORTAL STORM

MGM, 1940

Produced by Sidney Franklin; *Directed* by Frank Borzage; *Written* by Claudine West, Anderson Ellis and George Froeschel, based on the novel by Phyllis Bottom; *Photographed* by William Daniels; *Music* by Edward Kane; 100 minutes.

CAST:

Freya Roth, Margaret Sullavan; *Martin Breitner*, James Stewart; *Fritz Marberg*, Robert Young; *Professor Roth*, Frank Morgan; *Mrs. Roth*, Irene Rich; *Mrs. Brietner*, Maria Ouspenskaya; *Erich Von Rohn*, William Orr; *Otto Von Rohn*, Robert Stack; *Elsa*, Bonita Granville; *Rudi*, Gene Reynolds; *Rector*, Russell Hicks; *Lebman*, William Edmunds; *Professor Werner*, Thomas Ross; *Franz*, Ward Bond; *Marta*, Esther Dale; *Oppenheim*, Fritz Leiber; *Holl*, Dan Dailey; *Hartman*, Robert O. Davis; *Berg*, Granville Bates; *Theresa*, Sue Moore.

With Frank Morgan and Robert Young.

For their final film Margaret Sullavan and James Stewart became a part of Hollywood's forthright condemnation of Hitler and the Nazi regime. America may have been neutral in the two years prior to the attack on Pearl Harbor, but America's moviemakers left no doubt about their own sentiments regarding what was happening in Europe. It was almost as if they were preparing Americans for evenutal conflict with Nazi Germany. *The Mortal Storm* is a case in point. Released on June of 1940 the film was an indictment of the Nazis, as well as dramatic consideration of how people behave under a totalitarian government, of those who welcome it and those who do not. Seen today the film appears contrived and melodramatic, with a clearly MGM-backlot German setting and a cast of clearly American actors, especially Stewart, struggling to seem German.

Bavaria, late 1933. The Roth family are content and happy. Professor Roth (Frank Morgan) is a revered teacher and on his sixtieth birthday he is honored by his faculty, his students and his family. His daughter Freya (Sullavan) is courted by both Martin Breitner (Stewart) and Fritz Marberg (Robert Young), to the amusement of her friends Erich (William Orr) and Otto (Robert Stack). Freya prefers Fritz, until he shows his approval of the new Nazi moviement. Then her sentiments put her in line with Martin, who dislikes the political situation and quarrels with most of his friends about it. The situation worsens and Professor Roth is ousted from his college when it is learned he is not a pure Aryan. When he continues to voice criticism he is arrested and sent to a concentration camp, where he dies.

With Robert Stack, Margaret Sullavan, Robert
Young and William Orr.

With Maria Ouspenskaya and Bonita Granville.

With Maragaret Sullavan and Irene Rich.

With Dan Dailey and director Frank Borzage.

Martin moves to Austria when it is discovered that he has aided another professor to escape detection, and after the death of her father Freya proceeds to join Martin, in company with her mother (Irene Rich) and her young brother Rudi (Gene Reynolds). There is no reason to stay in Bavaria, now that former friends like Fritz and Otto are ardent Nazis and reason seems to have vanished. At the border, guards find a manuscript written by her father and accuse Freya of being an enemy of the state. Her mother and brother continue into Austria but Freya is detained. Learning of this Martin sneaks back across the border to rescue her. As they are about to cross the border they are caught by a patrol headed by Fritz. Freya is shot and dies in Martin's arms; sadly Fritz allows that it is a tragedy but one that could not be avoided under the circumstances.

The Mortal Storm is glossy MGM melodrama, circa 1940, and very much the work of that true romantic among film directors, Frank Borzage. In his book *The American Cinema*, Andrew Sarris makes an interesting point concerning Borzage's anti-Nazi films (*Little Man What Now* and *Three Comrades* were the others), that they were far ahead of their time, "emotionally if not politically. Borzage's objection to Hitler was a curious one. What Hitler and all tyrants represented most reprehensibly was an invasion of the emotional privacy of individuals, particularly lovers, those blessed creatures gifted with luminous rapport." The view applies particularly to Sullavan and Stewart in this film because of the definite luminous rapport they were able to achieve in their work together on screen. The Nazis do indeed seem to invade and violate their relationship, although Borzage overloads his message by having Stewart carry the dead Sullavan across the border as celestial music swells in the background. However, *The Mortal Storm* must be viewed in light of 1940 sentiments. Sullavan and Stewart are not merely lovers, they are symbols of human decency pitted against the onslaught of a dreadful reality, resisters of impending calamity. Apart from the fact that they are obviously not German, it is hard to deny the intense sincerity of their performances.

86

NO TIME FOR COMEDY

WARNER BROS., 1940

Produced by Jack L. Warner and Hal B. Wallis; *Directed* by William Keighley; *Written* by Julius J. and Philip G. Epstein, based on the play by S. N. Behrman; *Photographed* by Ernest Haller; *Music* by Heinz Roemheld; 93 minutes.

CAST:

Gaylord Esterbrook, James Stewart; *Linda Esterbrook*, Rosalind Russell; *Philo Swift*, Charles Ruggles; *Amanda Swift*, Genevieve Tobin; *Clementine*, Louise Beavers; *Morgan Carrell*, Allyn Joslyn; *Richard Benson*, Clarence Kolb; *Robert*, Robert Greig; *Jim*, Jm. M. Kerrigan; *Frank*, Lawrence Grosmith; *Desk Sergeant*, Robert Emmett O'Connor; *Doorman*, Herbert Heywood; *Can Driver*, Frank Faylen

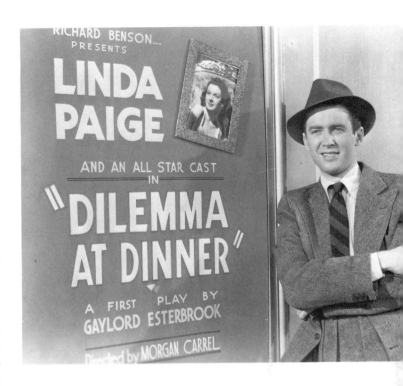

With Rosalind Russell.

With Rosalind Russell.

One of the hits on Broadway in 1939 was S. N. Behrman's comedy *No Time for Comedy*, starring Katharine Cornell and Lawrence Olivier, with the great Cornell's part being the dominant one. In adapting it for the screen for Warner Bros., their resident scenarists, the brothers Julius J. and Philip G. Epstein, had to swing the balance in favor of the actor who was about to get top billing—James Stewart, being loaned out by MGM for the eighth time—and was being paired with Rosalind Russell, whose open, bright style of acting worked well with Stewart's playing of a quiet, introspective playwright. The stage play was perhaps a little more intellectually sharp and edgier than the film, but Warners knew that what would bring in audiences would be the accent on romance. They also knew that material like this needed the taste and style of the right director, in this case the gentlemanly William Keighley.

Gaylord Esterbrook (Stewart) is a Minnesota newspaperman who writes a successful play about New York City, even though he has never been there. Invited to attend the staging of his play and to make some needed revisions, Gaylord becomes enchanted with the actress playing the lead, Linda Paige (Russell). They see more and more of each other and fall in love, which soon leads to marriage. It also leads to great success for Gaylord, who finds that he has a flair for comedy. He enjoys four hits in a row, but then starts to wonder if perhaps he is not wasting his talents writing light material. Abetting him in this reasoning is Amanda Swift (Genevieve Tobin), long a rival actress of Linda and also a lady much given to flirtation. She offers to be his patroness in his endeavors to be a serious dramatist, somewhat to the bemusement of her philosphical husband, Philo (Charles Ruggles), who has been through this hoop many times and shows no surprise when Linda starts to pay attention to him in retaliation for Amanda's going after Gaylord. Philo knows that it will all work itself out, and it does. Gaylord's drama is a dismal flop and its failure brings him to his senses.

If *No Time for Comedy* is describable as the kind of movie that is a thing of the past, it might be because Hollywood no longer seems to have witty writers like the Epstein brothers, sophisticated directors like Keighley and deftly comic character actors like Charles Ruggles. The film is fluff but it is amusing, and it did James Stewart no injury. In his review for *The New York Times*, Bosley Crowther said, "As usual Mr. Stewart is the best thing in the show—a completely ingratiating character who ranges from the charming clumsiness of a country playwright to the temperamental distraction of an established writer with complete and natural assurance."

THE PHIL- ADELPHIA STORY

MGM, 1940

Produced by Joseph L. Mankiewicz; *Directed* by George Cukor; *Written* by Donald Ogden Stewart, based on the play by Philip Barry; *Photographed* by Joseph Ruttenberg; *Music* by Franz Waxman; 112 minutes.

With Katharine Hepburn and John Howard.

CAST:

Dexter Haven, Cary Grant; *Tracy Lord,* Katharine Hepburn; *Mike Connor,* James Stewart; *Liz Imbrie,* Ruth Hussey; *George Kittredge,* John Howard; *Uncle Willie,* Roland Young; *Dinah Lord,* Virginia Weidler; *Set Lord,* John Halliday; *Margaret Lord,* Mary Nash; *Sidney Kidd,* Henry Daniell; *Edwards,* Lionel Pape; *Thomas,* Rex Evans; *John,* Russ Clark; *Librarian,* Hilda Plowright; *Manicurist,* Lita Chevret; *Bartender,* Lee Phelps.

The most romantic words ever spoken by James Stewart on the screen are these: "There's a magnificence in you, Tracy...the magnificence that comes out of your eyes and your voice and the way you stand there and the way you walk. You're lit from within, Tracy. You've got fires banked down in you, hearth fires and holocausts. You're made out of flesh and

With Katharine Hepburn.

With John Howard, Cary Grant and Katharine
Hepburn.

With Cary Grant and Ruth Hussey.

With Katharine Hepburn.

blood. That's the blank, unholy surprise of it! Why, you're the Golden Girl, Tracy—full of life and warmth and delight." Tracy is, of course, Katharine Hepburn and it's *The Philadelphia Story*. Stewart is reporter Mike Connor and both he and Tracy are a little drunk, which is probably the only circumstance in which the reporter—or James Stewart—would speak with such romantic grandiloquence.

The Philadelphia Story is the film for which Stewart won his Oscar, but neither he nor anyone else can regard it as being anything other than a Katharine Hepburn film. By 1939 she had been in the movies for seven years, with a popularity that suddenly went into decline. She withdrew from Hollywood and went to New York to look for a good stage vehicle. Playwright Philip Barry had an outline that intrigued Hepburn and with her encouragement he expanded it into a play. Together they took it to the Theatre Guild and they offered to put up half the money for its production. *The Philadelphia Story* opened at the Shubert Theatre on March 29, 1939, and ran for 415 performances, bringing Hepburn all the success she could have wanted. Several studios bid for the film rights and found the majority owner to be Hepburn. She drove a hard bargan—whoever made the picture would have to accept her as the star, with her right to choose the director and the two male leads. MGM made the best offer, and readily agreed to George Cukor as director. He had already made four films with Hepburn—*A Bill of Divorcement* (1932), *Little Women* (1933), *Sylvia Scarlett* (1936) and *Holiday* (1938)—and MGM were assured of a fine working relationship between the two. And since she had co-starred with Cary Grant in three films—*Sylvia Scarlett, Bringing Up Baby* (1938) and *Holiday*—he was therefore a logical choice to play C. K. Dexter Haven, the playboyish ex-husband of self-willed Tracy Lord. However, in hiring him, Hepburn discovered that his contract gave him the right to top billing. Several actors were discussed for the role of the reporter, but Hepburn made no objection to MGM's choice of Stewart.

The Philadelphia Story has its roots in *The Taming of the Shrew*, with Tracy finally calmed by the love of the man who has never stopped loving her, her ex-husband, and by Mike Connor, who spots the softness under Tracy's brash, aristocratic exterior. Connor and his photographer, Liz Imbrie (Ruth Hussey), have been assigned to cover the high society wedding of Tracy and a stuffy, self-made business tycoon, George Kittredge (John Howard), and neither of them care much for the assignment. Life in the upper social strata and the elegance of the Lord estate

With Katharine Hepburn.

are not much to their taste.

Mike and Liz have open access to the wedding because their publisher-employer threatens to expose Tracy's father (John Halliday) if he does not agree. It seems that Mr. Lord has not been too discreet with his extramarital love life. The man who has made this press access possible is C. K. Dexter Haven, who knows it will cause problems. He has his reasons, chief of which is the fact that he still loves Tracy and wants to keep her from marrying Kittredge. What he does not count on is Mike's falling in love with Tracy, which also comes as a surprise to Mike, since he despises this social set. One day in a library, as he researches the Lord family, he finds Tracy reading a book of his short stories. On the way back to the

house Mike talks to Tracy and discovers she is not quite the "rich, rapacious American female" he had at first thought.

Mike and Tracy spend more time together. They both get high on champagne at the party given by her Uncle Willie (Roland Young). Mike goes off to see Dexter, to talk about Tracy, and it becomes apparent that he is falling in love with her. Later that night he tells her so, and she is tipsy enough to be swept away by his compliments. They take a nude swim together in the pool, after which he carries her to her room. That, and further complications, cause Kittredge to back out of the marriage. When Mike offers to marry her she gently turns him down, knowing that Liz is in love with him. Dexter now makes the play he has been edging toward—the suggestion that he can solve the dilemma by again becoming her husband. Tracy is happy to accept.

93

With Katharine Hepburn, Ruth Hussey and director George Cukor.

Although the film is a study of Tracy Lord, it is also an examination of the various men in her life and the effect she has upon them. In the case of Mike Connor she causes a turnaround in his attitude toward the wealthy, which is one of contempt until she softens his heart. At first wary of her, he gradually sees the quality of her true nature underneath the bluster. He starts off their relationship as a snide commentator on the idle rich, "The prettiest sight in this fine, pretty world is the privileged class enjoying its privileges," but when she points out that he in his way is as snobbish as she in hers, he begins to take a more charitable view, and quotes a Spanish proverb, "With the rich and mighty, a little patience." And although he may be disappointed at not being able to marry this fine girl, contact with her will have altered his life for the better.

Stewart took the role of Mike Connor and gave it all the shadings and nuances it needed, bringing out the resentment of a journalist having to do a job he hates and the soul of a man who is a romantic at heart, once the clutter of prejudice is cleared from his mind. In the process he came up with one of the most romantic scenes in Hollywood history, which possibly surprised even his staunchest admirers. However, it was a small surprise compared to his own when he received the Oscar for Best Actor of 1940. He had not expected it, claiming that he himself had voted for his friend Henry Fonda in *The Grapes of Wrath*. It was Stewart's opinion that the award was a compensation for not winning for *Mr. Smith Goes to Washington*. He was not alone in that opinion.

COME LIVE WITH ME

MGM, 1941

Produced and *Directed* by Clarence Brown; *Written* by Patterson McNutt, based on a story by Virginia Van Upp; *Photographed* by George Folsey; *Music* by Herbert Stothart; 85 minutes.

CAST:

Bill Smith, James Stewart; *Johanna Janns*, Hedy Lamarr; *Barton Kendrick*, Ian Hunter; *Diana Kendrick*, Verree Teasdale; *Joe Darsie*, Donald Meek; *Barney Grogan*, Barton MacLane; *Arnold Stafford*, Edward Ashley; *Yvonne*, Ann Codee; *Doorman*, King Baggott; *Grandma*, Adeline de Walt Reynolds; *Farm Hand*, Sy Jenks; *Headwaiter*, Fritz Feld; *Chef*, Dewey Robinson.

With Hedy Lamarr.

Hedy Lamarr was a problem for MGM, whose commander-in-chief, Louis B. Mayer, regarded her as the most beautiful woman in the world. Beautiful she surely was, with a face that might have been created by Michelangelo. The problem was that she couldn't act, and the face seldom showed any expression beyond a come-hither kind of allure. She made her American film debut in 1938 with *Algiers*, at the age of twenty-four, and received good notices as a lovely new screen siren. Nothing much happened until MGM luckily scored two Lamarr hits in 1940, *Boom Town* and *Comrade X,* both of which paired her with Clark Gable. It then became James Stewart's pleasure to gaze into her beautiful face, in *Come Live With Me*, a title with which any red-blooded man could identify. In this film she was well cast, as a Viennese refugee who cannot return to Nazi Dusbria. Lamarr was born in Vienna as Hedwig Kiesler, although she was anything but a refugee, being the wife of millionaire Fritz Mandl, who took her to London in 1937. Being Jewish, a fact never alluded to in her years of stardom, she had no desire to return to Austria at this time. All in all, Lamarr had reason to understand the girl she was assigned to play in *Come Live With Me.*

With Ian Hunter.

With Hedy Lamarr.

In order to stay in America, Johanna Janns (Lamarr), or Johnny as she calls herself, is the mistress of publisher Barton Kendrick (Ian Hunter), whose wife Diane (Verree Teasdale) takes a liberal modern view of marriage and doesn't mind if her husband goes his way and she goes hers. This is not enough for Johnny, who is faced with deportation unless she can find a husband. In a cafe she comes across a penniless writer, Bill Smith (Stewart), and she suggests a marriage of convenience, in which she will pay his way until he finds success with his writing. He agrees and they set up separate residences, with the understanding that he cannot know her address. The situation is one that Bill decides to turn into a novel, one which comes to the attention of Kendrick, who buys it. Kendrick's wife agrees to a divorce and Johnny moves to divorce Bill in order to

marry Kendrick. Bill agrees only if Johnny will spend a day with him in the country, at the home of his grandmother (Adeline de Walt Reynolds). In this idyllic setting it dawns upon Johnny that Bill is the man she loves and that she cannot go through with the planned marriage to Kendrick. When Kendrick arrives at the house, having been asked by Johnny to pick her up, Bill suddenly realizes he is the other man, and he storms out of the house in anger. But when he comes back, he finds Johnny waiting, alone.

Come Live With Me is what it is—a glossy MGM romance, crafted with expertise. Hedy Lamarr is irresistible and Stewart plays the writer-husband with the kind of easy assurance and appeal that was now expected of him. Next up, another loan-out.

POT O' GOLD

UNITED ARTISTS, 1941

Produced by James Roosevelt; *Directed* by George Marshall; *Written* by Walter De Leon, based on a story by Monte Brice, Andrew Bennison and Harry Tugend; *Photographed* by Hal Mohr; *Music Director:* Lou Forbes; 86 minutes.

CAST:

Jimmy Haskell, James Stewart; *Molly McCorkle,* Paulette Goddard; *Horace Heidt,* Himself; *C. J. Haskell,* Charles Winninger; *Ma McCorkle,* Mary Gordon; *Jasper,* Frank Melton; *Mr. Louderman,* Jed Prouty; *Willie McCorkle,* Dick Hogan; *Lieutenant Grady,* James Burke; *Parks,* Charlie Arnt; *Donna McCorkle,* Donna Wood; *Larry Cotton,* Himself; *Samson,* Henry Roquemore; *Chalmers,* William Gould; *Judge Murray,* Aldrich Bowker.

While *Born to Dance* is the movie musical most associated with James Stewart, the largely forgotton *Pot o' Gold* is the one in which he is most involved with music. The film is an oddity, being the only one produced by James Roosevelt, the son of FDR, whose ambitions to be a movie producer ended with the failure of this picture. It would be the last time that MGM would have occasion to loan Stewart to another studio, and if they had gone on loaning him out for films such as this one, the relationship between home base and the actor would probably have become strained. He was, after all, an Oscar winner.

Pot o' Gold came about because of the NBC radio giveaway series of that name, sponsored by Tums, featuring Horace Heidt and his Orchestra, which is why Heidt has third billing in the film. Perhaps the worst comment on the film is that it contains seven musical numbers and that not one of them gained even the least popularity. The plot has Stewart as Jimmy Haskell, the music-obsessed manager of a music shop, but more interested in playing the harmonica than selling merchandise. He comes across a band of struggling musicians (Horace Heidt and his Orchestra) as they practice on the roof of a boarding house run by good-hearted Mom McCorkle (Mary Gordon), whose pretty daughter Molly (Paulette Goddard) also loves music.

With Horace Heidt and Paulette Goddard.

Jimmy and Molly combine forces to promote the career of Horace and the lads, a task made the more difficult because Jimmy's wealthy Uncle Charley (Charles Winninger) hates music and threatens to take legal action against Heidt unless he stops practicing. Everybody hates Uncle Charley and when, by a fluke, he is himself arrested and jailed, the inmates torture him with music. But Uncle Charley is a food manufacturer and a radio sponsor, and he listens when Jimmy comes up with a scheme for a radio program that will surely promote his products, a show featuring Heidt and his musicians, with audience participation and prizes. The show is a success and Jimmy goes on salary, enabling him to solve his problems and court Molly.

The plot machinations are many and improbable in this very minor entry in the Stewart catalog of films. Among the most improbable is a sequence in which Goddard fantasizes on a balcony and imagines herself a Juliet, courted by knights and troubadours. If nothing else, *Pot o' Gold* proves that Stewart did sing in a movie other than *Born to Dance,* and that he could do well playing the harmonica. Stewart is, in fact, a much more musical man than his career as an actor would indicate. However, after the experience of this particular film he was probably surprised that his next assignment would also find him deeply involved in the making of a movie musical.

ZIEGFELD GIRL

MGM, 1941

Produced by Pandro Berman; *Directed* by Robert Z. Leonard; *Written* by Marguerite Roberts and Sonya Levien, based on a story by William Anthony McGuire; *Photographed* by Ray June; *Music* by Herbert Stothart; *Music Director:* George Stoll; 131 minutes.

CAST:

Gilbert Young, James Stewart; *Susan Gallagher*, Judy Garland; *Sandra Kolter*, Hedy Lamarr; *Sheila Regan*, Lana Turner; *Frank Merton*, Tony Martin; *Jerry Regan*, Jackie Cooper; *Geoffrey Collins*, Ian Hunter; *Pop Gallagher*, Charles Winninger; *Noble Sage*, Edward Everett Horton; *Franz Kelter*, Philip Dorn; *John Slayton*, Paul Kelly; *Patsy Dixon*, Eve Arden: *Jimmy Walters*, Dan Dailey; *Al*, Al Shean; *Mrs. Regan*, Fay Holton; *Mischa*, Felix Bressart; *Mrs. Merton*, Rose Hobart; *Nick Capalini*, Bernard Nedell; *Officer Regan*, Ed McNamara; *Jenny*, Mae Busch; *Annie*, Rene Riano.

With Lana Turner.

Ziegfeld Girl is an immense backstage musical into which MGM poured tons of talent. It was the first production of Pandro S. Berman after his years of success at RKO and he spared no expense trying to out-Ziegfeld Ziegfeld, but why James Stewart should have received top billing is hard to fathom, since his is virtually a minor role in this lavish account of the adventures of three girls in show business. Robert Z. Leonard directed this two and a quarter hours of struggle, triumph, pain and music, but the two big production numbers, "Minnie from Trinidad" and

With Elliott Sullivan and James Flavin.

the finale built around the song "You Stepped Out of a Dream," were the work of the fabled wizard of cinematic choreography, Busby Berkeley. All Stewart had to do was suffer as the boyfriend of Lana Turner.

Susan Gallagher (Judy Garland), Sandra Koller (Hedy Lamarr) and Sheila Regan (Lana Turner) are chosen from hundreds to be Ziegfeld girls. Vaudeville singer Susan is persuaded by her father Pops Gallagher (Charles Winninger) to follow in his footsteps and for his efforts he is reunited with his old partner Al Shean (playing himself), and both are hired by Ziegfeld. Sandra is the wife of penniless violinist Franz Kolter (Philip Dorn), who is tormented when she seems to dally with Ziegfeld singer Frank Merton (Tony Martin). She eventually decides to give up her own career in favor of his, and with that his fortunes rise. Saddest of all is Sheila, whose dedicated boyfriend Gilbert Young (Stewart) is a truck driver. Sheila goes from being an elevator girl in a Brooklyn

department store to a life of theatrical glamour, including the attentions of socialite Geoffrey Collins (Ian Hunter). In his efforts to make money to keep up with Sheila's tastes, Gilbert takes to bootlegging liquor and winds up in jail. After he has served his sentence the repentant Sheila agrees to settle down in marriage but by now she has another problem—drink. Not wanting to miss the opening of the Ziegfeld show, the sick Sheila goes to the theatre, an experience that proves too much for her. She collapses and dies.

After playing the loser in *Ziegfeld Girl*, Stewart must have been wondering where his film career was going, especially following the frail *Pot O' Gold*. However, there was much more on his mind at this juncture. Military service was luring a willing recruit and he would be in the army before *Ziegfeld Girl* was released in April of 1941. A lot would happen in his own life and in the affairs of the world before his next movie was released in December of 1946.

IT'S A WONDER-FUL LIFE

RKO, 1946

Produced and *Directed* by Frank Capra; *Written* by Frances Goodrich, Albert Hackett and Frank Capra, based on the story "The Greatest Gift," by Philip Van Doren; *Photographed* by Joseph Walker and Joseph Biroc; *Music* by Dimitri Tiomkin; 129 minutes.

With Donna Reed and Carl "Alfalfa" Switzer.

CAST:

George Bailey, James Stewart; *Mary Hatch*, Donna Reed; *Mr. Potter*, Lionel Barrymore; *Uncle Billy*, Thomas Mitchell; *Clarence*, Henry Travers: *Mrs. Bailey*, Beulah Bondi; *Ernie*, Frank Faylen; *Bert*, Ward Bond; *Violet Bick*, Gloria Graham; *Mr. Gower*, H. B. Warner; *Sam Wainwright*, Frank Albertson; *Pa Bailey*, Samuel S. Hinds; *Harry Bailey*, Todd Karns; *Cousin*, Mary Treen; *Ruth Dakin*, Virgina Patton; *Cousin Eustace*, Charles Williams; *Mrs. Hatch*, Sarah Edwards; *Mr. Martini*, Bill Edmunds; *Annie*, Lillian Randolph; *Mrs. Martini*, Argentina Brunetti.

The changes in the world, in civilization and in humankind caused by the Second World War need no comment in these pages. Suffice to say that James Stewart was among those whose experiences during five years of military service had produced a more

mature, sharper and more astute human. No intelligent man who has been through years of war can be quite the same, and for Stewart those years helped forge greater ability as an actor. To begin with, he wanted to make his own way in the film business and not be subject to the dictates of a studio. He could have gone back to MGM, the arms of Louis B. Mayer were wide open. Instead he decided to join another man who had just returned from service, Frank Capra. Capra, also wanting to be independent, had formed Liberty Films, along with George Stevens, Williams Wyler and producer Samuel Briskin. Their first project would be *It's a Wonderful Life,* a solidly Capraesque affirmation of the values of American life. For such a picture there could only be one choice of actor for the leading role—James Stewart.

Even before he had the script written, Capra visited Stewart in order to give him a concept of what the film would be about. Stewart listened to Capra's rather confused yarn about a man who loses faith in life and wants to kill himself but is prevented from so

With Lionel Barrymore.   *With Donna Reed.*

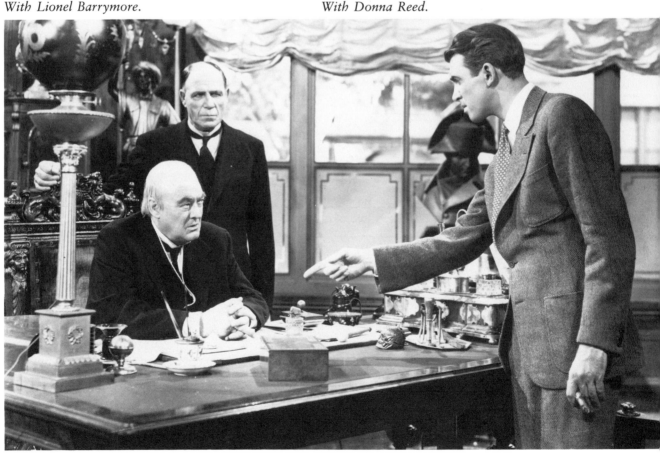

102

doing by a guardian angel named Clarence. Capra's account became increasingly muddled and he was about to withdraw when the actor said yes, he would be delighted to play the part. Whatever Capra wanted to do was all right with Stewart.

It's a Wonderful Life is quintessential Americana, a study of small town life, brimming over with Capra's optimism and vigor, although a somewhat too rosy-eyed view of the human condition. It might well be coupled with Dickens's *A Christmas Carol* as an exercise in presuading us that all is eventually well. The comparison with Dickens doesn't end there, since much of the Capra film centers around Christmas, and presents Lionel Barrymore as a very Scrooge-like, flinty-hearted banker named Henry Potter. However, Potter does not see the light of human kindness, he remains flinty-hearted amidst a sea of love and understanding, seemingly the only really rotten man in the town of Bedford Falls.

Bedford Falls is the hometown of George Bailey (Stewart), who thinks it's a nice but pretty dull place. He has a wife, Mary (Donna Reed), and four children, and he runs his father's building and loan

With player, Frank Faylen and Donna Reed.

company. When his father dies, George takes over and finds that a great many people in town have leaned heavily on his father's easygoing nature. But George is the same kind of man, which means that cash-flow is low and the hopes of keeping the company afloat are slim. In desperation he turns to Henry Potter for a loan. Since Potter wants to have the entire business life of Bedford Falls under his command, he does nothing to help George. In fact, George's collapse fits in with Potter's schemes.

The only really good thing in George's life is his family. He loves his wife and children, although he feels bad that he has never been able to keep his promise to Mary to take her traveling around the world. When his uncle (Thomas Mitchell) accidentally, and carelessly, loses the company funds, George is faced with ruin. His generous nature has been his undoing. One dark and snowy night he stands on the town bridge and tells himself he wishes he had never been born. Before George has a chance to jump, an old fellow named Clarence Oddbody (Henry Travers) throws himself in the river in order to be saved by George. Later he tells George he is his guardian angel and that before he kills himself he should take a look at Bedford Falls and what it would be like if he had

With Donna Reed and Thomas Mitchell.

With Frank Faylen, H.B. Warner, Sarah Edwards, Gloria Grahame, Donna Reed, Beulah Bondi and Lillian Randolph.

With Henry Travers.

MAGIC TOWN

RKO, 1947

Produced by Robert Riskin; *Directed* by William A. Wellman; *Written* by Robert Riskin, based on a story by Joseph Krumgold; *Photographed* by Joseph Biroc; *Music* by Roy Webb; 143 minutes.

CAST:

Lawrence "Rip" Smith, James Stewart; *Mary Peterman,* Jane Wyman; *Hoopendecker,* Kent Smith; *Ike Sloan,* Ned Sparks; *Lou Dicketts,* Wallace Ford; *Ed Weaver,* Regis Toomey; *Mrs. Weaver,* Ann Doran; *Mr. Twiddle,* Donald Meek; *Moody,* E. J. Ballantine; *Ma Peterson,* Ann Shoemaker; *Hank Nickleby,* Mickey Kuhn; *Richard Nickleby,* Howard Freeman; *Mayor,* Harry Holman; *Bob Peterman,* Mickey Roth; *Mrs. Frisby,* Mary Currier; *Senator Wilson,* George Irving; *Charlie Stringer,* Selmer Jackson; *Dickey,* Robert Dudley; *Mrs. Wilton,* Julia Dean.

With Kent Smith.

never lived. It would be a much different place. The despotic Potter would run everything and George's many friends would be leading dismal lives. Worst of all, Mary would be a sad and lonely widow. Returning to his home George finds that his friends have rallied to his support and collected enough money to save his business from falling into Potter's hands. Life, George realizes, is indeed wonderful.

Capra's glowingly optimistic movie emerged at Christmas 1946, and failed to become the smash hit Capra had hoped for. It seemed a little at variance with the cool postwar spirit and some critics hinted that this kind of cheerful Americana had slipped by the boards. But time and distance have lent enchantment. *It's a Wonderful Life* is generally regarded among filmmakers as a masterpiece and whenever it is shown today—it is a Christmas perennial—audiences respond to it as a beautiful evocation of former American values—with the hope that they have not entirely vanished. In the case of James Stewart and Frank Capra, both regard it as their favorite among their own movies.

James Stewart has ample reason to be greatful to Frank Capra. He told the authors of *The Films of Frank Capra* (Citadel Press, 1977), Victor Scherle and William Turner Levy, "In my opinion, Capra is one of the giants of the picture business and always will be. It is amazing the contribution that he made to the industry when it was young and just getting on its feet...Frank has had a great deal to do with the progress of my career over the years and I will always be grateful to him."

105

With director William Wellman and Jane Wyman.

With Jane Wyman.

Magic Town is among the least of James Stewart's films but it is an important one because its failure caused him to take stock of his movie image and reach beyond it. It was a movie that seemed to want to out-Capra Capra in revelling in American folkways. *Time* described it as "another of those serio-comic fables in favor of the American way of life which, it appears, cannot be made without James Stewart." With Robert Riskin as its producer and principal writer it could not escape being compared with Capra's work, since it was Riskin who scripted several of the great Capra pictures, including *You Can't Take It With You, Mr. Deeds Goes to Town* and *Meet John Doe.* Unfortunately, *Magic Town* proved that what had been great stuff in the pre-war years was not such good stuff in the post-war years, and that Stewart had best extricate himself from this kind of fantasy Americana.

In *Magic Town* he is Lawrence "Rip" Smith, a slick but failing public relations man who hits upon a scheme whereby he can make money as a pollster.

From his friend Hoopendecker (Kent Smith), he learns of a small town that is the perfect example of American opinions and manners and functions. So he goes to Grandview and sets up offices, with his cohorts Ike (Ned Sparks) and Lou (Wallace Ford). Having been right on every issue in the past fifty years, Grandview is a pollster's heaven. Rip makes money with his accurate statistics, posing all the while as an insurance man, and his plans work well until Mary Peterson (Jane Wyman) and her mother (Ann Shoemaker) begin to suspect that all is not what it should be. They run the local newspaper.

In order for his operation to work, Rip needs to have the town remain its complacent, unprogressive little self, which is counter to what Mary wants. She wants new enterprise, and in particular a new civic center, but her heart starts to warm toward Rip when he coaches the high-school basketball team and leads them to their first victory in many years. However, the budding romance goes awry when she discovers him giving out his polling figures. She exposes him in her newspaper the next day and Rip leaves town. The exposure in newspapers around the country brings all kinds of businesses to Grandview and the town goes poll-opinion crazy, resulting in chaos and collapse. When Rip hears of Mary's possible ruin, he comes back to Grandview and tells her of his regret and his love. Together they work out a scheme to get the town back on its feet and restore its former confidence and friendliness.

For Stewart, *Magic Town* was a mistake. Audiences were expecting him to be the affable, folksy and solidly honest fellow they had come to know in previous bits of Stewartian Americana. What they saw this time was a near con-man, even though he did reform at the end. But what the critics saw was an actor treading water in a movie that had set out to be a good-natured satire on life in small town America but instead seemed to be a mixture of sourness and sentimentality. Someone who really disliked the picture was its director, William Wellman. He went so far as to say that anyone who liked *Magic Town* was suspect. Some of the reviewers were kind in faintly praising it as an amusing bit of entertainment but there were a number who lambasted Stewart and suggested that he was on the verge of becoming a bore with this kind of characterization. One reviewer in particular asked how much longer would he have to put up with "this long beanstalk, hemming and hawing all over the place?" It was the kind of comment that would cause any intelligent actor to sit up and take notice. Stewart was, and is, an intelligent actor.

CALL NORTHSIDE 777

20TH CENTURY-FOX, 1948

Produced by Otto Lang; *Directed* by Henry Hathaway; *Written* by Jerome Cady and Jay Dratler, based on articles by James P. McGuire; *Photographed* by Joe MacDonald; *Music Director:* Alfred Newman; 111 minutes.

CAST:

McNeal, James Stewart; *Frank Wiecek,* Richard Conte; *Brian Kelly,* Lee J. Cobb; *Laura McNeal,* Helen Walker; *Wanda Skutnik,* Betty Garde; *Tillie,* Kasia Orzazeski; *Helen Wiecek-Rayska,* Joanne de Bergh; *Palmer,* Howard Smith; *Martin Burns,* Paul Harvey; *Sam Faxon,* John McIntire; *Parole Board Chairman,* Moroni Olsen; *Tomek Zaleska,* George Tyne; *Warden,* Richard Bishop; *Boris,* Otto Waldis; *Frank Wiecek, Jr.,* Michael Chapin; *Rayska,* E. G. Marshall; *Jan Gruska,* John Bleifer.

With Helen Walker.

After the somewhat disappointing reaction to *It's a Wonderful Life* and the poor response to *Magic Town,* James Stewart was in need of a good property, preferably one that would give him the chance to show a tougher image and get away from genial folksiness. *Call Northside 777* was an excellent choice, as was Stewart's decision to work with Henry Hathaway, a tough, no-nonsene kind of director. Hathaway felt the need in the post-war world to give films a better sense of reality, to get outside the studios and shoot in real locations. Just prior to this he had made the gritty crime film *Kiss of Death,* shooting much of it in New York, and for *Northside* he took his whole company to Chicago.

The film is based on a true story, that of Frank Wiecek (Richard Conte), who spent eleven years in jail for a crime he did not commit, and of the newspaperman, Mickey McNeal (Stewart), whose dogged efforts got him released. The case comes to his attention when his editor (Lee J. Cobb) spots a small ad in the Personal Notices column of his paper, offering $5000 for information about the killer of a police officer in 1932, and to call Tillie Wiecek (Kasia Orzazeski) at Northside 777. McNeal routinely follows up his editor's suggestion and becomes intrigued by the woman's dedication. She is a scrubwoman who has put aside most of her meager wages through the years in order to clear her son. McNeal goes to see the son and finds him to be a man resigned to his fate. He is not eager to be released and he has encouraged his wife Helen (Joanne de Bergh) to re-marry in order to provide a home for their son.

With Kasia Orzazeski.

With Richard Conte.

With Paul Harvey and Lee J. Cobb.

With Richard Conte, Michael Chapin, Kasia
Orzazeski, Joanne de Bergh and E.G. Marshall.

McNeal next visits the ex-wife and her new husband
(E. G. Marshall) and is struck by how devoted and
respectful they are of Frank. Encouraged by his own
wife (Helen Walker) and his editor McNeal starts to
dig into the research for his story.

The more he digs the more he becomes convinced of Wiecek's innocence. The key to the mystery
is a woman named Wanda Shutnik (Helen Garde),
who was the owner of the speakeasy in which the
policeman was killed. After much tracking McNeal
finds Wanda and discovers that she was a false
witness. He also discovers inaccuracies in police
records concerning the time of arrest and indictment,
and he is finally able to present sufficient evidence to
facilitate the release and pardoning of Frank Wiecek.
As Frank leaves the prison he is met by his son, his
ex-wife and her husband, and he is united with the

mother whose dedication has resulted in his
exoneration.

Henry Hathaway's use of actual locations
proved an asset in the making of *Call Northside 777*
and doubtlessly affected this style of filmmaking. He
involved the Polish community of Chicago and employed many of the local citizenry, but it is still
Stewart's performance that provides the film with its
spine. It was now apparent, more than ever, that
Stewart was a masterful film actor, and one particularly gifted with the ability to portray doggedness, to convey the character of the kind of man who
will not give up on something if he believes in it. By
now he had already played a newspaperman a half-
dozen times on the screen and he joked that he could
probably go into that profession if this one failed.
There was no cause for doubt. *Call Northside 777*
proved to everyone, Stewart included, that he had no
cause to worry about the course of his career in the
picture business.

ON OUR MERRY WAY

UNITED ARTISTS, 1948

Produced by Benedict Borgeaus; *Directed* by King Vidor and Leslie Fenton; *Written* by Lawrence Stallings, based on stories by John O'Hara, Arch Oboler and Lou Breslow; *Photographed* by John Seitz, Ernest Laszlo and Joseph Biroc; *Music* by Heinz Roemheld; 107 minutes.

CAST:

Martha Pease, Paulette Goddard; *Slim*, James Stewart; *Hank*, Henry Fonda; *Al*, Fred MacMurray; *Oliver Pease*, Burgess Meredith; *Gloria*, Dorothy Lamour; *Harry James*, Himself; *Floyd*, William Demarest; *Eli Hobbs*, Hugh Herbert; *Maxim*, Eduardo Ciannelli; *Ashton*, Victor Moore; *Mr. Sadd*, Charles D. Brown; *Lola*, Dorothy Ford; *Housekeeper*, Nana Bryant; *Cynthia*, Betty Caldwell; *Mr. Atwood*, John Qualen; *Bookie*, Frank Moran; *Zoot*, Carl Switzer; *Edgar Hobbs*, David Whorf; *Bank Teller*, Chester Clute.

With Burgess Meredith and Henry Fonda.

It is odd that it did not occur to anyone until 1948 to co-star James Stewart with his friend Henry Fonda. It was no secret that they had known each other since their fledgling days back East and by 1948 they were stars of virtual equal rank. *On Our Merry Way* brought them together on screen but in only one-third of a film. Like so many movies that feature a roster of stars in episodes of a story, this one failed to live up to a promise that probably seemed wonderful in the planning stages. It was filmed under the title *A Miracle Can Happen*, but the producer wisely dropped it lest it tempt critics to point out that in making the picture a miracle had not happened.

The thematic thread of the movie is the question, "What great influence has a little child had upon your life?" The question is the invention of Marth Pease (Paulette Goddard), who gives it to her husband Oliver (Burgess Meredith), a newspaperman who wants to write a good story. He roams around to get his material and the first people to whom he puts the question are a pair of footloose, down-on-their-luck musicians, a pianist called Slim (Stewart) and his chum, cornetist Lank (Fonda). After that Oliver interviews a pair of Hollywood extras (Dorothy Lamour and Victor Moore), and a couple of drifters (Fred MacMurray and William Demarest), who are at the mercy of a little boy who plays practical jokes on them. From these encounters Oliver is able to concoct a successful tale.

Almost everyone agreed that the best part of *On Our Merry Way* was the first episode, with

With Carl "Alfalfa" Switzer and Henry Fonda.

Stewart and Fonda as musicians trying to fix an amateur music contest in a California beach resort because of their desperate need for money. They try to arrange it so that the son of the mayor will win. The child of their story is a gorgeous six-foot-tall girl known as Babe (Dorothy Ford), who plays the saxophone and who wins their band away from them on a bet.

On Our Merry Way might have been better had the Stewart-Fonda section been enlarged into the whole film. Since this enjoyable material was written especially for the actors by the esteemed John O'Hara, the decision to limit it to an episode seems the more regrettable. While King Vidor and Leslie Fenton are listed as the directors, both John Huston and George Stevens were also involved. That they chose not to allow their names to be used in the credits suggests a problematic production, and possible reasons the movie did not make much of a merry way.

With Dorothy Ford.

ROPE

WARNER BROS., 1948

Produced by Sidney Bernstein and Alfred Hitchcock; *Directed* by Hitchcock; *Written* by Arthur Laurents, based on the play by Patrick Hamilton; *Photographed in color* by Joseph Valentine; *Music Director:* Leo F. Forbstein; 80 minutes.

CAST:

Rupert Cadell, James Stewart; *Shaw Brandon,* John Dall; *Philip,* Farley Granger; *Janet Walker,* Joan Chandler; *Mr. Kentley,* Sir Cedric Hardwicke; *Mrs. Atwater,* Constance Collier; *Mrs. Wilson,* Edith Evanson; *Kenneth Lawrence,* Douglas Dick; *David Kentley,* Dick Hogan.

Rope was James Stewart's thirty-third film but, except for the final sequences of *Ice Follies of 1939,* he

With Farley Granger and John Dall.

had not made one in color. *Rope* was also the first color film made by Alfred Hitchcock, as well as being his first as an independent director-producer. It was not, by 1948 movie practices, a logical choice for color, being a verbal play, filmed entirely on a single sound stage at Warner Bros. studios. However, the decision to shoot in color was a minor consideration compared to Hitchcock's much more radical one of filming it all as continuous action, with breaks only in the changeover from reel to reel. The film runs 80 minutes and that is also the length of the story. This was also the running time of Patrick Hamilton's play when it was originally presented in New York. Hitchcock gave himself the challenge of making the film as near to a play as he could get it, with sequences running the length of time of a canister of film, roughly ten minutes, with transitions accomplished by moving behind an actor's back or focusing on an object. Years later, in discussing it with French director Francois Truffaut, Hitchcock admitted that it was a gimmick. "I undertook *Rope* as a stunt. That's the only way I can describe it. I don't know how I came to indulge in it."

In the film Stewart is a professor at an elite school, a man who specializes in intellectual theory

With Sir Cedric Hardwicke and Farley Granger.

With Douglas Dick, Joan Chandler, Sir Cedric Hardwicke, Constance Collier, John Dall and Farley Granger.

With John Dall and Farley Granger.

On the set with Alfred Hitchcock (hands in pockets) and virtually the entire cast of the picture.

and who has just been lecturing on the Nietzschean philosophy of superhumankind. Two of his former students are themselves super intellectuals, Brandon (John Dall) and Philip (Farley Granger), both homosexuals and both men without human compassion and kindness. As a sheer intellectual exercise they murder a classmate and place his body in a chest. It is, they rationalize, a murder without motive and one that cannot be traced to them. To make the exercise more exciting they entertain a party in their swank apartment and invite their teacher, Rupert Cadell (Stewart); the murdered boy's father, Mr. Kentley (Sir Cedric Hardwicke); his fiancée, Janet Walker (Joan Chandler); and a few others. To make the experience even sharper for themselves, they hold a buffet supper with the chest as the serving table.

The party at first stimulates the two students, especially when they see the father holding a set of books bound together with the rope with which they have strangled his son. They continue their enjoyment by baiting Cadell with academic hints pointing to the crime that they have committed. What they do not count upon is the weakness in the nature of Philip. Brandon is a complete psychotic; Philip is not, and the strain gradually rattles his equilibrium. Eventually Cadell senses what has happened. After the party he returns to question the two students and accuse them of murder. He finds the body, calls the police and awaits their arrival.

Rope is a very clever parlor game of a murder mystery. It did not please a wide audience and must be rated among Hitchcock's least successful films. It is not without merit. The script and the acting are mostly excellent, and for filmmakers it is interesting to study in order to determine how Hitchcock constructed it all. For the actors it was almost like doing a play, requiring them to learn the dialogue for the ten-minute sequences. They had ten days of rehearsal, itself unusual in shooting films, and Hitchcock took eighteen days to shoot, much of that time being devoted to technical matters, such as the movements of the set on wheels.

Stewart was not pleased with his work in the film, and several critics pointed out something that had not been said about him before—that he seemed not entirely at ease in front of the cameras. In other words, a role much easier to play on stage than on film. He felt that the ingenuity of Hitchcock's devices were at variance with the nature of the material—an intellectual exercise forced to be technical. At one point in the filming Stewart ribbed Hitchcock: "You're really missing out on a wonderful opportunity here. You ought to charge people five bucks to come in and see the set rather than the movie, because the movements of the camera and the walls and everything is much more interesting than what we're saying."

YOU GOTTA STAY HAPPY

UNIVERSAL, 1948

Produced by Karl Tunberg; *Directed* by H. C. Potter; *Written* by Karl Tunberg, based on the story by Robert Carson; *Photographed* by Russell Metty; *Music* by Daniele Amfitheatrof; 100 minutes.

CAST:

Dee Dee Dillwood, Joan Fontaine; *Marvin Payne,* James Stewart; *Bullets Baker,* Eddie Albert; *Ralph Tutwiler,* Roland Young; *Henry Benson,* Willard Parker; *Mr. Racknell,* Percy Kilbride; *Mr. Caslon,* Porter Hall; *Georgia Goodrich,* Marcy McGuire; *Milton Goodrich,* Arthur Walsh; *Dr. Blucher,* Paul Cavanaugh; *Dick Hebert,* William Bakewell; *Martin,* Halliwell Hobbs; *Jack Samuels,* Stanley Prager; *Aunt Martha,* Mary Forbes; *Mrs. Racknell,* Edith Evanson; *Barnabas,* Peter Roman; *Jud Travis,* Housely Stevenson.

With Roland Young and Willard Parker.

Made a decade earlier, *You Gotta Stay Happy* would probably be a worthy item in the screwball comedy listing—provided it had starred Carole Lombard. In 1948 it was a rather obvious attempt to give Joan Fontaine a chance to have a little fun, in the wake of her heavy emoting in pictures like *Kiss the Blood Off My Hands* and *Letter from an Unknown Woman.* It came about because her then husband, William Dozier, was a high-ranking production executive at Universal and was therefore in a position to find his wife whatever kind of material she needed. His producer friend Karl Tunberg wanted to make a movie of a comedy he had partly scripted, and once Fontaine gave her nod of approval, Tunberg was in business. James Stewart, himself looking for something light to follow the lugubrious *Rope,* agreed to be the leading man, even though it meant second billing, but Stewart has never been an actor to fight over billing.

In this blithe little picture Fontaine is socialite-millionairess Dee Dee Dilworth, a lady about as light-headed as she is light-hearted, who finally marries at the urging of her psychiatrist, but who on her wedding night in a New York hotel finds she doesn't care to stay with her stuffy husband (Willard Parker). To escape him she ducks into another room, being occupied by Marvin Payne (Stewart), an ex-army pilot now trying to run his own freight air service and not having much luck. She wants Marvin to take her with him on his scheduled flight the next day to California and when he refuses she drugs herself with an overdose of aspirins, making it necessary for him

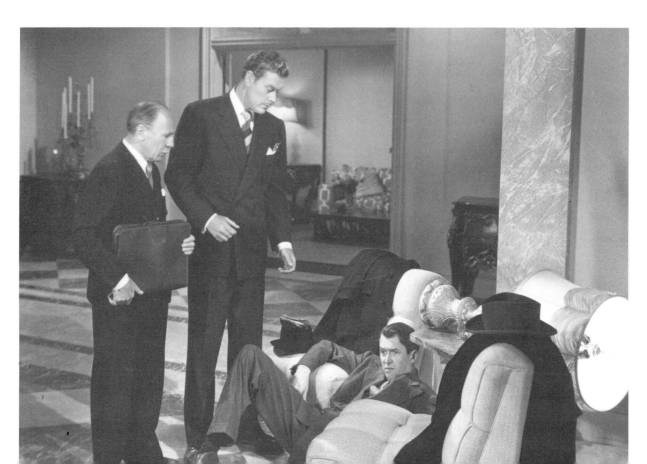

and his partner, Bullets Baker (Eddie Albert), to carry her onto the plane rather than desert her in such a strange condition. Marvin has only two planes in his company. This one has on its manifest—in a complement that could only come from the mind of a movie scenarist—a shipment of fish and sea food, a coffin containing a corpse, a chimpanzee with a taste for cigars, an escaped embezzler (Porter Hall), a GI and his bride (Arthur Walsh and Marcy McGuire) and a handful of other oddballs. Marvin resists the flirtatious Dee Dee, until they put down somewhere in the midwest and put up at a farm owned by kindly Mr. Racknell (Percy Kilbridge), a bumpkin with a very large family. By the time they get to California, Dee Dee has decided that this upright, struggling pilot is the man for her and not the dullard she left in New York. He is at first a little shocked to learn of her status in wealthy society, but finds he can adapt himself. With his initiative and her money, it seems a marriage made by the board room in heaven.

You Gotta Stay Happy was designed to amuse, and it did its job. Joan Fontaine failed to show any great talent as a comedienne but she did well enough. As for the leading man, *Time* made all the comment needed: "This is the kind of role that Jimmy Stewart could play blindfolded, hog-tied and in the bottom of a well." Enough said.

With Joan Fontaine.

With Joan Fontaine.

THE STRATTON STORY

MGM, 1949

Produced by Jack Cummings; *Directed* by Sam Wood; *Written* by Douglas Morrow and Guy Trosper; *Photographed* by Harold Rosson; *Music* by Adolphe Deutsch; 106 minutes.

CAST:

Monty Stratton, James Stewart; *Ethel Stratton*, June Allyson; *Barney Wile*, Frank Morgan; *Ma Stratton*, Agnes Moorehead; *Gene Watson*, Bill Williams; *Ted Lyons*, Bruce Cowling; *Pitcher*, Eugene Bearden; *Bill Dickey*, Himself; *Jimmy Dykes*, Himself; *Higgins*, Cliff Clark; *Dot*, Mary Lawrence; *Luke Appling*, Dean White; *Larnie*, Robert Gist.

With Frank Morgan and Agnes Moorehead.

Eight years after his last film at MGM, *Ziegfeld Girl* in 1941, James Stewart returned to the studio that had once been his film alma mater. The result, *The Stratton Story,* would be a personal and commercial triumph, one that would have *The New York Times* calling it "the best thing that has happened to Mr. Stewart in his post-war career." After several films of dubious merit he needed a winner. This was it, the story of Monty Stratton, a farmer with a passion for baseball, who became a major league player, and lost a leg in a hunting accident in 1938. Rather than quit the game, Stratton surmounted the obstacle of an artificial leg and continued his career as an ace pitcher. MGM had purchased the rights to Douglas Morrow's book about Stratton but Louis B. Mayer was doubtful about putting the film into production. Movies about sports figures had seldom been successful, and this one, about a crippled ball player, seemed to him an unlikely winner. He finally gave his approval, with the idea that Van Johnson would play Stratton opposite June Allyson, with whom he had already made five films. The choice of Johnson met with a lot of opposition from people who thought his playing would make the movie more of a tearjerker than it should be. The man Monty Stratton wanted to play himself was James Stewart, and once that fact became known there was no talk of any other actor.

Hedging his bets, Mayer assigned the job of directing the film to the solid old pro Sam Wood, who had already directed Stewart as a football-playing middie in *Navy Blue and Gold,* but, more important, had directed Gary Cooper in his superb performance as baseball legend Lou Gehrig in *The Pride of the Yankees* (1942). The success of the Stratton film would give Wood the distinction of having made the two finest baseball movies in Hollywood history. Wood was a tough, no-nonsense kind of director and his approach was the correct one for a movie that might easily have slipped into the maudlin in softer hands. And both he and Stewart had the advantage of having Stratton on hand during the production, with the actor getting daily workouts from the man he was portraying. Much of the filming was done in Wrigley Field in Chicago and in Hollywood's Gilmore Park, with additional shots in American League parks in Chicago, Cleveland, Detroit and Washington. Under Stratton's tutelage Stewart became thoroughly convincing with bat and ball.

The screenplay sticks closely to the facts. Stratton is discovered in a sandlot game by a once-famous

With June Allyson, Agnes Moorehead and Frank Morgan.

With Bill Williams.

With Frank Morgan, Bruce Cowling and June Allyson.

With June Allyson and the baby who inspired the father to walk.

With June Allyson.

With Frank Morgan and ballplayer.

a girl from Omaha, Ethel (Allyson), he bores her with talk about the game, although after a while she becomes impressed by his shy manner and his sincerity.

At the end of spring training Monty goes to Chicago with the White Sox but because he fares poorly he is farmed out to Omaha, which at least gives him access to Ethel. With her promise to marry him he becomes even more dedicated to baseball and is soon back with the White Sox. In Chicago Monty scores a hit by striking out Yankee slugger Bill Dickey (himself) and with time Monty's fame grows. After the final game the Strattons, now with a baby son, return to the Texas farm. One day on a hunting trip Monty accidentally shoots himself in the leg. Doctors advise that in order to save his life the leg must be amputated below the knee. To the ace baseballer it seems that his career has ended. He is bitter and despondent, until the day he sees his young son struggling in his first efforts to walk. The father takes inspiration from the child, and learns to walk himself. With an artificial leg Monty makes a great comeback in the game and in his first performance with his new limb he leads his team to a major victory.

The Stratton Story was an easy winner at the box office. It brought Stewart a raft of complimentary notices and, in a sense, his triumph, after a string of shaky movies, must have seemed a little like Stratton's own resumption of his career. It was a role that needed a fine actor to bring it to genuine film life and Stewart was perfect. In working with the actor, Sam Wood found, as had other directors, that Stewart was a committed worker, willing to put in any amount of time to master the physical requirements of the part. Monty Stratton himself was delighted with the film, especially with Stewart's hurling on the field. The *New Republic* said that Stewart played "the pitching phenomenon from the back country with a pleasant Will Rogers wit, and in the ball park sequences looks astonishingly professional."

As good as the baseball sequences might be, it is still Stewart's skill as an actor that gives *The Stratton Story* its real clout. The most crucial scene is the one in which he makes his resolve to walk again, after having sat around for a long time in gloom, refusing to use the artificial limb. When he sees his baby son master his first few steps he is shamed into trying to walk himself. Together in the backyard the crippled father and the infant hold hands and inch their way along. It is a touching and remarkable scene, and one of the many highlights in the film career of James Stewart.

and now down-on-his-heels player, Barney Wiles (Frank Morgan), who tells Stratton he has potential. Barney also has to convince Ma Stratton (Agnes Moorehead), who needs her son to help run their small Texas farm. Barney takes Monty to California, where the White Sox are in training and where he talks Jimmy Dykes (playing himself) into giving Monty a tryout. The young Stratton takes to pro baseball like a fish to water and on a blind date with

MALAYA

MGM, 1949

Produced by Edwin Knopf; *Directed* by Richard Thorpe; *Written* by Frank Fenton, based on a story by Manchester Boddy; *Photographed* by George Folsey; *Music* by Bronislau Kaper; 98 minutes.

CAST:

Carnahan, Spencer Tracy; *John Royer,* James Stewart; *Luana,* Valentina Cortesa; *Dutchman,* Sydney Greenstreet; *Kellar,* John Hodiak; *John Manchester,* Lionel Barrymore; *Romano,* Gilbert Roland; *Bruno Gruber,* Roland Winters; *Colonel Tomura,* Richard Loo; *Matisson,* Lester Matthews; *Carlos Tassuma,* Ian MacDonald; *Big Man,* Charles Meredith; *Carson,* James Todd; *Official,* Paul Kruger; *Secretary,* Anna Q. Nilsson.

With John Hodiak and Spencer Tracy.

James Stewart had to wait fifteen years before making his second film with Spencer Tracy, who by 1950 had become a kind of MGM Rock of Gibraltar. Despite Stewart's own considerable success, there was no doubt that he would have to take second billing, although it would be in a movie for which neither he nor Tracy would be much remembered. *Malaya* is perhaps of most interest to students of film acting, since it enables the student to examine the techniques of two highly individualistic actors, both masters of a slew of personal mannerisms. However, no actor, including Stewart, could pull a scene away from the mighty Tracy.

As he had in his first film with Tracy, Stewart again played a newspaperman, this time a correspondent involved in smuggling rubber out of the Malay jungles during the Second World War and getting it to the Allies. The story behind the making of the film is a little more interesting than the film itself. In 1942 newspaper editor Manchester Boddy, on whose story the film was based, wrote to President Roosevelt with a suggested plan to get badly needed rubber out of Japanese-occupied Malaya. Such a plan had already

With Spencer Tracy and Lester Matthews.

With Valentina Cortesa, Spencer Tracy and Sydney Greenstreet.

On the set with Valentina Cortesa.

been implemented but Boddy was able to contribute ideas. It was a successful operation and after the war Boddy sold the story to Dory Schary, then head of production at RKO. When Schary moved to MGM he took the story with him and discussed it with Tracy, who was so enthusiastic about the concept that he cancelled a vacation and asked Schary to set up immediate production. When Stewart heard about this he asked to see the script and after reading it he agreed to take the role of the newspaperman. He had always wanted to do another film with Tracy and suddenly the opportunity presented itself.

Manchester Boddy's own part in the story is played in the film by Lionel Barrymore, the name changed to John Manchester, a New York publisher who initiates the project. With government approval a reporter with much experience in the Far East, John Royer (Stewart) is called in to team up with a smuggler named Carnaham (Tracy), who is released from a life sentence in Alcatraz to proceed to Malaya. To facilitate the plans of infiltrating the rubber fields they hire a dealer known as The Dutchman (Sydney Greenstreet), a man interested only in money. But he

knows all the right contacts and methods, and with his help Royer and Carnaham start to ship out quantities of rubber from under the noses of the Japanese occupation forces. With the U.S. Navy's help they get out 150,000 tons of rubber in two shipments, but things go awry with the third shipment. The commander of the Japanese contingent (Richard Loo) in pursuit of the smugglers catches up with them as they move down a river toward the naval rendezvous. Royer is killed in the skirmish but the wounded Carnaham manages to get the shipment out, taking with him an Italian refugee (Valentina Cortesa) to whom he has taken a fancy.

Malaya is a good action melodrama, and a reminder of a little known operation in the Second World War. The principal actors are all better than their material, with Stewart playing his newspaper-man-adventurer as a rather dour and cynical type who has learned by hard experience to cast most of humankind in a suspicious light. It may not have been a difficult role to act, but with such renowned scene stealers as Tracy, Sydney Greenstreet and Lionel Barrymore he knew that he could not relax in the role for a single minute. Yes, *Malaya* is definitely an item for students of film acting.

WINCHESTER '73

UNIVERSAL, 1959

Produced by Aaron Rosenberg; *Directed* by Anthony Mann; *Written* by Robert Richards and Borden Chase, based on a story by Stuart Lake; *Photographed* by William Daniels; *Music Director,* Joseph Gershenson; 92 minutes.

CAST:

Lin McAdam, James Stewart; *Lola Manners,* Shelley Winters; *Waco Johnny Dean,* Dan Duryea; *Dutch Henry Brown,* Stephen McNally; *High Spade,* Millard Mitchell; *Steve Miller,* Charles Drake; *Joe Lamont,* John McIntire; *Wyatt Earp,* Will Geer; *Sergeant Wilkes,* Jay C. Flippen; *Young Bull,* Rock Hudson; *Jack Riker,* John Alexander; *Wesley,* Steve Brodie; *Wheeler,* James Millican; *Latigo Means,* Abner Biberman; *Doan,* Tony Curtis; *Crater,* James Best; *Mossman,* Gregg Martel.

With Millard Mitchell.

With Will Geer and Stephen McNally.

With Stephen McNally.   *With Millard Mitchell and Will Geer.*

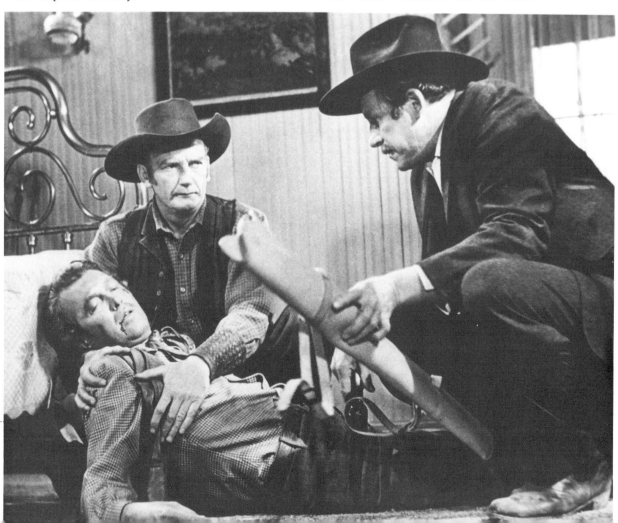

Ordinarily the sequence in which an actor's films is released is of no great importance. However, in the case of *Winchester '73* and *Broken Arrow*, the former may truly be regarded as the beginning of James Stewart's strong identity in westerns and not the latter, which was made first but released later. *Broken Arrow* is a good western but Stewart's hero is a mild man compared to the complex, driven Lin McAdam of *Winchester '73*. Stewart, essentially an Easterner, was not a likely candidate to become a first-rate movie Westerner, since his identity until 1950 was mostly as a conveyor of light comedy, with a few forays into drama. In the Stewart career, *Winchester '73* represents a definite breakthrough. Not only was it the first seen of his seventeen true westerns, including some of the finest ever made, but it revealed him as an actor capable of displaying anger, neurosis and ferocity. It was at this point that he ceased to be Jimmy Stewart and became James

With Dan Duryea.

Stewart. He would still be called upon now and then to be affable and boyishly charming, but there would now be pictures in which he would be anything *but* affable and boyishly charming.

This crucial turning point in Stewart's career came about through his teaming with director Anthony Mann. Stewart made four films with Alfred Hitchcock, three with Frank Capra and three with John Ford, and although these were all vital relationships with pantheon directors, his most productive partnership was with Mann, with whom he made eight films, five of them westerns. Mann (1906-1967) was a very masculine director. He had about him an air of tough authority and he seemed fascinated with the ambivalent nature of the human animal. And he saw in Stewart qualities that no other director had spotted—the ability to reveal the anger beneath the surface of even the most docile man, the containment of anger and temper, and the occasional bursting of that containment. Many of the men in the Mann westerns are those bent on revenge, and it is ironic that in Stewart, a man with probably not a

With Millard Mitchell, Tony Curtis, Charles Drake and Jay C. Flippen.

thread of such emotion in his makeup, he found an actor so capable of portraying it.

The weapon of the title is a rifle of exquisite precision, so perfect that it cannot be sold but won only in competition. In Dodge City on July 4, 1873, Lyn McAdam and his friend High Spade (Millard Mitchell) engage in such a competition, which boils down to just McAdam and Dutch Henry Brown (Stephen McNally). McAdam wins but Brown steals the prize rifle and flees, with McAdam in pursuit. McAdam now has two reasons to be after Brown—to retrieve the rifle but also, more important, to revenge the death of his father, who was killed by Brown. To make matters even more vicious, it so happens that McAdam and Brown are brothers.

Brown loses the rifle in a game of poker to a corrupt Indian agent (Joe Lamont), who sells guns to the Indians and rationalizes that they are used just for hunting. The rationale costs him his life when an Indian chief (Rock Hudson) kills him to get the rifle, which then falls into the hands of Steve Miller (Charles Drake) when a band of Indians are wiped out in conflict with a company of cavalry. Miller and his girlfriend, Lola (Shelley Winters), are riding in the group being protected by the soldiers. Shortly after-

wards Miller is killed by an outlaw, Waco Johnny Dean (Dan Duryea), who takes the rifle and gives it back to Brown. McAdam comes into conflict with Waco and kills him, but not before finding out where he can find Brown. He tracks him to a mountaintop and there, after a hard fight, kills the brother who killed his father, in addition to reclaiming the coveted rifle and taking up a relationship with Lola.

Winchester '73 is a western that does not lose its appeal. It is splendidly crafted, as is the rifle that is the centerpiece of its story. In essence the film is rather like a parable, with the rifle a mystical symbol of perfection for which men must strive, and in so doing reveal their character. In this story the rifle-symbol is the prize won by the decent son and the cause of death of the evil one. It was a dramatic theme of great appeal to Anthony Mann, who gravitated toward stories about social outsiders and loners and men bent on revenge, and who found he could best work with this kind of material in the setting of the western, with its stark characters and boundless landscapes. All five of the westerns Mann made with Stewart are of this ilk—Greek tragedy on the range—and in the history of the genre the relationship between Mann and Stewart compares favorably with that between John Wayne and John Ford, and between Randolph Scott and Budd Boetticher.

The success of *Winchester '73* was of great benefit to both Stewart and Mann, giving the director a spurt of confidence that set him on a higher level, and giving the actor the chance to broaden his style. Even Stewart's greatest admirers were probably surprised to see this new aspect of his screen persona, this ability to convey rage and disgust. In one scene with Dan Duryea in a saloon, Stewart, wanting to get information, grabs Duryea's right arm, twists it behind his back and slams his head down on the counter, with Duryea begging for mercy as Stewart loses his calm manner and turns ferocious. Stewart had possibly spent some time worrying about his screen image and the constant references to his nice folksiness. With *Winchester '73* he broke new ground, and came up with a portrayal of a tough, sinewy westerner of a kind who looked to the saddle born. Anthony Mann later said that one of the things that most impressed him about Stewart was the actor's attitude toward preparing a role, his willingness to work hard and take risks. He was impressed by the fact that Stewart spent hours studying rifle shooting in order to appear expert and more hours learning to ride a horse with skill and ease. In Stewart, Mann found a partner and a collaborator.

128

BROKEN ARROW

20TH CENTURY-FOX, 1950

Produced by Julian Blaustein; *Directed* by Delmer Daves; *Written* by Michael Blankfort, based on the novel *Blood Brother* by Elliott Arnold; *Photographed in color* by Ernest Palmer; *Music* by Hugo Friedhofer; 93 minutes.

CAST:

Tom Jeffords, James Stewart; *Cochise*, Jeff Chandler; *Sonseeahray*, Debra Paget; *General Howard*, Basil Ruysdael; *Ben Slade*, Will Geer; *Terry*, Joyce MacKenzie; *Duffield*, Arthur Hunnicutt; *Colonel Bernall*, Raymond Bramley; *Goklia*, Jay Silverheels; *Nalikadeya*, Argentina Brunnetti; *Bocher*, Jack Lee; *Lonergan*, Robert Adler; *Miner*, Harry Carter; *Lowrie*, Robert Griffin; *Juan*, Bill Wilkerson; *Chip Slade*, Mickey Kuhn.

With Basil Ruysdael.

Broken Arrow is often regarded as the first major film to deal respectfully with the American Indian and to show his role in the conflict with whites in the last century. Actually, that viewpoint had been touched upon in a number of films over the years, as far back as *The Vanishing American*, with Richard Dix, in 1925, and in the minor but excellent Tim McCoy western, *End of the Trail*, in 1932. Even the Errol Flynn Custer saga *They Died With Their Boots On*, with Anthony Quinn as Chief Crazy Horse, paid honor to the courage of Indians in battle and noted the raw deal they were given in their treaties with Washington. However, none of this need diminish the place of *Broken Arrow* in movie history. It does indeed reveal the Indians as people with structured lives and their own set of ideals. Historically it also has a place in Hollywood's attempts in the late 1940's to attack various forms of American bias, including anti-Semitism and the prejudice against blacks. A great deal of this new wave of morality in Hollywood was due to 20th Century-Fox chieftain Darryl F. Zanuck, under whose banner *Broken Arrow* was made.

James Stewart, whose own intolerance toward racial intolerance had been sharpened by his years of war service, readily accepted producer Julian Blaustein's offer to play the role of Tom Jefford, a scout who tries to promote peace between the whites in

With Jeff Chandler.

With Jeff Chandler.

Arizona and the Chiricahua Apaches, and who marries an Indian girl. It was a part some other leading men of the time may not have wished to play. The story takes place in 1870 and concerns Tom Jefford's decision to reach the leader of the Apaches, Cochise (Jeff Chandler), and try to bring peace between his people and the whites. Jefford finally manages to get to Cochise and convinces the Indian of his sincerity, having first learned something of the Apache dialect and customs. Cochise agrees that the continual warfare is futile, but it is hard for him to trust the whites, since so many of his family and tribesmen have died. As a token of good faith Cochise allows for the safe passage of U.S. Mail riders through his territory. Eager for peace, Washington sends General Howard (Basil Ruysdael) to negotiate a peace treaty.

The peace endures for a while, until renegade elements among both the whites and the Indians spoil it. In the meantime Jefford falls in love with the pretty Indian girl, Sonseeahray (Debra Paget), and receives Cochise's permission to marry her. He settles into the Indian village and all is well for a few months, until trouble is caused by Apaches from another tribe attacking and killing whites. They are driven off by Cochise and his men but this is unknown to the whites, who attack Cochise. In the conflict Sonseeahray is killed and Jefford is wounded. In his fury Jefford is willing to lead the Apaches against the whites, but the wise Cochise counsels him otherwise, pointing out that these whites were not authorized by their government to do what they did. He tells Jefford, "As I bear the murder of my people, so you will bear the murder of your wife."

Broken Arrow could easily have come off as pious and stilted, but instead, thanks to an intelligent screenplay and the firm hand of director Delmar Daves, it looks closely at its subject matter and contains much information about Apache culture. Daves took his crew of almost two hundred people into the stark Coconino Mountains, which are part

131

With Jeff Chandler and Debra Paget.

of the National Forest of Arizona, and employed several hundred Apaches. The film benefited from this authenticity and from the fine Technicolor photography of Ernest Palmer. Less effective was the casting of then seventeen-year-old Debra Paget as Sonseeahray. She is simply too pretty and refined of manner to be an Apache of the period. Jeff Chandler, an actor with slavic ancestry, fared much better as Cochise and the role caused his career to surge. But the point might be made that he is a shade too noble in his portrayal of the great Indian warrior.

The film met with mixed reactions from the critics, some of whom found it condescending in its treatment of the Indians and a little self-serving, but with time *Broken Arrow* has settled into somewhat better regard in the annals of westerns. The critical reaction to Stewart was also mixed, with some negative comments about his mannerisms being inappropriate to the role. *The New York Times* was especially critical in referring to his fumbling of words and his waving of hands in lazy gestures. Stewart has never been a man to disregard honest criticism and he doubtlessly pondered the New York comment. *Broken Arrow* was filmed in late 1949 but not released by Fox until August of 1950, by which time *Winchester '73* had been on the market for two months. The difference in the two performances is striking. Disregarding the essentially comic *Destry Rides Again*, *Broken Arrow* is Stewart's first genuine western and he clearly learned from it. Those critics who felt he was not completely at ease out West would have to eat their words when Stewart later appeared in a string of classic westerns.

132

THE JACKPOT

20TH CENTURY-FOX, 1950

Produced by Samuel G. Engel; *Directed* by Walter Lang; *Written* by Phoebe and Henry Ephron, based on an article by John McNulty; *Photographed* by Joseph La Shelle; *Music* by Lionel Newman; 87 minutes.

CAST:

Bill Lawrence, James Stewart; *Amy Lawrence*, Barbara Hale; *Harry Summers*, James Gleason; *Mr. Woodruff*, Fred Clark; *Leslie*, Alan Mowbray; *Hilda Jones*, Patricia Medina; *Phyllis Lawrence*, Natalie Wood; *Tommy Lawrence*, Tommy Rettig; *Pete Spooner*, Robert Gist; *Fred Burns*, Lyle Talbot; *Al Vogel*, Charles Tannen; *Captain Sullivan*, Bigelow Sayre; *Mr. Brown*, Dick Cogan; *Mrs. Brown*, Jewel Rose; *Mr. MacDougall*, Eddie Fireston; *Mrs. Mac-Dougall*, Estelle Ettere.

The Jackpot is a Jimmy Stewart picture. After several melodramas and a pair of westerns, it seemed necessary to remind the public of the Jimmy Stewart image—the image of slow-speaking, slightly confused, folksy charm. In short, the ingratiatingly ordinary fellow caught up in extraordinary circumstances. In this comic adventure he is a small town department store manager named Bill Lawrence, who is about to be made a vice president when he wins $24,000 on a radio quiz program. His life and that of his wife Amy (Barbara Hale) and their children Phyllis (Natalie Wood) and Tommy (Tommy Rettig) becomes all topsy-turvy.

Joy soon turns to concern. Bill's winnings take the form of merchandise and services, all of them serving the causes of the companies involved. Among the mountain of prizes are thousands of cans of soup, a Shetland pony, a portable swimming pool, electrical appliances, shrubbery and a station wagon. The Lawrence home becomes as busy with deliveries and callers as a railroad station. Matters worsen when an eccentric interior designer, Leslie (Alan Mowbray), arrives to completely alter the house's decor while ignoring the protestations of the occupants. Bill becomes even more distraught when his reporter friend Harry Summers (James Gleason) points out to him that income tax will have to be paid on all this newfound wealth and property. For

Bill, life now becomes something like a plush nightmare.

    With a $7000 tax bill staring him in the face, Bill sells off a few of his prizes, causing more people to descend upon his home. Among the prizes is the chance to have his portrait painted by a beautiful artist, Hilda (Patricia Medina), which provokes Amy's jealousy when Bill spends hours away from home in the artist's studio. She suspects an affair and banishes Bill to a separate bed, which happens to be out in the yard with lots of other stuff. In desperation Bill seeks out a fence in Chicago in order to sell off his prizes, and in so doing manages to get himself arrested in a police raid. Bill telephones his boss (Fred Clark) for help but finds instead that he has been fired because the boss has heard about some questionable transactions. Harry Summers gets Bill out of jail by proving his innocence, Hilda explains to Amy that there was nothing between her and Bill other than the painting of his portrait, the Chicago fence turns up with $5000 and Bill's boss admits to having misjudged Bill. After all the chaos the life of Bill Lawrence returns to something approaching normalcy.

    The Jackpot was released in December of 1950, at a time when radio quiz shows flooded the airwaves. The film easily found its audience and received mostly complimentary notices for its comic send-up of the giveaway business. It is among the best of Stewart's film comedies and allowed him plenty of range for his skill in this genre. Few actors have been able to so deftly balance geniality with confusion.

With Barbara Hale.

With James Gleason.

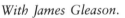

134

HARVEY

UNIVERSAL, 1951

Produced by John Beck; *Directed* by Henry Koster; *Written* by Mary Chase and Oscar Brodney, based on the play by Chase; *Photographed* by William Daniels; *Music* by Frank Skinner; 104 minutes.

CAST:

Elwood P Dowd, James Stewart; *Veta Louise Simmons*, Josephine Hull; *Miss Kelly*, Peggy Dow; *Dr. Sanderson*, Charles Drake; *Dr. Chumley*, Cecil Kellaway; *Myrtle Mae*, Victoria Horne; *Wilson*, Jesse White; *Judge Gaffney*, William Lynn; *Lofgren*, Wallace Ford; *Mrs. Chumley*, Nana Bryant; *Mrs. Chauvenet*, Grace Mills; *Herman*, Clem Bevans; *Mrs. McGiff*, Ida Moore; *Cracker*, Richard Wessell.

Cecil Kellaway, Jospehine Hull, Harvey and Elwood P. Dowd.

Harvey and its main character, a gentle, kindly alcoholic man named Elwood P. Dowd, is now so firmly linked with James Stewart that there is a tendency to think the part was created for him. It was not. The actor who originated the whimsical role was Frank Fay, who did very well as Elwood P. Dowd because he was not too far removed from the role in real life. It is not unkind to regard Fay as a fey character. Mary Chase won a Pulitizer Prize with *Harvey*, which opened on Broadway in November of 1944 and ran for more than twelve hundred performances. Stewart got his first crack at playing Dowd in 1947, as a summer replacement for Fay, and when Universal purchased the property for the screen, at the cost of one million dollars, the only actor considered for the part was Stewart. Certain New York critics said that Fay should have played the role but aside from the lack of film identification—he played a few leads and supporting roles in half a dozen films in the thirties—it is doubtful that the whimsy of his stage work would have translated to the screen. On film *Harvey* needed a man with command of film technique.

With Josephine Hull.

Elwood P. Dowd is a man in his early forties. Having inherited some money he has no need to make a living and neither has he any need to pay rent, since he lives with his sister Veta (Josephine Hull) and her daughter Myrtle Mae (Victoria Horne). But this in itself is something of a problem because Veta wants to marry off her daughter and what happens is that suitors get scared off by Elwood's talk of his friend Harvey, who is a six-foot-tall invisible rabbit. Elwood is forever telling of his first meeting with Harvey, of how he was just walking down the street and there was Harvey leaning against a lamppost, and how they just got to talking. Since Elwood is given to drinking it is assumed that alcohol has affected his mind. But it is hard to dislike him because he is not only invariably pleasant, he is also genuinely concerned about other people and always eager to help.

Veta decides she must have Elwood committed to a home for the mentally unstable but it is she who somehow ends up at the Chumley Rest Home, having admitted that she herself has seen Harvey. On his visits Elwood discusses Harvey at length with Dr. Chumley (Cecil Kellaway), until he too starts believ-

With Clem Bevans.
With Charles Drake and Peggy Dow.

ing. He even wants to know if it might be possible to hire Harvey. Later, when the doctor joins Elwood in a bar he gets tipsy and starts a conversation with the invisible rabbit, resulting in the doctor's getting thrown out.

Dr. Chumley is forced, by the family, to deal with the matter of Elwood's commitment. He recommends that a drug be administered that would free Elwood of his delusions. The ever obliging Elwood agrees to take it—anything to help Veta— but before Veta makes the decision she is advised by a taxi driver that she should think again. If Elwood is turned into a normal fellow he might not be anywhere near so nice, in fact he might turn out to be a crabby, mean sort of man, like so many others. Veta changes her mind. Better to have a loving, gentle brother and his rabbit comrade around the house than someone who could be a lot less agreeable to live with.

The simple plot is only a part of the point of *Harvey*. More to the point is the whole question of who is sane and who isn't, what is normal behavior and what isn't. And who is happier and the better adjusted—Elwood or his neurotic relatives? Or as Elwood puts it himself—he wrestled with reality for forty years and then, when he met Harvey, he won. For these and other reasons, it is difficult to make much of a case against Harvey, whether on stage or on film.

Stewart was nominated for an Oscar for his portrayal of Elwood P. Dowd but he lost to José Ferrer's *Cyrano de Bergerac*. He himself was not entirely pleased with his performance, feeling that it was a shade too pleasant. In later stage performances, and the television version of 1972, Stewart decided to make Elwood a little more complex and edgy. Josephine Hull, who had appeared in the stage version with Frank Fay, won the 1950 Best Supporting Actress for her screen portrayal of Veta.

Harvey did well at the box office and it has done much to give Stewart added identity. Critical reaction was generally in his favor but there were a few critics who felt that Stewart lacked some of the magic of Frank Fay, particularly the delicately deranged humor that Fay brought to the part. On the other hand some pointed out that Stewart's Elwood P. Dowd had a sweetness and a credibility lacked by Fay's Elwood. *Time* thought that in the movie Dowd "takes on the coloration of Stewart's movie personality: the gangling awkwardness, the fumbling, apologetic gestures, the verbal false starts." *Saturday Review* tended to favor Fay's interpretation, possibly because "Mr. Stewart just doesn't look like the kind of man who ever spent much time in a barroom. Then, too, as the years lurch on, Mr. Stewart has an increasing though understandable inclination just to be himself."

Saturday Review's comment that James Stewart now seemed inclined to be just himself on the screen is one that probably caused him to do a little thinking about his image and the future of his work. By 1950 he could easily have lapsed into a comfortable screen persona as folksy Jimmy Stewart. He chose not to do so, and in the next decade there would be some characterizations that would be far from folksy.

137

NO HIGHWAY IN THE SKY

20th CENTURY-FOX, 1951

Produced by Louis D. Lighton; *Directed* by Henry Koster; *Written* by R. C. Sherriff and Oscar Millard, based on the novel by Nevil Shute; *Photographed* by George Perinal; 98 minutes.

CAST:

Theodore Honey, James Stewart; *Monice Teasdale*, Marlene Dietrich; *Marjorie Corder*, Glynnis Johns; *Dennis Scott*, Jack Hawkins; *Elspeth Honey*, Janette

With Jack Hawkins.

Scott; *Shirley Scott*, Elizabeth Allan; *Sir John*, Ronald Squire; *Peggy*, Jill Crawford; *Captain Samuelson*, Niall MacGinnis; *Dobson*, Kenneth More; *Fisher*, Wilfred Hyde-White; *Major Pearl*, Maurice Denham; *Penworthy*, David Hutcheson; *Sir David Moon*, Hugh Wakefield.

Twelve years after *Destry Rides Again* James Stewart and Marlene Dietrich were re-teamed for *No Highway in the Sky*, a film with none of the glamour or the flair of the famed comic western. The natures of the characters in this film relate in not the slightest way to Tom Destry and Frenchy. In fact, this time the pairing is tame to the point of being lackluster, and it is a little difficult to believe that Stewart and Dietrich in *No Highway* are the same actors who were once locked in delirious and delicious combat in 1939.

In this rather gloomy outing Stewart is known as Mr. Honey, a brilliant but eccentric aviation scientist, who believes the tail of the air liner on which he is flying will break away after 1,440 hours of flying. Honey is being sent from England to Labrador to investigate an air crash and he becomes alarmed, and causes everyone else to become

With Glynis Johns and Niall MacGinnis.

With Glynis Johns, Kenneth More and David Hutcheson.

With Maurice Denham and Jack Hawkins.

With Marlene Dietrich.

alarmed, when he finds this plane has already logged 1,420 miles. He tells the pilot, who ignores him, that he must turn back. Someone who takes him more seriously is famed Monica Teasdale (Dietrich). She knows nothing of the technical problems but she feels she understands people, and senses the urgency of what he is saying. So does stewardess Marjorie Corder (Glynis Johns). When the plane reaches Gander, Newfoundland, Honey demands that the plane be inspected. It is, but nothing is found and the pilot decides to take off. Honey then wrecks the plane by pulling the lever to release the undercarriage.

In England Honey is called to account by his employers and he explains that "energy caused vibration must be absorbed by the metal itself." He pleads with them to allow him to conduct extensive testing on the problem of metal fatigue. They are about to dismiss him as having become mentally unreliable when Monica visits the plant and convinces the owners that Honey is in her opinion of sound mind and that he should be allowed to proceed with his tests. With this they give him the go-ahead.

Monica and the stewardess, intrigued by the strength of Honey's convictions, become concerned about his private life and find that there is not much else in his life except for the love of his daughter Elspeth (Janette Scott). It appears that following the death of his wife, Honey has submerged himself in his work, to the detriment of his daughter, who has not been getting much attention from her otherwise loving father. The two women decide to take Elspeth under their wings while Honey devotes himself to his testing. His research proves him to be entirely correct in his concerns and measures are adopted that will be of benefit to aviation.

No Highway in the Sky was filmed in England and benefited from the casting of a fine range of British character actors. Dietrich was perfect as a celebrated actress, all decked out in Dior suits and furs, and Stewart was an almost textbook example of the absent-minded scientist, quietly but doggedly propounding his beliefs. His Mr. Honey is an appealing sort of fuddy-duddy and the critic for the New York *Herald Tribune* commented that he played the role as if walking in a "bent-over position as though approaching a microscope to peer into it and in like manner loads his acting with all the fussy paraphernalia of such a character." Having recently seen Stewart as Elwood P. Dowd in *Harvey*, viewers could be forgiven for thinking that Mr. Honey might perhaps be a distant relative. However, *No Highway in the Sky*, the first film made by Stewart outside of the United States, did not find a wide audience, then or now.

THE GREATEST SHOW ON EARTH

PARAMOUNT, 1952

Produced and *Directed* by Cecil B. DeMille; *Written* by Fredric M. Frank and Barre Lyndon, based on a story by Fredric M. Frank and Frank Cavett; *Photographed in color* by George Barnes, J. Peverell Marley and Wallace Kelley; *Music* by Victor Young; 153 minutes.

CAST:

Holly, Betty Hutton; *Sebastian,* Cornel Wilde; *Brad,* Charlton Heston; *Phyllis,* Dorothy Lamour; *Angel,* Gloria Grahame; *Buttons,* James Stewart; *Detective,* Henry Wilcoxon; *Emmett Kelly,* Himself; *Klaus,* Lyle Bettger; *Henderson,* Lawrence Tierney; *Harry,* John Kellogg; *Jack Steelman,* John Ridgely; *Doctor,* Frank Wilcox; *Ringmaster,* Bob Carson.

With Betty Hutton.

Anyone can be forgiven for not remembering *The Greatest Show on Earth* as one of James Stewart's movies. Not only is he but one of a cluster of stars who populate this mammoth circus extravaganza but he spends almost all of his screen time heavily made up as a clown. The make-up makes him virtually impossible to recognize, which fact is intrinsic to the story line because he plays a man who does not want to be recognized. *The Greatest Show on Earth* is well titled. It is a circus gospel according to Cecil B. DeMille, made between his *Samson and Delilah* (1949) and his *The Ten Commandments* (1956) and produced with almost as much religious zeal—a rich and ripe two and a half hours of circus spectacle that might have made Barnum, Bailey and the Ringling Brothers green with envy.

Woven among the many acts are some story lines, mostly about a hard, tough circus boss, Brad (Charlton Heston), who seems not to notice that his glamorous aerialist Holly (Betty Hutton) is madly in love with him, or that The Great Sebastian (Cornel Wilde) has more than a professional eye on Holly. Angel (Gloria Grahame) has her eyes on Sebastian, when not performing her stunts with elephants, which causes elephant trainer Klaus (Lyle Bettger) not only to leave the circus but to cause a wreck of the train carrying the company and the animals. Brad is seriously hurt and pinned under the wreckage, and badly needs a doctor. To the amazement of his co-workers Buttons (Stewart) steps forward and reveals that he is a surgeon. In doing so he also reveals himself as a man wanted for the mercy killing of his wife. He has been known in the circus as

With Henry Wilcoxon and Charlton Heston.

On the set with marine guests.

a clown who never takes off his make-up, and now they know why. After Buttons has been arrested by the detective (Henry Wilcoxon) who has been tracking him, hopefully to meet a compassionate sentence, Brad realizes how much he is loved by Holly, and Sebastian and Angel decide to get married.

The Greatest Show on Earth almost defies criticism. It is the circus movie to end all circus movies and easily falls into the "they don't make them like that anymore" category. A number of critics took pleasure in describing it as super kitsch and "run of DeMille," but the great moviemaker had the laugh on them when it won an Oscar as the best film of 1952. Stewart's role as the sweet-natured but sad clown with the dark past was about the only genuinely appealing character in the film and he claims having enjoyed learning about the life of circus clowns, and especially working with the great Emmett Kelly, who coached Stewart in his part as well as playing a role himself.

BEND OF THE RIVER

UNIVERSAL, 1952

Produced by Aaron Rosenberg; *Directed* by Anthony Mann; *Written* by Borden Chase; *Photographed in color* by Irving Glassberg; *Music* by Hans J. Salter; 91 minutes.

CAST:

Glyn McLyntock, James Stewart; *Cole Garrett*, Arthur Kennedy; *Laura Baile*, Julia Adams; *Trey Wilson*, Rock Hudson; *Marjie Baile*, Lori Nelson; *Jeremy Baile*, Jay C. Flippen; *Shorty*, Harry Morgan; *Cap'n Mello*, Chubby Johnson; *Tom Hendricks*, Howard Petrie; *Long Tom*, Royal Dano; *Adam*, Stepin Fetchit; *Red*, Jack Lambert; *Don Grundy*, Frank Ferguson; *Mrs. Prentiss*, Frances Bavier; *Willie*, Cliff Lyons; *Lock*, Jennings Miles; *Wasco*, Frank Chase; *Aunt Tildy*, Lillian Randolph.

In going to see James Stewart in *Winchester '73* some people had expected a comedy along the lines of *Destry Rides Again*. They were not expecting a rough, tough Stewart. With *Bend of the River*, anyone who had thought *Winshester '73* was an aberration in style from the generally soft-spoken, warm Stewart image of old now learned that the actor had found another screen persona, that of the quiet man with an air of edginess, who, when leaned on too heavily, erupts in anger. There had been indications of it along the way, even as far back as *Mr. Smith Goes to Washington*, when the angered hero goes into his frenzied filibuster, and after *Bend in the River* audiences would be looking for Stewart to turn furious when overcome by frustration or injustice. The director who most utilized this aspect of Stewart's range was Anthony Mann, and most conspicuously in all five of the westerns the two made together.

In *Bend of the River* Stewart is Glyn McLyntock, a wagon train guide hired to lead a band of settlers to their destination in Oregon. He is also an ex-outlaw, once a Missouri border raider in the years after the Civil War, a past he would like to forget but which crops up with his rescue of Emerson Cole (Arthur Kennedy) from a lynching party. Cole has

With Julia Adams.   With Julia Adams and Arthur Kennedy.

With Jay C. Flippen and Arthur Kennedy.

been accused of stealing horses and is about to pay for it with his life when McLyntock saves him, a decision mostly due to the two men having been comrades in Missouri days. Cole swears that he has reformed and that he would like to join the group and settle down. McLyntock has his doubts but he is willing to give the charming Cole a chance, even though the man is a reminder of a past he is trying to deny. Among other things, McLyntock keeps his neck covered to hide the scars of a near-hanging. But Cole is a tough scrapper and his presence is felt when the time comes to fight off Indian attacks.

Once the settlers arrive in Portland, the leader of the farmers, Jeremy Baile (Jay C. Flippen), arranges with merchant Tom Hendricks (Howard Petrie) for transportation up the river to the land they wish to occupy and to afterwards send the food supplies that will sustain them through the winter. The party reaches the destination by riverboat and build their settlement, but the supplies never arrive. McLyntock and Baile ride to Portland to find out what has happened and discover the town has gone crazy due to a gold boom. Hendricks decides not to turn over the supplies because he can make an enormous profit from them by selling to the miners. McLyntock and his men steal the supplies and commandeer a boat, with Hendricks and his men in pursuit.

McLyntock is now faced with an even bigger problem—the character of his old friend Cole, who has not changed at all with the years. Realizing the

money he can make by throwing in with Hendricks, Cole turns on McLyntock and deserts him, taking not only the supplies but Baile and his daughter Laura (Julia Adams) as hostages, so that McLyntock will not follow. In a brutal fight Cole beats McLyntock and leaves him to die amid the stark mountain terrain. But McLyntock recovers, and full of determination and fury he tracks Cole, finally facing him in a fight that ends in Cole's death and his body being washed away downriver—symbolically purging McLyntock of his past. After that he is accepted by the settlers, especially Laura, as one of them.

Bend of the River invariably turns up in any discussion among western connoisseurs of the best examples of the genre. Among its virtues is the magnificent color photography of Oregon, in the region around Mount Hood, with the beautiful foothills and the Snake River serving as a kind of Eden that makes the trek of hardship understandable. However, it is the focusing on character that gives Borden Chase's screenplay its real quality, that and the playing of Stewart and Arthur Kennedy as the men linked by the past but separated by the difference in objectives. This is the crux of the story and the one Anthony Mann was particularly adept at developing. It would also be the nature of all Stewart-Mann westerns, causing later evaluation from even the most intellectual movie critics. One French critic went so far as to call Mann the Virgil of the West. On the more mundane and pragmatic Hollywood level, the success of *Bend of the River* simply meant that there would likely be a lot more projects being handed to James Stewart and Anthony Mann as a means of getting them to work together again.

CARBINE WILLIAMS

MGM, 1952

Produced by Armand Deutsch; *Directed* by Richard Thorpe; *Written* by Art Cohn; *Photographed* by William Mellor; *Music* by Conrad Salinger; 91 minutes.

CAST:

Marsh Williams, James Stewart; *Maggie Williams*, Jean Hagen; *Captain H. T. Peeples*, Wendell Corey; *Claude Williams*, Carl Benton Reid; *Dutch Kruger*, Paul Stewart; *Mobley*, Otto Hulett; *Redwick Karson*, Rhys Williams; *Lionel Daniels*, Herbert Heyes; *Leon Williams*, James Arness; *Sam Markley*, Porter Hall; *District Attorney*, Fay Roope; *Andrew White*, Ralph Dumke; *Feder*, Leif Erickson; *Bill Stockton*, Henry Corden; *Sheriff*, Howard Petrie; *Truex*, Frank Richards; *Tom Venner*, Stuart Randall; *Jesse Rimmer*, Dan Riss; *David Williams*, Bobby Hyatt; *Mitchell*, Willis Bouchey.

James Stewart has made four biographical films, three of them about highly admirable and likeable men—Monty Stratton, Glenn MIller and Charles Lindbergh—and the other about an oddball who perfected a piece of gun mechanism while in jail. Of the four *Carbine Williams* is clearly the odd man out, but ironically it is the story of a man whose invention had even more impact on history than the beloved baseball player, the great bandsman and the celebrated aviator. It was during his time in prison that David Marshall Williams conceived the short-stroke piston, which became the integral part of the M-I carbine, which, when developed by Winchester, became the first new rifle adopted by the United Staes Army in forty years. Eight million were manufactured during the Second World War and General MacArthur referred to the weapon as being "one of the strongest contributing factors to our victory in the Pacific."

In July of 1921, Williams was a North Carolinian metalworker making money on the side with the construction of stills and the selling of moonshine liquor. In producing a film about his life MGM consulted Williams, who afterwards vouched for its authenticity. In the opening sequence Williams and

With Rhys Williams.

With Jean Hagen.

146

On the set with the real David Marshall "Carbine" Williams and his son David, played by Bobby Hyatt (right).

With Wendell Corey.

with him to give himself up rather than become a hunted renegade. Williams is tried but the result is a hung decision on the question of first-degree murder and, rather than risk a second trial which could send him to his death, Williams agrees to plead guilty to a charge of second-degree murder.

Williams is shocked to find himself sentenced to thirty years of life as a convict. He becomes bitter, confused and stubborn and when he rebels against prison authority he finds himself on a chain gang. One of his outbursts costs him thirty days in solitary confinement. The prison warden, Captain H. T. Peeples (Wendell Corey) becomes interested in this strange man, and since Williams is a metalworker he allows him to work in the machine shop. It is here that the prisoner becomes tractable and starts to reveal his ingenuity as an inventor. And during all his years in jail his wife and his father (Carl Benton Reid) never stop their efforts to get him pardoned.

Williams, with a minimum of material—a pipe, wire and bits of metal—devises a system for a short-stroke rifle and convinces Peeples of its probable worth. Peeples allows him to go ahead with its development and later gives his permission for the rifle to be tested. This causes Peeples to be summoned for inquiry by the State Prison Board and charged with irresponsibility. He irately defends his position and brings in the shackled Williams to explain his invention. When the panel wavers, Peeples dramatically announces, "If he escapes, I'll serve out his thirty-year sentence." With this the board gives its consent for the testing and, under simulated battle conditions, Williams proves his rifle all that he believes it to be. He is offered a contract by the Winchester Repeating Arms Company, which offer is dwarfed by the even better news that his case has been reviewed by the governor and that a pardon has been granted. After eight years in prison Williams walks out a free man, to be greeted by his loving wife and a son he has rarely seen.

Carbine Williams is the story of a remarkable man, especially in view of the fact that he went on to earn more than sixty United States patents. For all that, the film met with only modest success, perhaps with many people feeling that Stewart might best have let some other actor play the admirable but not very nice convict. For one thing the film never resolved the question of Williams being guilty or not of killing a man, and Williams himself never discussed the matter. For Stewart it was another chance to create an interesting piece of acting, but for audiences expecting something like *The Stratton Story,* it was a disappointment.

his cohorts are raided by Revenue agents, who smash the stills and arrest as many of the men as they can grab. In the fracas one of the agents is shot and killed, but with no one knowing exactly which shot might have caused the death. Williams eludes capture but his worried wife Maggie (Jean Hagen) pleads

148

THE NAKED SPUR

MGM, 1953

Produced by William H. Wright; *Directed* by Anthony Mann; *Written* by Sam Rolfe and Harold Jack Bloom; *Photographed in color* by William Mellor; *Music* by Bronislau Kaper; 91 minutes.

CAST:

Howard Kemp, James Stewart; *Lina Patch,* Janet Leigh; *Ben Vandergroat,* Robert Ryan; *Roy Anderson,* Ralph Meeker; *Jesse Tate,* Millard Mitchell.

Of the James Stewart-Anthony Mann westerns, the connoisseur's item is *The Naked Spur.* It is the one referred to as being adult and full of psychological undercurrents, and it is without doubt the film in which Stewart gives his most intense, bordering-on-hysterical performance. Having explored his ability to portray a certain edginess in *Winchester '73* and *Bend of the River,* Stewart and Mann here went a step further and dealt with a westerner almost consumed with bitterness and revenge. In *The Naked Spur,* Stewart's Howard Kemp is a man who has suffered bad luck, someone shoved to the sidelines of human society and desperate to get back in. It is among the most unusual westerns ever made, dealing as it does with only five characters and dwelling on the interplay between them.

Kemp is a bounty hunter with a fierce need to make money. He wants to reclaim the land that was taken from him while he was away fighting in the Civil War. Seething with resentment, Kemp sees bounty hunting as the fastest way to get what he wants. Posing as a sheriff he proceeds to Colorado, on the trail of Ben Vandergroat (Robert Ryan), an escaped killer with a reward tag of $5000 on his head, dead or alive. Traveling with Vandergroat is Lina Patch (Janet Leigh), who knows him as a friend of her father, an outlaw who has been killed. Now without family of any kind, Lina tags along with Vandergroat because he promises to take her to California. In the mountains Kemp comes across a grizzled old prospector, Jesse Tate (Millard Mitchell), and a cashiered army lieutenant, Roy Anderson (Ralph Meeker). Believing him to be a sheriff, they help Kemp track and capture Vandergroat, but when

With Ralph Meeker.

they find out he is a bounty hunter they demand their share of the reward. Vandergroat needs to be delivered to Abilene, Kansas, a trip that is likely to take a week.

The trip becomes ever more tense, as the wily Vandergroat astutely sums up the nature of his captors and explores their weaknesses, exploiting their greed and distrust, and setting them on edge. He taunts them, and the man who most feels the strain is Kemp, who, unlike Vandergroat and Anderson, still has a spark of compassion in his soul. Vandergroat uses Lina as a ploy between the ex-soldier and the bounty hunter. Indians begin to track the party, and when the reason becomes apparent—that they are after Anderson for raping and killing an

149

With Robert Ryan, Ralph Meeker, Janet Leigh and Millard Michell.

Robert Ryan, Ralph Meeker, Janet Leigh and Millard Mitchell.

With Janet Leigh and Ralph Meeker.

With Robert Ryan.

Indian woman—the others order him to leave. He rides ahead and sets an ambush, which results in the Indians being killed but also causes Kemp to take a bullet in his right leg. For Kemp, the trip is now more and more arduous.

Vandergroat plays upon Tate's love of gold, telling him where they can find a strike. With Lina they sneak out at night, but the next morning Vandergroat kills Tate with a shot from his rifle and then fires another shot in the air to make certain the pursuing Kemp and Anderson can find him. Perched atop a rocky ledge overlooking a twisted gorge in the Colorado River, Vandergroat takes aim as the two men approach. As he is about to fire, Lina deflects his shot. She has come to feel affection for Kemp, having learned to understand his motives while listening to him mutter during his delirium the previous night, and she also knows by now Vandergroat will do only what is good for him and not for her. Vandergroat is killed by a shot from Anderson and the body falls into the river. Anderson crosses to the other side to retrieve the corpse, but he is killed when a tree stump rams him in the swiftly flowing water. Kemp frantically pulls in the roped body of Vandergroat and throws it across the back of a horse. As he does so Lina pleads with him to forget about taking the body back for the reward. The distraught, confused Kemp cries, "But why? Tell me why. I'm gonna sell him for money!" Now realizing the inhumanity of it all, Kemp breaks down and cries. Lina tells him she loves him, and as he makes ready to bury Vandergroat, he asks, "Still wanna go to California?"

The final scene of *The Naked Spur* is like the break-up of a logjam. Howard Kemp, the former decent citizen returns, after years of misfortune and bitterness, to his true nature—he gives up the past and moves on to the future. Now, after all the misery and the pain of his pursuit of Vandergroat, he can let go. With the love of Lina, revenge suddenly has no meaning. It is a splendid last scene and the culmination of a splendid performance by Stewart of a difficult role, possibly among the half-dozen best of his career. Credit also goes to Robert Ryan, an actor yet to be fully appreciated, for his playing of Vandergroat—smiling, devious, desperate and deadly. It is the tension between the two actors that gives the film an added sting, abetted all the way by the brilliance of Mann's direction. To regard *The Naked Spur* as simply a western is to do it an injustice. What it really is is an incisive study of human nature in the raw.

THUNDER BAY

UNIVERSAL, 1953

Produced by Aaron Rosenberg; *Directed* by Anthony Mann; *Written* by Gil Doud and John Michael Hayes, based on ideas by George W. George and George F. Slavin; *Photographed in color* by William Daniels; *Music* by Frank Skinner; 103 minutes.

CAST:

Steve Martin, James Stewart; *Stella Rigaud*, Joanne Dru; *Teche Bossier*, Gilbert Roland; *Johnny Gambi*, Dan Duryea; *Francesca Rigaud*, Marcia Henderson; *Phillippe Bayard*, Robert Monet; *Kermit Mac-Donald*, Jay C. Flippen; *Dominique Rigaud*, Antonio Moreno; *Rawlings*, Harry Morgan; *Sheriff*, Fortunio Bonanova; *Louis Chighizola*, Mario Siletti; *Joe Sephalu*, Antonio Filauri.

With Dan Duryea.

With Gilbert Roland.

With Harry Morgan, Jay C. Flippen, Joanne Dru,
Gilbert Roland and Dan Duryea.

With Joanne Dru.

begrimed and laconic as the indomitable wildcatter whose dream finally comes true."

Among the points in favor of *Thunder Bay* is that it was, in 1953, the first Hollywood movie to set its adventures amid the drilling of tideland oil. And the producers were obviously aware that the subject was a hot one with the public, due to the congressional hearings and the controversy over off-shore drilling. To make *Thunder Bay* as effective as possible Mann and his company went to the Louisiana bayou town of Morgan City, with further shooting—in Technicolor by the masterly William Daniels—thirty miles out in the Gulf of Mexico on an oil barge. The story revolves around a pair of expert oil drillers, Steve Martin (Stewart) and Johnny Gambi (Dan Duryea), who have invented a stormproof drilling platform for use in the off-shore search for oil. They persuade an oil tycoon, Kermit MacDonald (Jay C. Flippen), to financially back them in what seems like a risky enterprise and one that will cost a fortune. This provokes immediate hostility from the local shrimp fishermen, who have been having a hard time recently in locating fresh beds of shrimp and who fear oil drilling will only make matters worse for them. Johnny adds to the conflict by paying attention to Francesca (Marcia Henderson), the girlfriend of fisherman Phillippe Bayard (Robert Monet), while Francesca's sister Stella (Joanne Dru) finds herself leaning toward Steve. When a furious storm breaks out, Steve decides to stay on his oil platform to find out how it will behave, and Stella joins him. Phillippe now attempts to blow up the platform with dynamite, but Steve catches him in time, which results in Phillippe's losing his life following a fight with Steve, and further results in Steve believing that Stella was part of the attempt.

Life becomes harder for Steve and Johnny when MacDonald withdraws his support, thinking that the enterprise is both too costly and also not likely to succeed. The irresponsible Johnny chooses this inappropriate time to elope with Francesca, which brings on the fury of her father (Antonio Moreno) and the fishermen, who attack Steve's platform-derrick with the idea of wrecking it. But this is the moment when Steve's luck dawns. The driller not only strikes oil but he uncovers a huge shrimp bed, which mollifies the depressed fishing community and proves that the two industries can exist side by side—and also bring happiness to Steve and Stella, not to mention the happiness it brought to the gentlemen in the front offices at Universal Studios, Universal City, California, who found they had struck oil with *Thunder Bay.*

Perhaps feeling that as a pair they might be becoming over-identified with westerns, James Stewart and Anthony Mann decided to do something different with their next two projects, although the first, *Thunder Bay,* may easily be regarded as a modern western about oil drillers. It was not a film that required any acting subtlety from its star. In reviewing the picture, *The New York Times* summed it up easily: "James Stewart is properly tough, harried,

154

THE GLENN MILLER STORY

UNIVERSAL, 1954

Produced by Aaron Rosenberg; *Directed* by Anthony Mann; *Written* by Valentine Davies and Oscar Brodney, *Photographed in color* by William Daniels, *Music Director:* Joseph Gershenson, 116 minutes.

CAST:

Glenn Miller, James Stewart; *Helen Burger,* June Allyson; *Don Haynes,* Charles Drake; *Chummy,* Harry Morgan; *Si Schribman,* George Tobias; *General Arnold,* Barton MacLane; *Kranz,* Sig Rumann; *Mr. Miller,* Irving Bacon; *Mr. Burger,* James Bell; *Mrs. Miller,* Kathleen Lockhart; *Mrs. Burger,* Kathleen Warren; *Colonel Spaulding,* Dayton Lummis; *Polly Haynes,* Marian Ross; *John Becker,* Phil Garris; *Jonnie Dee,* Deborah Sydes; with Frances Langford, Louis Armstrong, Gene Krupa, Ben Pollack, The Modernaires, and The Archie Savage Dancers as themselves.

The actor and the subject.

Ten years after his tragic death in 1944 at the age of forty, Glenn Miller was still as highly regarded, if not more so, as during his lifetime. A film about him was inevitable, and it would have had to have been a bad one in order not to have been successful. Fortunately Universal gave their version all the backing it needed, and even more fortunately it gave James Stewart one of his biggest successes. He was an excellent choice to play the legendary bandsman and his own musical training enabled him to simulate the playing of Miller's own instrument, the trombone. Stewart clearly used his observation of trombonists to convey the stance and the way this kind of musician picks up the instrument and prepares to play, especially the movements of the mouth and lips. For the soundtrack Joe Yuki was hired to do the actual playing but if Universal had claimed Stewart as the performer it would not have been difficult to believe.

The Glenn Miller Story is a limited kind of story. Aside from the shock of his death there was not much to tell about him beyond his ambition to create a new and different sound in dance music, his courting of Helen Burger (June Allyson) and his success on all counts. The film opens with his years as a bandsman in Los Angeles in the early 1930's. He

With Charles Drake, June Allyson and George Tobias.

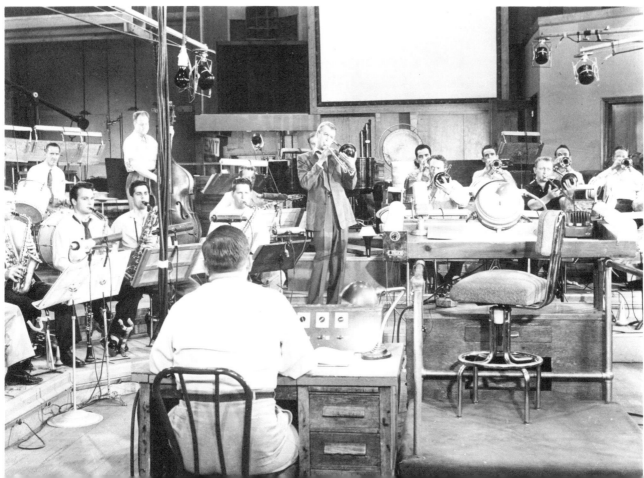

With band leader Ben Pollack and Henry Morgan.
With June Allyson.

occasionally picks up jobs playing trombone, but his overwhelming concern is getting his work as an arranger accepted. He has studied serious music and he believes a more interesting sound can be brought to dance band music. He is constantly hocking his instrument with kindly pawnbroker Kranz (Sig Rumann) in order to get money to sustain him through the time he devotes himself to his arrangements. His closest friend is pianist Chummy Mac-Gregor (Harry Morgan)—MacGregor was hired as the advisor on the making of the film—and they land an engagement with Ben Pollack (playing himself) and his band in Santa Monica. Pollack at first shows no interest in new arrangements but Chummy tricks him into hearing one of them, and with this Miller begins his trek on the road to success.

Two years prior to the Pollack job, Glenn had dated Helen in Denver. He has kept her in mind as the girl he wants, but he has been casual in the courting, sending only a Christmas card in all this time. Booked to play in Colorado, Glenn telephones Helen, who has difficulty in placing him and who also has difficulty in resisting him when it becomes plain that he has set out with the idea of winning her. She breaks her engagement to another man when Glenn asks her to come to New York, where he is appearing with Pollack, and to marry him. Unlike Glenn, who is casual with money, she is a penny pincher, which proves a boon when he wants to start his own band. Where, he wonders, can he get the $1800 he needs to do it? He finds that in a couple of years of marriage Helen has been putting aside small change, knowing that it would be needed for this very purpose. The account contains $1842.

With his own band, including the reliable Chummy, Glenn goes through the usual struggles of a new, touring dance band leader. In time his arrangements lead to acceptance. People like the new sound, the smooth, soft orchestrations balancing brass and woodwinds, especially in Miller's own composition "Moonlight Serenade," and they also enjoy his spirited rhythm numbers. The only problem in the life of the Millers is Helen's inability to have children, so they adopt a boy and a girl. Broadcasts, recordings and engagements swell the coffers, until the outbreak of war and Glenn's need to be involved. He applies for a commission in the army as a music director and becomes Captain Glenn Miller.

Glenn's military ideas are as revolutionary as the civilian ones that had set him apart from all the other band leaders. He feels there is a need for a newer sound in military music—to break away from the use of standard parade marches and bring in jazz-

157

accented rhythms. His immediate superiors are appalled by this departure from tradition, but General Arnold (Barton MacLane) is intrigued by it and gives his approval. Glenn takes advantage of the general and asks him for permission to form a separate band, the American Expeditionary Forces Orchestra, and to be sent to England, there to broadcast and to stage shows for the armed services. The enterprise is a great success, but it costs him his life. In mid-December of 1944, Glenn, now promoted to major, gets into a small plane for passage across the foggy English Channel and is never seen again.

The facts in the life of Glenn Miller are respectfully followed in this broad and pleasing movie, which became a major success at the box office. Among the many movies made about entertainment celebrities, this one ranks with the best. The accent is on music, of course, and the arrangements, the playing and the recordings are all top-notch. The film is one of the early credits of Henry Mancini, who had had plenty of experience in dance band arranging. All the famous Miller hit numbers, such as "Little Brown Jug," "String of Pearls," "In the Mood," and "Pennsylvania 6-5000," were included, and Universal wisely included the presence of stalwarts like Louis Armstrong, Gene Krupa, Ben Pollack, the Modernaires and Frank Langford. It was a film that could hardly fail. The choice of Anthony Mann as director seemed like an odd one, in view of the tough nature of the three films he had made with Stewart prior to this and the three he would make afterwards, but it is the firmness of Mann's direction that keeps the Miller film from slipping into excess sentiment and wallowing. The death of Miller, in particular, is treated in a straightforward manner.

As for the performance of Stewart as Miller, it is a finely crafted piece of work. As the New York *Herald Tribune* put it, "James Stewart plays the role of the scholarly looking band leader with discretion and clarity and the shy good humor which clings to most of his roles."

158

REAR WINDOW

PARAMOUNT, 1954

Produced and *Directed* by Alfred Hitchcock; *Written* by John Michael Hayes, based on the novelette by Cornell Woolrich; *Photographed in color* by Robert Burks; *Music* by Franz Waxman; 122 minutes.

CAST:

L. B. Jeffries, James Stewart; *Lisa Fremont,* Grace Kelly; *Thomas J. Doyle,* Wendell Corey; *Stella,* Thelma Ritter; *Lars Thorwald,* Raymond Burr; *Miss Lonely Hearts,* Judith Evelyn; *Song Writer,* Ross Bagdasarian; *Miss Torso,* Georgine Darcy; *Woman on Fire Escape,* Sara Berner; *Fire Escape Man,* Frank Cady; *Miss Hearing Aid,* Jesslyn Fax; *Honeymooner,* Rand Harper; *Mrs. Thorwald,* Irene Winston; *Newlywed,* Harris Davenport.

With Grace Kelly.

Working with Alfred Hitchcock in *Rope* had not been a particularly enjoyable experience for James Stewart, and with the lackluster reception given it by both the critics and the public there was little reason to imagine the actor and the director would work together again. But the movie business, like life itself, is full of surprises and Stewart and Hitchcock would end up making together three of the finest films in both their careers—*Rear Window, The Man Who Knew Too Much* and *Vertigo.* Each film would draw from Stewart a fully developed characterization of a man subjected to extraordinary circumstances and each would further his reputation as a film actor of extraordinary intelligence. In the first he is a top-notch professional photographer, who has broken his left leg and is confined to his Manhattan apartment, sitting in a wheelchair and whiling away his time staring out his window, watching his neighbors in the courtyard of his apartment building. Few actors have given such a riveting performance from such a limited position.

L. B. (Jeff) Jeffries (Stewart), a man used to world travel as a magazine photographer, is bored as he sits in his apartment on a summer day, with the windows wide open, looking out into the courtyard and into the windows of the apartments on the

With Thelma Ritter.   With Thelma Ritter and Grace Kelly.

With Wendell Corey and Grace Kelly.

opposite side of the complex. Now and then he smiles with amusement at the antics of the neighbors. He gets to know their activities. There are some newly-weds, a song writer who does health exercises when not working at the piano, there is a lady who lives alone and whom Jeff dubs Miss Lonely Heart, there is a young girl of fine shape whom he calls Torso, there are couples who sleep out on the fire escape and another couple who walk their dog in the courtyard, and there is a heavy-set, sad-looking man named Lars Thorwald (Raymond Burr), who always seems to be arguing with his wife. Jeff discusses all these types with his elegant, fashion-model girlfriend Lisa Fre-mont (Grace Kelly), police detective chum Thomas J. Doyle (Wendell Corey) and his nurse-therapist Stella (Thelma Ritter), a lady of caustic tongue, who tells him he ought to be ashamed of himself peering at the neighbors through binoculars.

Partly through boredom and partly because of being an award-winning photographer, Jeff turns into a Peeping Tom. He becomes more and more curious about the people upon whom he is spying, and Stella snorts in disgust. "You should just see yourself." Jeff's attention starts to focus on the windows of Lars Thorwald, as his movements become hard to understand. Thorwald's wife is ill and apparently cantankerous, and Jeff notices that Thorwald, a salesman by trade, is leaving his apartment at odd hours during the night and carrying his sample case. There seems to be no evidence anymore of the presence of the wife and yet Jeff has not seen her leave. With his high-powered binoculars Jeff observes Thorwald's wrapping carving knives and a saw in newspaper, and he begins to suspect the worst.

Jeff's theory of foul play isn't accepted by Doyle, but with time both Lisa and Stella begin to believe there is something to it. Lisa agrees to enter Thorwald's apartment when the salesman is out, but she can find nothing, although she is spotted by Thorwald leaving his part of the building. After a

With Raymond Burr.

while Thorwald realizes that Jeff is tracking him and probably realizes that he has murdered his wife. He now comes after Jeff, breaking into the apartment intent on killing him. Jeff, stuck in his wheelchair, stretches out the conflict by blinding Thorwarld with flashbulb explosions. By the time Doyle arrives to save him, Jeff is hanging on to his window ledge, with Thorwald pounding on his hands. Doyle captures Thorwald but not in time to save Jeff from falling three floors to the courtyard and breaking his other leg, thereby requiring more convalescence and possibly more time sitting at his window.

Rear Window is a fine piece of work on all counts, with major credit going to Hitchcock for his skill in building suspense in such a claustrophobic setting. The set itself is impressive, seemingly filling an entire sound stage at Paramount, with a landscaped courtyard and a four-story building on each side. When the film was described as a voyeur's delight, Hitchcock pointed out that the art of cinema is largely voyeurism and that the role played by Stewart allows the audience to be voyeurs through his eyes. The film is really an exercise in the nature of human curiosity. In visually prying into the lives of his neighbors, Stewart sees life in all its daily functions, including happiness, sadness, loneliness, hope, despair and death. A kaleidoscope of everyday activities.

The casting could not be better. Raymond Burr makes the morose killer as pitiable as he is frightening, Thelma Ritter is a tart-tongued but soft-hearted commentator and the relationship between the patrician Grace Kelly and her frustrated lover-photographer is, thanks to Hitchcock's slyness, a good deal more earthy than might at first be assumed. Stewart's performance as an active man confined to a wheelchair is superb, with a great deal of the emoting done with his eyes. This is an amiable man but also one a lot more nervous and vulnerable than even he himself might have expected. The success of their collaboration on *Rear Window* made another Stewart-Hitchcock film almost inevitable.

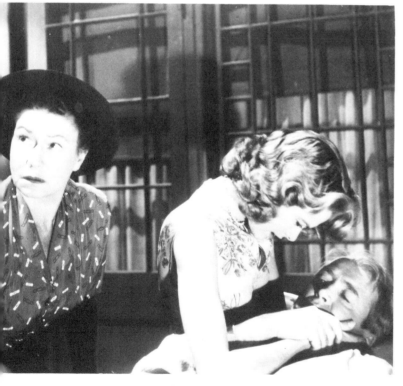

With Thelma Ritter and Grace Kelly.

162

THE FAR COUNTRY

UNIVERSAL, 1955

Produced by Aaron Rosenberg; *Directed* by Anthony Mann; *Written* by Borden Chase; *Photographed in color* by William Daniels; *Music Director:* Joseph Gershenson; 96 minutes.

CAST:

Jeff Webster, James Stewart; *Ronda Castle,* Ruth Roman; *Renee Vallon,* Corinne Calvet; *Ben Tatem,* Walter Brennan; *Gannon,* John McIntire; *Rube,* Jay C. Flippen; *Ketchum,* Harry Morgan; *Ives,* Steve Brodie; *Hominy,* Connie Gilchrist; *Madden,* Bob Wilke; *Dusty,* Chubby Johnson; *Luke,* Royal Dano; *Newberry,* Jack Elam; *Grits,* Kathleen Freeman; *Tanana Pete,* Guy Wilkerson; *Bosun,* Allan Ray; *Yukon Sam,* Eddy Waller; *Dr. Vallon,* Eugene Borden; *Miner,* John Doucette; *Kingman,* Robert Foulk; *Sheriff,* Paul Bryar.

The Far Country is perhaps the most conventional of the James Stewart-Anthony Mann westerns in terms of plot and action but the least conventional in its settings. The title refers to Alaska and the Klondike during the years of the gold rush (1897-98), with much of the footage shot in the Canadian Rockies, particularly Alberta's Jasper National Park, all of it finely captured on Technicolor stock by William Daniels. Making it even more unusual for a western, the footage included shots taken on the massive Columbia Ice Fields. Had it failed as a feature film, Universal could easily have turned *The Far Country* into a travelogue. However, there was no need. The movie did very well for itself.

In this original screenplay by the expert teller of western tales, Borden Chase, Stewart is a Wyoming wrangler named Jeff Webster, a hardbitten man with a reputation as a quick-on-the-draw gunman and one who always has his own interests at heart. His primary interest at this point in his life is to raise enough money to buy his own ranch. To this end he and his eccentric old sidekick, Ben Tatum (Walter Brennan), take a herd of livestock by land and sea to the Canadian town of Dawson in the Yukon Territory, by way of Skagway, Alaska. These are times in which there is money to be made. On the boat Jeff

With Walter Brennan, Jay C. Flippen and John McIntire.

With Harry Morgan, Ruth Roman, Steve Brodie and Walter Brennan.

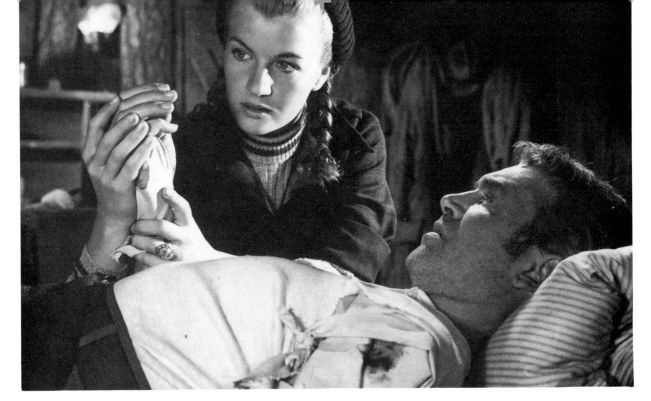

With Corinne Calvet.

meets Ronda Castle (Ruth Roman), a beautiful lady with talent as a barroom gambler and shill. Since she is about as self-centered as Jeff, the two find immediate rapport.

Skagway is a wide-open, wild town of easy money, and the only apparent law is that administered by the corrupt, self-appointed sheriff known as Mr. Gannon (John McIntire). With his own version of legal procedure Gannon appropriates Jeff's cattle, which causes Jeff to devise his own means of getting the cattle back and across the Canadian line. The only thing he has enjoyed about Skagway is meeting a nice French-Canadian girl, Renee Vallon (Corinne Calvet), who gets him to thinking about possibly changing his ways and settling down, except that life with the more exciting Ronda is also something to think about. Jeff delivers his cattle and makes his sale in Dawson, and is pleased to find it a town trying to be civilized—until Gannon and his men arrive in pursuit. With the cattle beyond his reach the vindictive Gannon now goes after the gold claim Jeff has staked, and in defending it Ben is shot to death. The loss of Ben sets Jeff to more thinking. Rather than continue his selfish ways he decides to band together with the townspeople and help rid them of the deprivations of Gannon and his like. He kills Gannon, but in the process of trying to warn Jeff, Ronda loses her life, leaving him to the understanding Renee.

The use of the spectacular Northwest landscapes gives *The Far Country* an enormous edge over westerns with similar story lines, and in terms of visual drama it is interesting to see how Mann uses these breathtaking backdrops in a foreboding kind of way, the land very much dwarfing the people and their struggles. The scenery is beautiful but it is also frightening. Also frightening is the villain played by John McIntire, a seemingly jovial fellow, unshaven and wearing a battered plug-hat, but with a heart as cold as ice. In creating this role Chase had in mind a fascinating Alaskan bad man called Soapy Smith, whose story had often been considered for filming. In drumming up the other characters Chase had obviously familiarized himself with the writings of Robert Service and his stories about the Klondike. Ruth Roman's part as a barroom lady is also clearly the result of research, especially in the scenes where she jostles drunken miners, causing them to spill gold dust, which is later panned from the sawdust on the floor. Mann himself must have studied photographs of life in the Klondike because so many of his characters look as if they had stepped from them.

In this, the fourth of his westerns with Mann, Stewart was able to sketch yet another raw-boned westerner, driven by the need to be a self-sustainer in a hard lifestyle, mostly a loner but never without some basic core of decency, no matter how badly treated by his fellow man. Amidst all the thousands of westerns that have been made since *The Great Train Robbery* in 1903, no other actor has mined western character more interestingly than Stewart.

STRATEGIC AIR COMMAND

PARAMOUNT, 1955

Produced by Samuel J. Briskin; *Directed* by Anthony Mann; *Written* by Valentine Davies and Beirne Lay; *Photographed in color* by William Daniels, *with aerial photography* by Thomas Tutweiler and Paul Mantz; *Music* by Victor Young; 114 minutes.

CAST:

Lt. Col. Robert "Dutch" Holland, James Stewart; *Sally Howland,* June Allyson; *General Ennis C. Hawkes,* Frank Lovejoy; *Lt. Col. Rocky Samford,* Barry Sullivan; *Ike Knowland,* Alex Nicol; *General Espy,* Bruce Bennett; *Doyle,* Jay C. Flippen; *General Castle,* James Millican; *Reverend Thorne,* James Bell; *Aircraft Commander,* Richard Shannon; *Mrs. Thorne,* Rosemary De Camp; *Captain Symington,* John McKee; *Major Patrol Commander,* Don Haggerty.

With John McKee.

That James Stewart should make a film in tribute to the Air Force came as a surprise to no one with any knowledge of his lifelong interest in aviation, his wartime service record or his rank in the U.S. Air Force Reserve. And neither should it be much of a surprise that the film *Strategic Air Command* came into being at the behest of Brigadier General James Maitland Stewart. Having spent time with General Curtis LeMay, the SAC chief, and convinced that the public should know more about this vital defense operation, Stewart persuaded Paramount to make the film. At the time he said that SAC was "the biggest single factor in the security of the world." Paramount, of course, received all the cooperation it needed from the Air Force, with access to filming at the Carswell Air Force Base at Fort Worth, Texas, and the MacDill Air Force Base at Tampa, Florida.

To make the picture as appealing as possible to a wide audience, Paramount hired June Allyson to reprise the role of Stewart's wife, following their successful pairing in *The Stratton Story* and *The Glenn Miller Story;* and with Stewart playing a big-time baseball player named Robert Holland, *Strategic Air Command* looked a little like a spin-off of *The Stratton Story,* which is probably what the producers had in mind. The story, like that of Stewart himself, is about a man in the public eye, who serves with distinction during the war but who, unlike Stewart, wants to put the Air Force behind him.

Robert Holland is a third baseman with the St. Louis Cardinals, drawing a $70,000 salary, when he

With Barry Sullivan.   With Henry Morgan.

With June Allyson.

is recalled by the Air Force because of the shortage of pilots with his particular experience in flying heavy bombers. Holland is reluctant to go, feeling he has done his share, and because his wife Sally is pregnant. The Hollands are happy with life the way it is. He is reinstated with the rank of lieutenant colonel and comes under the command of General Ennis C. Hawkes (Frank Lovejoy), a hard-driving man who demands the utmost in performance from his officers. As a part of SAC, Holland quickly comes to appreciate the importance of the project and its meaning to the safety of America. By the end of his tour of duty Holland is committed to SAC and chooses to stay on as a full-time officer, somewhat to the dismay of Sally, who has to be coaxed into realizing the importance of his position.

The story lines of *Strategic Air Command* are obviously secondary to the visual impact of the picture, with its skies full of majestic old B-36's and hornet-like B-47 jet fighters spinning through the air, along with the lumbering C-124 Globemaster transports, full of tanks and trucks and masses of equipment. All of this, especially the stratospheric refuelling of the huge bombers by the KC-97 tanker planes, was new and thrilling to 1955 audiences, much as *Top Gun* was in 1986. The film was shot in the impressive VistaVision process in Technicolor by William Daniels, with added aerial footage by Thomas Tutweiler, and supervision by Hollywood's foremost aviation authority Paul Mantz. In short, it was in the hands of experts, including those of director Anthony Mann, who Stewart almost demanded be assigned to the film. The role of General Ennis, well played by Frank Lovejoy, was patterned after the tough, dedicated Curtis LeMay, a man much admired by Stewart. However, for all its sincerity and technical excellence, *Strategic Air Command* is very much a movie of the past, its planes long consigned to aviation history books and its men, like Stewart, long retired from the service.

THE MAN FROM LARAMIE

COLUMBIA, 1955

Produced by William Goetz; *Directed* by Anthony Mann; *Written* by Philip Yordan and Frank Burt, based on the story by Thomas T. Flynn; *Photographed in color* by Charles Lang; *Music* by George Duning; 101 minutes.

CAST:

Will Lockhart, James Stewart; *Vic Hansbro,* Arthur Kennedy; *Alec Waggoman,* Donald Crisp; *Barbara Waggoman,* Cathy O'Donnell; *Dave Waggoman,* Alex Nicol; *Kate Canaday,* Aline MacMahon; *Charley O'Leary,* Wallace Ford; *Chris Boldt,* Jack Elam; *Frank Darrah,* John War Eagle; *Tom Quigby,* James Millican; *Fritz,* Gregg Barton; *Spud Oxton,* Boyd Stockman; *Padre,* Frank de Kova.

With Alex Nicol.

All seven of the films Anthony Mann had so far made with James Stewart had been for Universal. Now having completed his contract, he was free to follow his own course. He first signed with Columbia, to make two movies, both of which he chose to be westerns, *The Man from Laramie,* with James Stewart, and *The Last Frontier,* with Victor Mature. In making the one with Stewart he wanted to further pursue the hero-as-avenger concept and perhaps summarize all that he and Stewart had accomplished in their previous westerns. With *The Man from Laramie* there is reason to believe that Mann succeeded. He had spoken for some time of doing a western version of *King Lear,* and *Laramie* would seem to be a bold step in that Shakespearean direction. As Will Lockhart, the man from Laramie, Wyoming, Stewart rides into a county of New Mexico which seems like a feudal kingdom, ruled over by a land baron named Alec Waggoman (Donald Crisp), whose one weakness appears to be his inordinate love for his son Dave (Alex Nicol), whom he has spoiled rotten. The boy is amoral and he will be the death of his father.

Will Lockhart poses as a freighter but he is actually an army officer out to discover the people who sold guns to the Indians and indirectly caused the death of his young brother, himself an army officer. As he nears his destination he stops at the site of the massacre and he muses on the scene, picking

With Alex Nicol (nearest horseman) and Wallace Ford (bearded).

With Cathy O'Connell, Arthur Kennedy and Frank de Kova.

With Arthur Kennedy.

up the battered hat of one of the dead soldiers and wonders how his brother might have died. In the county town of Coronado, Lockhart meets Barbara Waggoman (Cathy O'Donnell), the niece of Alec Waggoman, whose influence on the community seems near complete. After unloading his merchandise Lockhart moves out of town for another trip and stops on some salt flats, assuming their use to be free. He is attacked by Dave and a bunch of his henchmen, and Lockhart is lassoed and dragged through a fire, his mules are shot and his wagon burned. When he asks the identity of his assailants, Dave, who clearly relishes in indulgence in brutality, points to a horse brand and says, "That's the only introduction you need, mister."

Lockhart might have been killed by Dave had it not been for the intervention of Vic Hansboro (Arthur Kennedy), the foreman and foster son of Waggoman. Hansboro appears to be less vicious than Dave and later acts in a friendly manner toward Lockhart, who is somewhat relieved when he meets Waggoman and finds him to be a civilized man. Waggoman pays Lockhart for his damages but warns him to get out of town. Lockhart decides he would rather stay, mostly because of Barbara and partly because a friendly rancher, Kate Canaday (Aline MacMahon), offers him a job. This will also give him time to conduct his investigation.

Lockhart and Hansboro come to have a degree of respect for one another but Hansboro becomes furious when he learns he has no chance of taking over the Waggoman empire when the old man dies. Waggoman, even though he knows his son is a weakling, names Dave as his sole inheritor. Hansboro becomes even more disgusted when he witnesses a gun fight between Dave and Lockhart. Lockhart gets the best of the younger man but is punished in return when Dave tells some of his men to hold Lockhart

while he pumps a bullet into his right hand. In agony Lockhart screams, "You scum!" When he recovers from the wound he pursues his investigation more earnestly, but it is Waggoman himself who discovers that the gunrunners are Dave and Hansboro. In a struggle with his son he falls off a cliff, but he lives long enough to tell Lockhart what he knows. Hansboro kills Dave in a quarrel and tries to pin the blame on Lockhart, but Hansboro's life comes to its inevitable end when Lockhart tracks him down.

By 1955 standards *The Man from Laramie* was a notably brutal western. Nothing quite so severe as Stewart getting shot in the hand point blank had ever been seen in such a film, although the sequence was dramatically logical. In terms of life in the old West, incapacitating a man by ruining his right hand was almost like castration, and well in keeping with the psychopath played by Alex Nicol. It is a film with many fine performances, especially those of the ever-reliable Arthur Kennedy as a rogue not entirely without a sense of decency, and the then 73-year-old Scotsman Donald Crisp as a hard landowner, blinded by his love of a wayward son. It is an almost Shakespearean character, an old man going blind and who in the end tries to somewhat atone for his sins by telling the truth. Crisp has one scene in which he tells Stewart about his nightmares, and it is a memorable piece of acting by a man who by that time had already been in films for forty years.

The Man from Laramie is very much to the credit of Anthony Mann, who took his cast and crew to New Mexico and filmed on various locations within a hundred miles of Santa Fe. As with his other westerns, Mann used the land as part of his drama, the images sharpening the action. Now that they had worked together so many times the chemistry between Mann and Stewart made this fine western that much finer. And Mann again voiced his high regard for the actor's willingness to subject himself to rough work. Wherever possible Stewart chose to do his own stunts, such as riding down a steep slope and allowing himself to be knocked under the hooves of horses during a brawl, and most noticeably the scene in which he is dragged through a fire. He considered all this part of the job of giving a credible characterization. These are all reasons that contributed to Stewart's being the finest actor among the major stars who made westerns. John Wayne, Joel McCrea and Randolph Scott were all superb movie westerners but none had Stewart's dramatic range. What a pity that *The Man from Laramie* became the final Stewart-Mann western. And yet, as a final collaboration, it is hard to imagine a better one.

THE MAN WHO KNEW TOO MUCH

PARAMOUNT, 1956

Produced and *Directed* by Alfred Hitchcock; *Written* by John Michael Hayes and Angus McPhail, based on a story by Charles Bennett and D. B. Wyndham-Lewis; *Photographed in color* by Robert Burks; *Music* by Bernard Herrmann; 120 minutes.

CAST:

Ben McKenna, James Stewart; *Jo McKenna*, Doris Day; *Mrs. Drayton*, Brenda de Banzie; *Mr. Drayton*, Bernard Miles; *Buchanan*, Ralph Truman; *Louis Bernard*, Daniel Gelin; *Ambassador*, Mogens Wieth; *Val Parnell*, Alan Mowbray; *Jan Peterson*, Hilary Brooke; *Hank McKenna*, Christopher Olsen; *Rien*, Reggie Nalder; *Woburn*, Noel Willman; *Manager*, Richard Wattis; *Helen Parnell*, Alix Talton; *Police Inspector*, Yves Brainville; *Cindy Fontaine*, Carolyn Jones.

With Doris Day.

With the combination of ego and humor that was characteristic of Alfred Hitchcock, he explained the difference between his 1934 filming of *The Man Who Knew Too Much* and the 1956 re-make as the first being the work of a gifted amateur and the second the work of a professional. There is no reason to quibble. Filmmaking doesn't get to be much more professional than the expertly crafted 1956 version. For James Stewart it was another opportunity to portray the decent, ordinary American man caught up in extraordinary and dangerous circumstances and responding with a mixture of courage, confusion and most of all a dogged determination to figure out what is going on. Few actors have been able to convey this guise as well as Stewart. Here, as the man who gets to know too much about a planned political assassination, he is Dr. Ben McKenna, a surgeon on vacation in Morocco with his wife Jo (Doris Day) and his son Hank (Christopher Olsen). They are American tourists having a nice time, until certain events turn their trip into a frightening experience.

While sightseeing in Morocco, the McKennas make the aquaintance of a gentlemanly Frenchman, Louis Bernard (Daniel Gelin), and a nice, ordinary English couple, Mr. and Mrs. Drayton (Bernard Miles and Brenda de Banzie). The Frenchman invites them all to dinner but mysteriously cancels it and the McKennas end up dining with the Draytons. The next day, in the marketplace of Marrakesh, an Arab comes staggering toward McKenna. He has a dagger stuck in his back and when he collapses at McKenna's

With Doris Day, Bernard Miles and Brenda de
Branzie.

With Daniel Gelin.

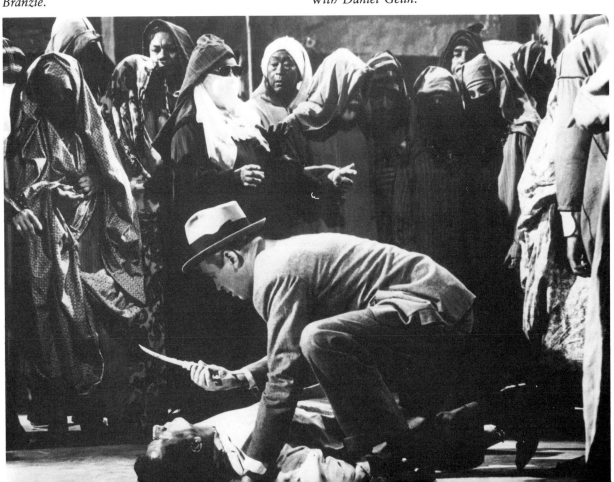

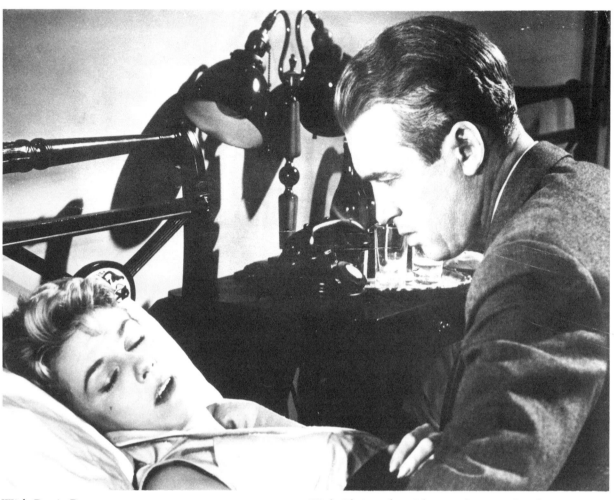

With Doris Day.　　　　　　　　　　　　With Christopher Olsen and Bernard Miles.

pistol appearing between the folds of a curtain as the moment approaches and she screams. Her scream causes the assassin to miss and when later chased by the police he falls to his death from a high box to the floor of the hall.

The failure of the attempt on the diplomat's life does not give the McKennas back their son, but a ruse occurs to Jo. Spotting a piano in an office she plays and loudly sings a song that Hank knows, "Que Sera Sera," which reaches his ears and has him eluding the Draytons and running toward his mother. Life goes back to normalcy for the McKennas after their upsetting adventures.

The Man Who Knew Too Much was a commercial winner, although few critics seem to hold it in high regard. In financing the film Paramount told Hitchcock they wanted a family picture, no matter how suspenseful or no matter how many twists and turns of plot he might devise. They were well satisfied. So were the song writing team of Jay Livingstone and Ray Evans, who won an Oscar for "Que Sera Sera," which also became a hit record for Doris Day. The casting of Day in a Hitchcock film raised a few eyebrows when it was first announced but it made sense in view of her role being that of a former singer and the song being a part of the dramatic structure. Although known mostly as a singer, she had given a fine performance in *Love Me or Leave Me* just prior to this, and Hitchcock was impressed. Unfortunately she had few opportunities thereafter to use the dramatic side of her talent.

In writing the music score, Bernard Herrmann agreed with Hitchcock that it was wise to re-use the dramatic cantata that Arthur Benjamin had written for the 1934 version. It does indeed work perfectly and Hitchcock kept the same dramatic devices in the assassination attempt that he had used before. Comparisons between the two versions are pointless, since the former ran 75 minutes and the re-make clocks in at exactly two hours, and with production values unavailable to Hitchcock in 1934. For Stewart it was a chance to play a doctor whose life is drastically turned upside down and whose rather smugly confident posture is badly bruised. He is a man forced to come to terms with matters that strain his courage and temporarily shatter his life of well-measured success, and in the process comes to realize his wife is a stronger and more courageous human than he had known before. His Dr. Ben McKenna is a thoroughly believable man. And now, with this Hitchcockian success neatly tucked in his belt, Stewart set about making a movie he had been longing to make.

feet, the doctor sees that it is the Frenchman in disguise. Louis Bernard whispers into McKenna's ear and then dies, while the Draytons look on. Later, when the McKennas get back to their hotel they find that the Draytons have kidnapped Hank. The English couple are involved in espionage and their intention is to give McKenna something urgent to occupy his mind, instead of relating what he has learned from the Frenchman to the proper authorities.

The McKennas rush to London because part of the information given by the dying Frenchman concerns a London name—Ambrose Chapel. McKenna assumes it to be the name of a man and he manages to locate one, a taxidermist, who knows nothing about kidnapping and assassination but who suggests that what McKenna is really looking for is a small church called Ambrose Chapel. It is there that McKenna finds his son, the Draytons and their colleagues, all involved in a plot to kill a certain diplomat during a concert at the Royal Albert Hall. McKenna is unable to extricate Hank from Ambrose Chapel and the boy is taken by the assassins to the concert. In the meantime McKenna tries to convince the police of the planned murder but he receives only limited cooperation, although enough to get some policemen to go with him to the Albert Hall. Once there Jo is approached by one of the assassins and told to keep quiet or her son will be killed. At Ambrose Chapel McKenna has learned how the murder will be committed and he tells Jo: during the climax of the composition "Storm Clouds Cantata," at the moment of a cymbal crash, the assassin will fire at the diplomat. Seated in the audience, Jo spots a

THE SPIRIT OF ST. LOUIS

WARNER BROS., 1957

Produced by Leland Hayward; *Directed* by Billy Wilder; *Written* by Wilder and Wendell Mayes, based on the book by Charles Lederer; *Photographed in color* by Robert Burks and J. Peverell Marley; *Music* by Franz Waxman; 135 minutes.

CAST:

Charles A. Lindbergh, James Stewart; *Bud Gurney,* Murray Hamilton; *Mirror Girl,* Patricia Smith; *B. F. Mahoney,* Bartlett Robinson; *Knight,* Robert Cornwaithe; *Model,* Sheila Bond; *Father Hussman,* Marc Connelly; *Donald Hall,* Arthur Space; *Boedecker,* Harlan Warde; *Goldsborough,* Dabbs Greer; *Blythe,* Paul Birch; *Harold Bixby,* David Orrick; *Major Lambert,* Robert Burton; *William Robertson,* James L. Robertson; *E. Lansing Ray,* Maurice Manson; *Earl Thompson,* James O'Rear; *Lane,* David McMahon; *Old Farmer,* Griff Barnett.

James Stewart well remembers May 20, 1927. It was his nineteenth birthday but it was also the day Charles A. Lindbergh made his solo flight across the Atlantic and carved himself a niche in the history of aviation. As a child Stewart had already been keenly interested in airplanes (he made models) and like the rest of his community he avidly listened for news of Lindbergh and his adventure. Another young man named Billy Wilder also followed the news. When he became a filmmaker he resolved that he would one day make a film about Lindbergh, just as Stewart resolved that if anyone made such a film he would want to be first in line to play Lucky Lindy. The resolve emerged in 1957 as *The Spirit of St. Louis,* a splendid, earnest and painstaking account of the famed aviator. Sadly it was not to be a very successful film, and the reasons for its failure are due in large part to Stewart and Wilder. Stewart, forty-eight at the time of filming, was simply too old to play Lindbergh at twenty-five. Wilder, who has always excelled with satire and the quirks of human nature, was not quite the right man for the job of directing, and partly

With Harlan Warde.

In his ruminations Lindbergh imagines himself landing in Paris and being met by a single gendarme.

scripting, a story devoid of satire. In short, *The Spirit of St. Louis* is more admirable than entertaining.

The film presents the facts clearly. As an airmail pilot Lindbergh senses the possibility of making the long trip across the Atlantic and eventually finds the backers for the project. A plane is specially built to his specifications and in the period while he is waiting for the weather to clear in order to take off—and at points during the flight—he recalls scenes of former days as a barnstorming pilot in circuses, flying the mail, and his adventures learning how to fly. As he flies the Atlantic he fights the temptation to sleep and grows fearful when ice forms on his wings. He loses the use of his compass for a while and has to fly by the stars. Then, thirty-three and a half hours after leaving Roosevelt Field, Long Island, Lindbergh touches down at Le Bourget Field, Paris, shortly before eight o'clock on the morning of May 20, 1927, to be greeted by thousands of admirers. Later, in New York, many more thousands of admirers welcome him with a ticker-tape parade of triumph.

Lindbergh wrote *The Spirit of St. Louis* in 1953 and he sold the film rights to Warner Bros. for one million dollars. Warner then spent another five million making the picture. Production began in August of 1955 and stretched over the next eight months, with the film not being released until March of 1957. Three copies of Lindbergh's plane, a Ryan N-X-211 single-seater, were made for the film and other planes were built for the circus sequences. Most of the location filming was done at the Santa Monica Airport, about twenty miles from Warners' Burbank studios, at the airport on Long Island where Lindbergh had taken off and at Guyancourt, near Versailles. Thousands of miles were flown by aerial photographers to get the CinemaScope color shots of

Lindbergh's flight path over Cape Cod, Nova Scotia, the Atlantic, Ireland, England and France. The producers were able to persuade the City of Paris to turn on the city lights an hour ahead of schedule, such was the French support for the project, and they had no trouble finding thousands of extras to flood Le Bourget for Lindy's arrival.

The skill and the effort that went into the making of *The Spirit of St. Louis* is wholly admirable, but the public does not go to see movies because they are admirably made. *St. Louis* did not recoup its costs and Billy Wilder afterwards said that the concept was wrong, that he should not have focussed the film entirely on the famous flight but that it should have told the whole story of Lindbergh's life, with a build-up to the infamous kidnapping case, a major tragedy that changed Lindbergh's life. Wilder admitted that he had wanted a younger actor for the role—John Kerr would probably have been his choice—but he knew such a film needed a major name in order to have any box office clout, and that Stewart was the obvious man for the job.

As disappointing as the results were for Wilder and the producers, it was a personal failure for Stewart, who dearly wanted to do the film and worked very hard at it. The make-up was expert and the actor certainly looks years younger, but it was impossible to convey the aura of a twenty-five-year-old. Almost every critic picked up on the age factor, although most were willing to admire Stewart's work. Most felt that it was a sincere and appealing characterization, although by its very nature a standardized portrait of heroism. *Time* made a generous assessment, "Stewart, for all his professional, 48-year-old boyishness, succeeds almost continuously in suggesting what all the world sensed at the time: that Lindbergh's flight was not the mere physical adventure of a rash young 'flying fool,' but rather a journey of the spirit, in which, as in the pattern of all progress, one brave man proved himself for all mankind as the paraclete of a new possibility."

Despite its failure, *The Spirit of St. Louis* is a film well worth studying, especially for anyone with an interest in aviation. It also has much to offer students of cinematography, to say nothing of watching an actor like Stewart meticulously define a characterization in a different setting. It was not only a solo flight but it was largely a solo acting performance. And in one respect the film is an absolute masterpiece—the musical score of Franz Waxman, which virtually accompanies the flyer and speaks his thoughts and anxieties. A landmark in the art of film music.

NIGHT PASSAGE

UNIVERSAL, 1957

Produced by Aaron Rosenberg; *Directed* by James Neilson; *Written* by Borden Chase, based on a story by Norman A. Fox; *Photographed in color* by William Daniels; *Music* by Dimitri Tiomkin; 90 minutes.

CAST:

Grant McLaine, James Stewart; *The Utica Kid*, Audie Murphy; *Whitey Harbin*, Dan Duryea; *Charlotte Drew*, Diane Foster; *Verna Kimball*, Elaine Stewart; *Joey Adams*, Brandon de Wilde; *Ben Kimball*, Jay C. Flippen; *Will Renner*, Herbert Anderson; *Concho*, Robert J. Wilke; *Jeff Kurth*, Hugh Beaumont; *Shotgun*, Jack Elam; *Howdy Sladen*, Tommy Cook; *Mr. Feeney*, Paul Fix; *Miss VIttles*, Olive Carey; *Tim Eiley*, James Flavin; *Jubilee*, Donald Curtis; *Mrs. Feeney*, Ellen Corby.

With Olive Carey.

The role called for Stewart to play the accordion, and with no need to fake it.

With Brandon de Wilde.

With Diane Foster, Brandon de Wilde and Audie Murphy.

Night Passage is among the least of the James Stewart westerns. The most important point to be made about it is a sad one, that it caused a rift in the working relationship between Stewart and Anthony Mann. Mann had agreed to direct it but he backed out shortly before the film went into production, claiming that the script by Borden Chase, with whom he had worked on *Winchester '73, Bend of the River* and *The Far Country,* was not strong enough or interesting enough. Mann decided instead to direct Henry Fonda in *The Tin Star,* which had a script by Dudley Nichols, about ambiguous characters in conflict, that was far more to Mann's liking. Stewart was annoyed with Mann but refused to cancel his commitment to make *Night Passage,* although there were people who suggested to him that he should. There is about Stewart quite a bit of the doggedness that marks many of his screen characters.

Producer Aaron Rosenberg and Stewart—this was their sixth film together—decided to use James Neilson as director, thereby giving him his first screen credit in that capacity. Neilson, who had made

a good reputation as a war photographer, proved to be a straightforward kind of a director and after this assignment his work would be almost entirely with Walt Disney Productions. How much better *Night Passage* might have been with Mann as director is open to question, other than that he would have derived more from the quirkiness of the characters. There was not much he could have done with the rather mundane plot.

The film opens with Grant McLaine (Stewart) riding through beautiful mountain scenery and arriving at a railroad camp. He wears no gunbelt but he carries an accordion. For the past five years he has been making a meagre living as an itinerant musician, following his dismissal as a railroad employee for his involvement in theft. There are those who believe he took the blame for others. Railroad owner Ben Kimball (Jay C. Flippen) decides to give Grant a chance to prove his honesty, largely through the coaxing of his lovely, young wife Verna (Elaine Stewart), and assigns him the job of getting the payroll through to his field workers, who are on the verge of quitting. Every attempt so far has failed, due to the raiding of Whitey Harbin (Dan Duryea) and his gang. One of the members of that gang is the

181

Robert Wilke takes it on the chin.

Utica Kid (Audie Murphy), who happens to be Grant's kid brother, for whose previous crimes Grant has taken the rap.

Grant befriends an orphaned teenager, Joey Adams (Brandon de Wilde), and when Harbin and his men board the train, Grant takes the money and puts it into the shoe box Joey is carrying. The money is therefore within sight of the bandits all the time they are frantically looking everywhere else for it. Eventually the Utica Kid sides with his older brother when he sees that he will probably be killed by Harbin. In the final battle Harbin and most of his men are wiped out, but the Utica Kid takes a bullet and dies in Grant's arms. And the girl (Diane Foster) who has been faithfully waiting for the Kid all these years, now walks away hand-in-hand with Grant, presumably to help him rebuild his life.

Night Passage met with only mild response and had it not been marketable as a James Stewart western it is safe to assume the response would have been milder still. It is easy to see why Anthony Mann backed away from it and sad to think that it caused the actor and the director to part company on a sour note. Some time later they resumed their friendship, but they never again had the chance to work together. After making two more westerns, the remarkable *Man of the West,* with Gary Cooper, and the disappointing re-make of *Cimarron,* with Glenn Ford, Mann became involved in the time-consuming epics *El Cid, The Fall of the Roman Empire* and *The Heroes of Telemark,* and died in 1967 from a heart attack, at the age of sixty-one.

The best things about *Night Passage* are the color photography of northern New Mexico by William Daniels and the music score by Dimitri Tiomkin, which included two songs with lyrics by Ned Washington. Both songs are sung by Stewart—"Follow the River" and "You Can't Get Far Without a Railroad"—giving him the most singing he has ever done on film. He also accompanies himself on the accordion, the instrument he mastered as a boy, and this opportunity to show his skill with the squeeze-box may have been a factor in his wanting to make the movie. However, following the dissapointing reception given *The Spirit of St. Louis* and the even poorer response to *Night Passage,* Stewart was now in need of a boost. Thanks to Alfred Hitchcock he was about to get one.

VERTIGO

PARAMOUNT, 1958

Produced and *Directed* by Alfred Hitchcock; *Written* by Alex Coppel and Samuel Taylor, based on the novel *D'Entre Les Morts* by Pierre Boileau; *Photographed in color* by Robert Burks; *Music* by Bernard Herrmann; 120 minutes.

CAST:

John "Scottie" Ferguson, James Stewart; *Madeline Elster/Judy Barton,* Kim Novak; *Midge,* Barbara Bell Geddes; *Gavin Elster,* Tom Helmore; *Official,* Henry Jones; *Doctor,* Raymond Bailey; *Manageress,* Ellen Corby; *Pop Leibel,* Konstantin Shayne; *Mistaken Identity,* Lee Patrick; *Captain Hansen,* Paul Bryar; *Saleswoman,* Margaret Brayton; *Jury Foreman,* William Remick; *Flower Vendor,* Julian Petruzzi; *Nun,* Sara Taft; *Policeman,* Fred Graham.

Vertigo is a film now so highly regarded that it is difficult to understand why it did not meet with greater critical regard when first seen in May of 1958, which, incidentally, happened to be the month of James Stewart's fiftieth birthday. It was well received at the time by critics and public alike as a typically good Hitchcock suspense thriller but with time *Vertigo* has slowly gathered a mystique, and if it is not the greatest film made by Alfred Hitchcock it surely stands among the first half dozen. However, there is little doubt that it is the most studied and discussed of his movies, and the one that bears seeing over and over again. What is it about *Vertigo*? In many ways it is not typical Hitchcock. It has little suspense and it reveals its mystery about two-thirds of the way through its labyrinth of a plot. It is bizarre, hypnotic and tragic. The hero is a neurotic loser and the heroine ends up dead. The only winner is the villain, who plans the perfect murder and gets away with it. Aside from all this it is the film in which Stewart gives one of the cleverest and most complex performances of his career.

In *Vertigo*, Stewart is San Francisco policeman John "Scottie" Ferguson, who takes early retirement from the force because of his acute acrophobia, his petrifying fear of heights. The decision is brought about when a policeman plunges to his death while trying to rescue Scottie from a roof gutter from which he is hanging a dozen or so floors above a street. How Scottie survives this predicament is

With Tom Helmore.   With Kim Novak.

something Hitchcock chooses not to explain. Scottie finds comfort in the company of his understanding girlfriend Midge (Barbara Bel Geddes), although not enough to want to marry her. Deciding to strike out as a private detective, he is hired by an old friend, shipping tycoon Gavin Elster (Tom Helmore), who wants him to track his wife Madeleine (Kim Novak) because she seems suicidal, perhaps as the result of being obsessed with her great grandmother, Carlotta, who went mad and killed herself. "Do you believe that someone out of the past, someone dead, can enter and take possession of a living being?" Scottie is a pragmatic cop and not given to occult consideration, but he is intrigued enough to take the case.

As Scottie trails the beautiful Madeleine all over San Francisco he becomes puzzled by her strange behavior. She seems to be in a trance. He follows her to a point just under the San Francisco Bridge, where after moments of apparent meditation she throws herself into the water. He saves her and then takes her unconscious body back to his apartment. She wakes up unclothed in his bed, having been tenderly cared for. As they afterwards get to know each other, Scottie begins to fall in love with this enigmatic beauty. She tells him she has a strange compulsion to visit the Mission at San Juan Batista. He takes her there but as soon as she arrives she joyfully races up the stairs of the tall bell tower. He tries to follow but his acrophobia makes it difficult. Halfway up he is horrified by a scream and the sight of her body pitching past a window to her death. But why does the body look as if it is already dead?

The shock causes Scottie to lapse into a nervous breakdown, through which he is nursed by the faithful, motherly Midge. Months pass and he almost has Madeleine out of his mind when he spots a girl on the street who looks just like her. He follows her and persists in getting to know her. Her name is Judy Barton, a dark-haired and more common version of the beauteous Madeleine. Scottie falls in love with her and starts to groom her to look like Madeleine, until it becomes apparent that this is exactly who she is, except that in actuality she is a girl hired by Elster to pretend to be Madeleine—the real wife having been killed by him and thrown off the bell tower. In rage and confusion, Scottie takes Judy back to the mission in order to try and understand why and how he had been tricked. He forces her up the steps of the tower and in his fury he overcomes his acrophobia. But the price he pays is heavy and cruel. After admitting her collusion with Elster and that she loves Scottie, Judy is startled by a black-clad figure emerging from the shadows in the dark top of the tower—

With Kim Novak.

actually a nun—and she falls to her death when she stumbles at the edge, where Scottie has made her stand in order to frighten the truth out of her. The nun murmers, "God have mercy," but the words have little meaning for Scottie, a man who has loved and lost the same girl twice.

Vertigo is one of those rare films that can be

185

With Kim Novak.

seen again and again, in the same way that any genuine work of art never loses its fascination. This is Hitchcock at the height of his skill, plus the goodly amount of luck that sometimes descends upon film-makers when everything works even better than planned. The color photography of San Francisco and its environs by Robert Burks is an enormous plus for the film, as is the masterly music by Bernard Herrmann, with gives added dimensions of yearnings and tragedy. Hitchcock had at first resisted the idea of using Kim Novak, preferring Vera Miles, but Paramount fortunately changed his mind. It is Novak's rather blank beauty that adds to the enigma of Madeleine and the confusion of Judy. Like the film itself her performance is a mystery—is it or is it not acting? Whatever it is, it is perfect. As for James Stewart, it is possibly one of the finest pieces of acting ever given by a major Hollywood star. It is a study in romantic obsession, in the anguish of a disturbed man, in his anger and bafflement, with the curse of his acrophobia becoming a symbol of the pain in his heart. A truly remarkable performance.

BELL, BOOK AND CANDLE

COLUMBIA, 1958

Produced by Julian Blaustein; *Directed* by Richard Quine; *Written* by Daniel Taradash, based on the play by John Van Druten; *Photographed in color* by James Wong Howe; *Music* by George Duning; 103 minutes.

CAST:

Shepard Henderson, James Stewart; *Gillian Holrody,* Kim Novak; *Mickey Holrody,* Jack Lemmon; *Sidney Redlitch,* Ernie Kovacs; *Mrs. De Pass,* Hermione Gingold; *Queenie,* Elsa Lanchester; *Merle Kittridge,* Janice Rule; *French Singer,* Phillippe Clay; *Secretary,* Bek Nelson; *Andy White,* Howard McNear.

Only five months after appearing in *Vertigo,* James Stewart and Kim Novak were re-teamed for *Bell, Book and Candle,* but whereas they will always be remembered for their work together in the Hitchcock picture it requires a nudge to recall that they appeared in a second film. For Hitchcock, Stewart was required to play a complicated human being. For *Bell, Book and Candle* he was required to perform as a genial, fumblingly charming Jimmy Stewart. On stage the John Van Druten play had served the then-married Rex Harrison and Lilli Palmer well, but Novak was no Palmer. For the film the accent was placed on the visual charms of Novak, supported by the gorgeous color photography of James Wong Howe and a witty music score by George Duning. The end result was a very nice little comedy about witches, magic and spells.

Gillian Holroyd (Novak) is a witch, a sleek and elegant one who runs an art shop and keeps company with a beautiful Siamese cat called Pyewacket. Gillian is a girl of amorous disposition and she yearns for a normal life. One day into her life comes publisher Shepard Henderson (Stewart) and she decides he is the man for her. After spending a few hours with her in her apartment, Henderson starts to feel amorous himself and he postpones his planned marriage to Merle Kittridge (Janice Rule). He has no idea that Gillian is a witch and that her jazz-loving

With Elsa Lanchester and Kim Novak.

With Janice Rule.

With Kim Novak.

With Janice Rule, Jack Lemmon, Elsa Lanchester and Kim Novak.

brother Nicky (Jack Lemon) is a warlock, and that both of them can do things like walk through walls and cause street lights to turn off and on. He also has no way of knowing that she has him under a spell and that despite her yearnings for love, she, as a witch, is incapable of loving. Henderson does, however, suspect that he is among rather strange people. Nicky is in the process of helping an alcoholic author, Sidney Redlitch (Ernie Kovacs), to write a book about witchcraft, which worries Gillian, lest it cause Henderson to find out about her true status. She tries to make Nicky give it up but he promises to expose her if she interferes.

Gillian decides to tackle her problem head on, and tell Henderson herself just what she is. With this knowledge he goes to see the leader of Manhattan witches, the flamboyant Mrs. De Pass (Hermione Gingold), to ask if it is possible to release Gillian from her spell and become a normal human. This causes a rift between the lovers and it looks as if it is all over, except that Gillian's delightfully giddy Aunt Queenie (Elsa Lanchester) believes that love should conquer all. She maneuvers to get the couple together again, and when Henderson sees that Gillian can both blush and cry—things that witches cannot do—he knows he has a real girl for a lover.

Such is the stuff of *Bell, Book and Candle*, pleasant fluff made into entertainment by skillful moviemaking, the beauty of Kim Novak and the droll talents of the likes of Jack Lemon, Ernie Kovacs and Hermione Gingold. For Stewart it was a pleasant and relatively easy assignment, and in the listing of his films important only as the point where he ceased to be a romantic leading man. In his movies, he would court no more. With the exception of *The Man Who Shot Liberty Valance*, in which he would win and marry Vera Miles, although without much apparent romance, James Stewart would now be either a family man on screen or an adventurous loner. He was fifty and he agreed with the critics that it was a little off-putting for actors of that age to be cast opposite much obviously younger actresses.

With Kim Novak.

ANATOMY OF A MURDER

COLUMBIA, 1959

Produced and directed by Otto Preminger; *Written* by Wendell Mayes, based on the novel by Robert Traver; *Photographed* by Sam Leavitt; *Music* by Duke Ellington; 160 minutes.

CAST:

Paul Biegler, James Stewart; *Laura Manion,* Lee Remick; *Frederick Manion,* Ben Gazzara; *Parnell McCarthy,* Arthur O'Connell; *Maida,* Eve Arden; *Mary Pilant,* Kathryn Grant; *Judge Weaver,* Judge Joseph N. Welch; *Mitch Lodwick,* Brooks West; *Claude Dancer,* George C. Scott; *Alphonse Pacquette,* Murray Hamilton; *Dr. Smith,* Orson Bean; *Dr. Harcourt,* Alexander Bell; *Photographer,* Joseph Kearns; *Caretaker,* Russ Brown; *Dr. Dompierre,* Howard McNear; *Dr. Raschild,* Ned Weaver; *Madigan,* Jimmy Conlin; *Police Sergeant,* Ken Lynch.

Opinions vary as to which is James Stewart's best film performance, but there are many who place his work in *Anatomy of a Murder* at the top of the list.

With Lee Remick.

The New York Film Critics Association named him their choice for Best Actor of the Year and he was so nominated, for the last time, by the Academy of Motion Picture Arts and Sciences. But 1959 was the year of *Ben-Hur,* which swept up ten Oscars, including one for Charlton Heston as Best Actor. However, the consensus was that Stewart's performance as a small-town Michigan lawyer named Paul Biegler was what held the unusually long (two hours and forty minutes) picture together, and that it was an unusually crafty piece of acting. Perhaps, like Stewart himself, Biegler is much more than what he at first seems. This is a lawyer who appears amiable and easygoing but who actually has a mind like a steel trap.

Anatomy of a Murder was produced and directed by Otto Preminger, a man with a reputation for handling a film cast and crew with martial command. His teaming with Stewart, a man with a reputation for knowing exactly how he wants to play a role, was not a likely one but both men respected each other and the results were excellent. Stewart had expected his co-star to be Lana Turner, but when she started making demands about costumes, insisting that Jean Louis design her wardrobe, Preminger dumped her and gave the part to Lee Remick, who had been slated for the small role then handed to Kathryn Crosby.

Preminger shot most of the film on location in Michigan and chose to shoot in black-and-white, feeling that color might tend to glamorize what was basically a rather sordid story. It is about an army lieutenant, Frederick Manion (Ben Gazzara), who kills a bartender, claiming that the man had beaten and raped his wife, Laura (Remick). She supports her

With Eve Arden and Arthur O'Connell.　　　With Lee Remick and Ben Gazzara.

husband's story and takes a lie detector test to help substantiate his case. However, the police surgeon who examines her can find no evidence of rape, her bruises being mostly confined to her face. Manion is assigned the rather shabby-looking Biegler for his defender and the state appoints the sharp Claude Dancer (George C. Scott) as the prosecutor. In the course of interviewing his client, Biegler finds him to be a man with a violently possessive nature, and he digs up evidence that Laura is morally lax and may possibly have had affairs with other men. He knows that this is the tack likely to be taken by the prosecution.

And it is. Dancer grinds away at the charge of probable immorality. He points out that the bartender was a well-liked man in the town and that Laura had enticed him into intercourse, with her husband thrashing her after he had killed the man. Biegler knows he is on rough ground and asks his associate, Parnell McCarthy (Arthur O'Connell), to come up with some ideas. McCarthy has a brilliant legal mind but one that is too often besotted with drink. With the help of his faithful secretary, Maida (Eve Arden), McCarthy stays sober and manages to dig up the findings of an old case in which a man had been acquitted because of acting on "irresistible impulse." Biegler uses this to help his client, but the tactic that wins him the case is the placing on the stand of the bartender's illegitimate daughter, Mary Pilant (Crosby), who confirms Biegler's theory that her father was a man of questionable moral character. Manion is cleared but Biegler immediately learns something about his client's own moral character—he and his wife leave town without paying him his fee.

Anatomy of a Murder benefits greatly from having been filmed in Michigan and from Preminger's astute use of real settings and glimpses of small-town life. His players are all first class— Gazzara, Remick, O'Connell, Scott and Arden perform the parts to the letter—but it is still Stewart who provides the spine of the film. This is a laid-back, not very ambitious lawyer, content to make a modest living, play a little jazz piano and hunt and fish, but who, when presented with a challenge, rises to the occasion. Stewart must surely have drawn upon his own early experiences of small-town life to give himself the nuances of character of this man. His Paul Biegler is just about the last word in defining quiet doggedness and deviousness. He had his doubts about the nature of his client but he is bound and determined to get him cleared.

The only major criticism of the film lies in Preminger's odd choice of Duke Ellington to provide the score. The great jazzman's music simply does not fit the picture. However, there is much to be said in favor of the production, including a candor that was new in 1959. Michigan Supreme Court Justice John D. Voelker wrote the story using the pseudonym Robert Traver and it contained a great deal of specific terminology about rape and carnal knowledge. To his credit Preminger opted for using much of it. He also came up with a brilliant piece of casting, using Judge Joseph N. Welch as the judge in his film. The eminent Bostonian had come to public acclaim as the man who cut Senator Joseph McCarthy down to size in the televised hearings in which Welch defended those being attacked by the ravenous senator—and as an actor Welch did very well in this, his only movie. About the star of the picture he said, with tongue in cheek, "It's almost immoral for Jimmy Stewart to become such a good lawyer without having to work at it as I did."

In *The New York Times*, Bosley Crowther stated that it was as good a courtroom drama as he had ever seen, and he praised Stewart for the manner in which the actor revealed the character of Biegler: "Slowly and subtly, he presents us a warm, clever, adroit and complex man, and, most particularly, a portrait of a trial lawyer in action which will be difficult for anyone to surpass." Ironically, the task would fall to Stewart himself fourteen years later when he used the Biegler characterization as the basis for his series of telefilms as small-town lawyer Billie Joe Hawkins.

With Arthur O'Connell.

THE FBI STORY

WARNER BROS., 1959

Produced and *directed* by Mervyn LeRoy; *Written* by Richard L. Breen and John Twist, based on the book by Don Whitehead; *Photographed in color* by Joseph Biroc; *Music* by Max Steiner, 149 minutes.

CAST:

Chip Hardesty, James Stewart; *Lucy Hardesty*, Vera Miles; *Sam Crandall*, Murray Hamilton; *George Crandall*, Larry Pennell; *Jack Graham*, Nick Adams; *Jennie*, Diane Jergens; *Anna Sage*, Jean Willis; *Anne*, Joyce Taylor; *Mario*, Victor Millan; *Harry Dakins*, Parley Baer; *McCutcheon*, Fay Roope; *U.S. Marshall*, Ed Prentiss; *Medicine Salesman*, Robert Gist; *Mike*, Buzz Martin; *Casket Salesman*, Kenneth Mayer; *Suspect*, Paul Genge; *Mrs. Ballard*, Ann Doran; *Minister*, Forrest Taylor; *Dillinger*, Scott Peters; *William Phipps*, Baby Face Nelson.

The story of the Federal Bureau of Investigation was not unfamiliar to moviegoers by 1959. Nevertheless, Warner Bros. decided to give the history of America's national police body a thorough going-over, tracing its development through the career of a pioneer member named Chip Hardesty, a pillar of dedication to the service. Such a character needed a stalwart kind of screen presence. Who better to represent the best of American values than James Stewart? The FBI had previously been the subject of movie shorts such as *The March of Time*, which always managed to do justice to a worthy subject in a quarter of an hour. *The FBI Story* is rather like an episode of *The March of Time* spread over two and a half hours. Admirable, respectful and plodding.

In 1924, at the FBI office in Knoxville, Tennessee, Chip Hardesty, Sam Crandall (Murray Hamilton) and Harry Dakins (Parlet Baer) receive orders to report to a new bureau chief in Washington. Before leaving, Chip marries Lucy Ballard (Vera Miles), who doesn't like his dangerous line of work and would prefer him to be a lawyer. When Chip hears what J. Edgar Hoover has to say about his plans for improving, enlarging and making the FBI more efficient, he realizes that this is the career he must follow. Lucy understands, but in the years to

With Vera Miles.

come she has many reasons to regret her husband's insistence on devoting himself to the prevention of crime.

Under the new leadership, Chip, with Lucy, is sent to combat the violence of the Ku Klux Klan in Louisiana. Next he is assigned to the Middle West, at a time when such gangsters as Dillinger, Baby Face Nelson and Pretty Boy Floyd ran riot. Tracing and fighting all these and other hoods causes Chip to be away from home for days at a time, and causes Lucy

With Parley Baer.

to do a lot of worrying. The worrying continues when they are posted to the oil fields of Oklahoma, where Chip goes after the murderers of oil-rich Indians. In time Lucy gives birth to three children and her concern, and anger, about her husband and his work increases. She leaves him, but, after a separation that she finally decides she cannot maintain, she returns.

With the outbreak of the Second World War the FBI increases its membership to five thousand men. Chip's duties expand, what with the rounding up of enemy aliens and being sent to South America to track German agents. On the homefront Sam Crandall's son George (Larry Pennell) becomes an FBI man himself and marries the girl he loves—Chip's daughter Anne (Joyce Taylor). On their first anniversary, as the family celebrates with the parents, a telegram arrives to inform Chip and Lucy that their

son Mike (Buzz Martin) has been killed in action. After the war Chip and his agents find themselves with a new enemy—international communism. More dangerous adventures and so on until 1959, when Chip is given the less hazardous job of lecturing new recruits, to the final relief of his faithful wife.

The FBI Story is a long two and a half hours. It tells a great deal about the famed Bureau in an earnest manner but it lacks excitement and spirit. It is the work of a director, Mervyn LeRoy, respected for craftsmanship but never praised for being sparkling in style. Stewart's performance is all that could be expected in such a picture. He is credible, restrained, intelligent and occasionally even a little wryly humorous. The film proved a good investment for Warners and lead to their long-running TV series about the FBI, starring another restrained and intelligent gentleman star—Efrem Zimbalist, Jr.

196

THE MOUNTAIN ROAD

COLUMBIA, 1960

Produced by William Goetz; *Directed* by Daniel Mann; *Written* by Alfred Hayes, based on the novel by Theodore White; *Photographed* by Burnett Guffey; *Music* by Jerome Moross; 102 minutes.

CAST:

Major Baldwin, James Stewart; *Madame Sue-Mei Hung*, Lisa Lu; *Collins*, Glenn Corbett; *Michaelson*, Harry Morgan; *General Kwan*, Frank Silvera; *Niergaard*, James Best; *Miller*, Rudy Bond; *Prince*, Mike Kellin; *Ballo*, Frank Maxwell; *Lewis*, Eddie Firestone; *Colonel Li*, Leo Chen; *General Loomis*, Alan Baxter; *Colonel Magnusson*, Bill Quinn; *Chinese Colonel*, Peter Chong; *Chinese General*, P. C. Lee.

In the listing of war films *The Mountain Road* seems to have drifted to the sidelines. It was a film that made little impact on 1960 audiences, since it appeared to have little to say about the pain and distress of war that had not been better said before. The most interesting thing about the film is that it deals with a little-covered aspect of World War II, the 1944 operation of the U.S. Army in China, in the operation to delay the Japanese advance from the east coast toward the Chinese military headquarters in the interior. For James Stewart it was an opportunity to portray an army major named Baldwin, who is eager for a command of his own, apparently because he wants to test his own character and find out how he will behave in directing a dangerous situation.

Baldwin is given the job for which he volunteers, to lead an eight-man demolition team, picked from the last American garrison of an airfield, as the Japanese come to within fifty miles. Baldwin's assignment is to destroy anything that might help the enemy—to tear up roads, destroy bridges and set explosive traps. Baldwin seems intrigued with the fact that he has this kind of power at his command, but he believes he is using it with proper discretion and military effectiveness. That he might not be

With Frank Silvera, Lisa Lu and Glenn Corbett.

With Lisa Lu.

behaving with human understanding is a consideration that comes from his meeting with a cultured, American-educated Chinese lady, Madame Sue-Mei Hung (Lisa Lu).

After blowing up a mountain bridge, Baldwin takes Madame Hung into his custody, along with a Chinese general, Kwan (Frank Silvera), who has been separated from his command and who offers to help

Baldwin. The destruction of the bridge isolates thousands of Chinese, who now become homeless and hungry. Madame Hung expresses her disgust at this needless destruction, but Baldwin rationalizes that it was necessary. His sympathy for the Chinese greatly lessens when a starving group brutally kill one of his men, Collins (Glenn Corbett), who has offered food to the ravenous mob. This embitters Baldwin because

With Frank Silvera, Peter Chong and Harry Morgan.

By the end of the film the major has come to the point of doubting his decisions under fire. From the Chinese lady, with whom he had started to feel affection, he has learned something about compassion and he admits that he has not used his power as wisely as he might have done. He also knows he has missed a possible love relationship with a worthy lady. In other words, Major Baldwin has found out what being in command of a war operation is all about, and how it reveals a man's character. He has to admit that it was a bit too much for him.

In making Stewart the only name attraction in an off-beat war movie, Columbia took a doubtful chance, and found that it was not a good investment. This was not the kind of film in which most people expected or wanted to see James Stewart. There is little to criticize in his performance, it simply is not a role that offered a chance to say anything new about soldiers under the strain of combat in an alien environment and encountering situations that are as bewildering as they are frightening. *The Mountain Road* is not without merit. Filmed in stark black-and-white in Arizona, in the mountains near Phoenix, the warfare is chillingly depicted and the plight of the Chinese populace well conveyed. But it is not a James Stewart movie. His admirers had long grown accustomed to his being bewildered on the screen, but not bewildered and unsympathetic.

Collins had shown interest and compassion toward the Chinese. He becomes even more bitter later when Chinese renegade soldiers murder two of his men. Baldwin starts to wonder why he should be helping people who seem no better than the enemy. In anger he orders a village destroyed, causing the death of many people, and also causing Madame Hung to refuse to go any further with Baldwin.

199

TWO RODE TOGETHER

COLUMBIA, 1961

Produced by Stan Shpetner; *Directed* by John Ford; *Written* by Frank Nugent, based on the novel *Comanche Captives* by Will Cook; *Photographed in color* by Charles Lawton, Jr.; *Music* by George Duning; 108 minutes.

CAST:

Guthrie McCabe, James Stewart; *Lt. Jim Gary*, Richard Widmark; *Marty Purcell*, Shirley Jones; *Elena*, Linda Christal; *Sergeant Posey*, Andy Devine; *Major Frazer*, John McIntire; *Edward Purcell*, Paul Birch; *Mr. Wringle*, Willis Bouchey; *Quannah*, Henry Brandon; *Jackson Cole*, Harry Carey, Jr.; *Abby Frazer*, Olive Carey; *Boone Clay*, Ken Curtis; *Ward Corbey*, Chet Douglas; *Belle Aragon*, Annelle Hayes; *Running Wolf*, David Kent; *Mrs. Malaprop*, Anna Lee; *Mrs. McCandless*, Jeanette Nolan; *Ole Knudsen*, John Qualen; *Henry Clay*, Ford Rainey; *Stone Calf*, Woody Strode.

With Richard Widmark and John McIntire.

In her book *The Western Films of John Ford* (Citadel Press, 1974), J. A. Place makes a vital point: "James Stewart has been used in more different ways by directors than any other actor of his stature." Few other commentators have picked up on this interesting aspect of Stewart's long film career. He is, indeed, whatever his director has wanted him to be. For Frank Capra he had been the ideal American Everyman. For Alfred Hitchcock Stewart was a more complicated version of the Capra figure, with hints of neurosis. For Anthony Mann he was a man driven by various forms of torment, and for John Ford he was all these figures in combination, to be manipulated whichever way Ford fancied. The oddity of the Ford-Stewart association, in their three films together, is that no other director ever used the actor to portray the negative side of the American persona to quite the same extent. This might have something to do with Stewart's having come into Ford's professional life late in the day, when the director's attitudes had become harder and more cynical.

Two Rode Together is thematically the same as *The Searchers* (1956), with two men setting out to rescue white women and children from Indian capture. But in the six years between the two films Ford's idealism about the West seemed to have changed. In the former, John Wayne's Ethan Edwards is a man out to find his relatives, without any talk of money. In *Two Rode Together* Stewart's Guthrie McCabe is a venal character whose creed is "What's in it for me?"

and who sets out on the mission when he is assured $500 for each white he can bring back. McCabe is a sheriff brought into the search by army lieutenant Jim Gary (Richard Widmark), who at first thinks little of the corrupt lawman but who warms a little when he finds McCabe himself has been the victim of human failings and that he does not lack courage. They ride into the camp of an Indian chief, Quannah Parker (Henry Brandon), and find a white woman with Indian children, plus an older woman who is too full of shame to want to return to her people and a wild white boy who has become a proud member of the tribe. They trade for the boy and haul him away but they are also given a Spanish lady, Elena (Linda Christal), the woman of Stone Calf (Woody Strode), Quannah's rival for power.

On the way back Stone Calf comes after his woman and is killed by McCabe, who then proceeds to the fort where he was hired by Major Frazer (John McIntire). At the fort the wild boy kills a crazed woman who believes he is her son and the boy is lynched, to the horror of Marty Purcell (Shirley Jones), who has proof the boy is her brother. However, the death relieves the feelings of guilt that she has harbored for being responsible for her brother's being captured by the Indians and she now decides to accept Gary's offer of marriage.

Romance also comes to Guthrie McCabe at this point in his life. The seemingly hard-hearted mercenary jumps to the defense of Elena when she is treated with veiled contempt by the wives of the officers. Elena is a lady of good family but because she is Spanish and because she has been the forced woman of an Indian she is looked upon as trash. This does not sit well with McCabe, and he tells the assembled guests at a dance what he thinks of their moral fibre. Compassion turns to love and McCabe takes Elena with him back to town. There he finds he is no longer sheriff. With that he expresses another piece of his mind and decides to set out for California with Elena.

John Ford was never more cynical about the West than he was in *Two Rode Together*, and James Stewart never appeared in any film in which he was so morally ambiguous and furtive. There is nothing Capraesque about his Guthrie McCabe. This is a character who has always demanded ten percent of any business within his grasp and who takes a dim view of humankind in general. McCabe is a complicated character and Stewart mined all the various strata of the man. He agreed with Ford that the character should have about him a bit of humor and rough charm, and not be an entirely unlikeable man.

With Richard Widmark.
With Linda Cristal.

With Richard Widmark, Shirley Jones, Linda Cristal, John McIntire and Anna Lee.

It is one of the most complex of Stewart's performances, but unfortunately not in one of Ford's best westerns.

Stewart was cast in the film before it was offered to Ford by Columbia's Harry Cohn. Ford apparently owed Cohn a film and agreed to do it even though he regarded the script as "lousy." Ford would make only two more westerns, but he would use Stewart in both of them. This would make Stewart the last major star to be involved with the great director, and it is regrettable that these two stalwarts could not have discovered their working affinity earlier.

With Shirley Jones and Richard Widmark.

202

THE MAN WHO SHOT LIBERTY VALANCE

PARAMOUNT, 1962

Produced by Willis Goldbeck; *Directed* by John Ford; *Written* by James Warner Bellah and Willis Goldbeck, based on a short story by Dorothy M. Johnson; *Photographed* by William H. Clothier; *Music* by Cyril Mockridge; 123 minutes.

CAST:

Tom Doniphon, John Wayne; *Ranson Stoddard*, James Stewart; *Hallie Stoddard*, Vera Miles; *Liberty Valance*, Lee Marvin; *Dutton Peabody*, Edmond O'Brien; *Link Appleyard*, Andy Devine; *Dr. Willoughby*, Ken Murray; *Nora*, Jeanette Nolan; *Peter*, John Qualen; *Jason Tully*, Willis Bouchey;

With Vera Miles and Andy Devine.

Maxwell Scott, Carleton Young; *Pompey*, Woody Strode; *Amos Carruthers*, Denver Pile; *Floyd*, Strother Martin; *Reese*, Lee Van Cleef; *Handy Strong*, Robert F. Simon; *Ben Carruthers*, O. Z. Whitehead; *Mayor Winders*, Paul Birch; *Hasbrouck*, Joseph Hoover.

Senator Ranse Stoddard and his wife Hallie (Vera Miles) return after a long absence to the town of Shinbone, to attend the funeral of Tom Doniphon (Wayne), a derelict who has died in poverty. A reporter asks Stoddard why he would come all the way from Washington for this. Stoddard muses for a moment and then decides it is time he told his story. It begins with his arriving in Shinbone as a young man but being beaten up by an outlaw named Liberty Valance (Lee Marvin) just before his coach gets to town. Valance is a brutal, swaggering, grinning gunman whose presence is tolerated in Shinbone because he is a hireling of ranchers who oppose statehood for the territory. Just about the only man he doesn't choose to treat with contempt is Doniphon, a small-time cattleman. It is Doniphon who finds the beaten Stoddard and brings him into town.

Stoddard's aim is to set up a law practice but, because of being robbed by Valance, he has no money. Doniphon takes him to the cafe run by a kindly Swedish couple (John Qualen and Jeanette Nolan), whose daughter Hallie is fond of Doniphon but who finds her affections switching to the idealistic young lawyer. Stoddard takes on a job as a

With Lee Marvin.

With Lee Marvin and John Wayne.

waiter and he is again abused by Valance when he has occasion to serve the outlaw. And again Doniphon comes to the rescue. With enough money saved, Stoddard sets up a shingle at the offices of newspaper editor Dutton Peabody (Edmond O'Brien) and lets it be known that it is his intention to bring law and order to the town and do everything he can to bring the territory into statehood. Peabody supports Stoddard and for so doing he is almost killed in a brutal beating by Valance. In retaliation Stoddard sets out after Valance with a pistol he barely knows how to

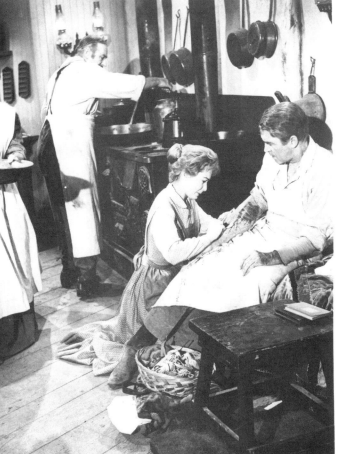

With Jeanette Nolan, John Qualen and Vera Miles.

205

With Edmond O'Brien.

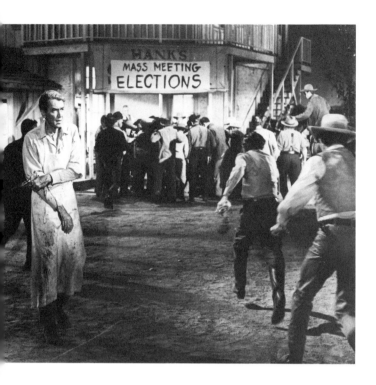

use. The two men face each other on a sidewalk at night. Valance aims with contempt at the lawyer but a shot rings out and he falls dead. Stoddard assumes that his own shot has killed Valance, and so does everybody else.

Valance has actually been killed by Doniphon, who has responded to Hallie's plea to help Stoddard. It is a noble act for Doniphon, because he has long been in love with Hallie and had wanted to marry her. He gets drunk and in his bitter confusion he sets fire to the ranch house he had built for her. On the strength of being the man who killed Valance, Stoddard is lionized and nominated for government office. Feeling that he cannot build a career on having killed a man, he declines, until Doniphon lets him know that it was he who shot Valance, and that he did it for Hallie. He also points out that if Stoddard wants to marry Hallie and become the man she and everybody wants him to become, he has no choice but to be known as the man who shot Liberty Valance.

Stoddard goes on to great success in politics and brings the territory into statehood. And it is as a much-respected senator that he returns to Shinbone for the funeral of Doniphon. After telling his story to the reporter he is surprised to find the reporter tearing up his notes. Stoddard wants to know why. "You're not going to use my story?" Says the reporter, "No, sir. As our late and great editor Dutton Peabody used to say, 'It ain't news. This is the West. When the legend becomes fact, print the legend.'"

The Man Who Shot Liberty Valance is about as fine a thesis on the intermingling of western fact and fiction as has ever been filmed. It is also yet another commentary on the merging of the old Wild West into the new one, skillfully guided by the leathery spirit of John Ford. It is truly a black-and-white western, and was so shot by William Clothier, and it is largely a study of character, mostly filmed on studio stages and not in the great outdoors. The two stars appear in almost quintessential guise—John Wayne as the indomitable westerner and James Stewart as a kind of western version of Jefferson Smith, albeit a Smith who has to learn that politics is a mutable craft. It is among the best of Stewart's performances, particularly in the early scenes in which he conveys an almost frenzied sense of outrage at the glib brutality of Liberty Valance. And it is no mean accomplishment that in these scenes the then fifty-four-year-old Stewart has to play the role of a young man. *The Man Who Shot Liberty Valance* is a major item in the careers of Stewart, Wayne and Ford.

The Man Who Shot Liberty Valance is the film in which occurs the famous line, "When the legend becomes fact, print the legend." In any study of the history of western movies this one is essential because its whole premise is an exploration of that line, and since it is the work of John Ford it is more than essential, it is required. The great maker of westerns, in the last phase of his career, here seemed to be summing up his work in the mighty genre, but not without a little cynicism. His former concepts of western bravery and chivalry were still strong but they were now tempered with the wisdom of age, with a strong implication in this film that even the most moral of men need be pragmatic in winning whatever it is they are after. The man who shot Liberty Valance, for example, is a thoroughly decent politician whose success has come about by default.

It is a tribute to James Stewart's professionalism that he readily accepted second billing in what is clearly a John Wayne western. As with any true pro, for him it was the work that mattered, not the billing. He had enjoyed working with the crusty Ford on *Two Rode Together* and he was eager to make another film with him. That plus the fact that the part in *Valance* offered a challenge. Whereas in *Two Rode Together* Stewart's Guthrie McCabe is a mostly selfish rogue, his Ranse Stoddard is an idealist with a genuine desire to serve his fellow humans.

MR. HOBBS TAKES A VACATION

20TH CENTURY-FOX, 1962

Produced by Jerry Wald; *Directed* by Henry Koster; *Written* by Nunnally Johnson, based on the novel *Hobbs' Vacation* by Edward Streeter; *Photographed in color* by William C. Mellor; *Music* by Henry Mancini; 116 minutes.

CAST:

Roger Hobbs, James Stewart; *Peggy Hobbs*, Maureen O'Hara; *Joe*, Fabian; *Byron*, John Saxon; *Mrs. Turner*, Marie Wilson; *Reggie McHugh*, Reginald Gardiner; *Katey*, Lauri Peters; *Marika*, Valerie Varda; *Janie*, Lili Gentle; *Mr. Turner*, John McGiver; *Susan*, Natalie Trundy; *Stan*, Josh Peine; *Brenda*, Minerva Urecal; *Danny Hobbs*, Michael Burns; *Mr. Saltonstall*, Richard Collier; *Peter Carver*, Peter Oliphant; *Freddie*, Thomas Lowell; *Carl*, Stephen Mines; *Dick*, Dennis Whitcomb; *Phil*, Michael Sean.

With Michael Burns, Maureen O'Hara, Lauri Peters, and Natalie Trundy.

After the rigors and travail of working with the cantankerous John Ford in *Two Rode Together* and *The Man Who Shot Liberty Valance*, James Stewart was in need of somewhat lighter-hearted labor. He teamed up with veteran director Henry Koster for three comedies to be made at 20th Century-Fox, all of them of a family nature and each presenting him as a father trying to keep his sanity amid chaos. In the first he is Roger Hobbs, a banker who yearns for a quiet summer vacation somewhere on the California coast with just his pretty wife Peggy (Maureen O'Hara). The Nunnally Johnson screenplay guarantees that it will be anything but quiet.

Roger's first problem is that Peggy is devoted to all the members of her family and can't bear to be parted from any of them. Rather than the little place by the sea for which he had hoped, Roger finds himself driving up to a huge, gothic, gingerbread horror of a house, with plenty of room, as Peggy beams, for everyone, which includes not only their children Katey (Lauri Peters) and son Danny (Michael Burns) but their married daughters, their husbands and small children, plus a cook (Minerva

Urecal), who soon quits in disgust. Nothing in the house works as it should and Roger spends his time fixing things, while Katey sulks and Danny does nothing but watch television. Then eldest daughter Susan (Natalie Trundy) and husband Stanley (Josh Peine) arrive with their children, and it is clear they are having marital problems.

Next daughter Janie (Lili Gentle) and her stuffy

208

With Maureen O'Hara.

husband Bryon (John Saxon) arrive, with baby, and the result is more commotion, especially when Bryon becomes interested in a bikini-wearer, Marika (Valerie Varda), on the beach. At a dance Roger manages to introduce Katey to a nice young boy named Joe (Fabian) and he also manages to pull Danny out of the depression caused by the exploding TV set by

With Maureen O'Hara and Lauri Peters.

introducing him to the joys of sailing. A telegram arrives to inform Stanley that he has gained an important job and he asks the Hobbses to entertain his new employers. They do, and regret it. They turn out to be a couple who don't drink, swim, sunbathe or play games of any kind. They are birdwatchers, and Roger finds himself drawn into a birdwatching excursion. But this tiresome pair, Martin (John McGiver) and Emily Turner (Marie Wilson) have a chink in their armor. They are secret drinkers and after they leave the Hobbs vacation house in a huff of disgust it is assumed that Stanley will not get the job. But he does because his employers are too embarrassed to have their vice exposed. Stanley and Susan are happy, Katey loves Joe and Roger has a new rapport with Danny. The vacation has been a success, except that Roger is aghast to learn that Peggy has booked the same house for next summer.

Mr. Hobbs Takes a Vacation happily did the kind of business 20th Century-Fox had hoped for and the review in *Variety* neatly put its finger on the reason why: "The picture has its staunchest ally in Stewart, whose acting instincts are so remarkably keen that he can instill amusement into scenes that otherwise threaten to fall flat." They might have added that as a father-husband bombarded by every conceivable calamity known to family life he should have been nominated for a special Oscar.

HOW THE WEST WAS WON

MGM, 1963

Produced by Bernard Smith; *Directed* by Henry Hathaway, John Ford and George Marshall; *Written* by James R. Webb, based on the *Life* magazine series; *Photographed in color* by William H. Daniels and Milton Krasner; *Music* by Alfred Newman; 155 minutes.

CAST:

Narrator, Spencer Tracy; *Eve Prescott*, Carroll Baker; *Marshall*, Lee J. Cobb; *Jethro Stuart*, Henry Fonda; *Julie Rawlings*, Carolyn Jones; *Zebulon Prescott*, Karl Malden; *Cleve Van Valen*, Gregory Peck; *Zeb Rawlings*, George Peppard; *Roger Morgan*, Robert Preston; *Lilith Prescott*, Debbie Reynolds; *Linus Rawlings*, James Stewart; *Charlie Gant*, Eli Wallach; *General Sherman*, John Wayne; *Mike King*, Richard Widmark; *Dora*, Brigid Bazlen; *Colonel Hawkins*, Walter Brennan; *Attorney*, David Brian; *Peterson*, Andy Devine; *Abraham Lincoln*, Raymond Massey; *Rebecca Prescott*, Agnes Moorehead; *General Grant*, Harry Morgan; *Agathe Clegg*, Thelma Ritter.

James Stewart was one of a dozen major stars, hundreds of actors and thousands of extras who filled out the immense Cinerama canvas of *How the West Was Won*, surely the most epic of all the epic westerns. Even without the impressive photographic effects of Cinerama—and only the most jaded viewer could fail to be impressed—the film tells a respectable story with flair and excitement. However, anyone who did not, or cannot, see the original theatrical presentation will never experience the huge images and vivid clarity of the film's visual values—the raft hurtling down the rapids of the Ohio River, the buffalo stampede in the Rockies and the battle on a runaway train amid spectacular Arizona scenery.

The story spans the fifty years between 1839 and 1889 and traces the adventures of a single family, the Prescotts, as they make their way west through the Ohio Valley. As they camp alongside the Ohio

With Carroll Baker.

With Carroll Baker, Kimm Charney, Brian Russell and Karl Malden.

Battling river pirates.

River they meet a trapper-trader named Linus Rawlings (Stewart), who becomes smitten with one of the two daughters, Eve (Carroll Baker), and she with him. The next day Linus comes across a storekeeper who calls himself Colonel Hawkins (Walter Brennan), who is actually a river pirate. Hawkins tries to kill Linus in order to steal his furs but Linus survives and shortly thereafter leads an attack on Hawkins and his men and wipes them out, thereby saving the Prescotts from the murderous plans of Hawkins. The Prescotts then set off down the river on their raft but they are caught in the rapids and the parents drown. Linus, who has decided he wants to marry Eve, buries the parents. Eve tells him that this is where they should build the farm her parents had in mind when they left New England.

Linus and Eve settle down and raise a family. They have two sons, Zeb (George Peppard) and Jeremiah (Claude Johnson), and all is well until the outbreak of the Civil War, when Linus leaves to serve in the Union Army. He never returns. Eve is heartbroken when Zeb later makes the same decision but realizes she cannot stop him. Zeb survives the war but finds his mother has died by the time he returns home.

The remainder of *How the West Was Won* focuses mostly on what happens to Zeb during his lifetime, also with the fortunes of Eve's sister Lilith (Debbie Reynolds), who marries a handsome gambler (Gregory Peck), rises to great wealth but loses it and ends up going to live with Zeb and his family in Arizona. Stewart's role occupies only the first half hour of the film and this section was directed by Henry Hathaway. Fifty-five at the time of filming, Stewart, decked out in buckskins, had to play a man some twenty years younger. With expert make-up and his own quirky kind of energy he brought the part off with conviction. His Linus Rawlings is a feisty frontiersman. He looks very much like the kind of man who helped win the West.

TAKE HER, SHE'S MINE

20TH CENTURY-FOX, 1963

Produced and *Directed* by Henry Koster; *Written* by Nunnally Johnson, based on the play by Phoebe and Henry Ephron; *Photographed in color* by Lucien Ballard; *Music* by Jerry Goldsmith; 98 minutes.

CAST:

Frank Michaelson, James Stewart; *Mollie Michaelson*, Sandra Dee; *Anne Michael*, Audrey Meadows; *Pope-Jones*, Robert Morley; *Henri Bonnet*, Philippe Forquet; *Hector G. Ivor*, John McGiver; *Alex*, Robert Denver; *Linda*, Monica Moran; *Sarah*, Jenny Maxwell; *Adele*, Cynthia Pepper; *M. Bonnet*, Maurice Marsac; *Miss Wu*, Irene Tsu; *Liz Michaelson*, Charla Doherty; *Policeman*, Marcel Hillaire; *Stanley*, Charles Robinson; *Mme. Bonnet*, Janine Grandel.

With Audrey Meadows and Charla Doherty.

Take Her, She's Mine was the second of James Stewart's comedies with producer-director Henry Koster and writer Nunnally Johnson, and the first movie to be filmed at 20th Century-Fox following the near-debacle of *Cleopatra*. At the time of filming it was the only picture in production on the vast Fox lot, which might account for a certain air of desperation about its humor. Darryl F. Zanuck had just begun his new regime at the studio and the moderate success of this Stewart vehicle helped him to get the studio back on its feet. On Broadway the play by Phoebe and Henry Ephron had starred Art Carney. In adapting it for the screen, Johnson obviously tailored it to the Stewart image, even to the extent of working in a gag about the character played by Stewart, a lawyer and father named Frank Michaelson, always being mistaken for movie star James Stewart. Since the character in the film is the quintessential Stewart of bumbling, hesitant charm and bafflement, his claims of "No, I'm not" become hard to accept. There couldn't be two men like this in the world.

The film opens with Frank Michaelson facing the school board of which he is the chairman and trying to explain his strange behavior and escapades at another school, all of which have found their way into newspaper coverage. Flashback. Frank and his patient wife, Anne (Audrey Meadows), are worried about their pretty young daughter, Mollie (Sandra

With Sandra Dee.

With John McGiver and player.

ith Sandra Dee.

Dee), who, in her letters from college, writes mainly about boys and social activities, and little about her studies. Frank decides to pay a visit to the college and see just what it is his daughter is involved in. It is more than his fears had imagined. Among other things Mollie is a part of demonstrations against the use of atomic weapons, which puts her into contact with beatnicks and sit-down strikes at the city hall. In trying to extricate her, Frank is himself swept up in the turmoil and seized by the police, which results in newspaper stories.

The Michaelsons are more than a little relieved when Mollie flunks her college courses and returns home. But the relief is short-lived. Their lively daughter now decides to fly to Paris, where she has accepted an art scholarship. Her letters from Paris make her letters from college seem mild in comparison. Once again father sets off to check on his irrepressible offspring. The first thing he finds is that Mollie is romantically involved with a handsome young painter, Henri Bonnet (Philippe Forquet), and once again Frank runs afoul of the law. Gendarmes arrest him when he visits a wild tavern frequented by strange artistic types. In order to meet Henri, Frank accepts Mollie's invitation to attend a fancy dress ball, at which he appears as Daniel Boone. The costume falls apart and to add to his embarrassment he falls into the Seine. Some measure of order appears in his life with the announcement that Mollie and Henri will get married, but the prospect of similar troubles to come loom up when Frank realizes his daughter Liz (Charla Doherty) is now a teenager and about to go off to college.

Take Her, She's Mine might also be titled *Mr. Hobbs Takes a Vacation, Part Two*, since it is clearly from the same comic pot, and full of the deftly witty touches that characterized Nunnally Johnson's scripts. Once again Stewart was required to be a father put through the mill of modern life, with all its frantic complications. And that he would do it with all the comic innocence and astonishment that the role could possibly allow is something that his employers and his audience had come to expect. Anything less would in itself have been astonishing.

215

CHEYENNE AUTUMN

WARNER BROS., 1964

Produced by Bernard Smith; *Directed* by John Ford; *Written* by James R. Webb, based on the novel by Mari Sandoz; *Photographed in color* by William H. Clothier; *Music* by Alex North; 156 minutes.

CAST:

Wyatt Earp, James Stewart; *Carl Schurz*, Edward G. Robinson; *Captain Thomas Archer*, Richard Widmark; *Deborah Wright*, Carroll Baker; *Captain Oscar Wessels*, Karl Malden; *Red Shirt*, Sal Mineo; *Spanish Woman*, Dolores Del Rio; *Little Wolf*, Ricardo Montalban; *Dull Knife*, Gilbert Roland; *Doc Holliday*, Arthur Kennedy; *Lt. Scott*, Patrick Wayne; *Guinevere Plantagenet*, Elizabeth Allen; *Major Jeff Blair*, John Carradine; *Tall Tree*, Victor Jory; *Major Dog Kelly*, Judson Pratt; *Sergeant Wichowsky*, Mike Mazurki; *Homer*, Ken Curtis; *Major Braden*, George O'Brien; *Trail Boss*, Shug Fisher.

John Ford's final western was his most expensive, longest, most heartfelt and, unfortunately, least successful. *Cheyenne Autumn* drew all his many admirers when it was released in December of 1964 and reviewers wrote miles of copy in discussing it, but to audiences looking for the excitement associated with Ford westerns it seemed more like a lecture than an entertainment. And anyone expecting James Stewart to be one of the leading players had to be content with an extended cameo, and a rather odd cameo at that. Here he is Wyatt Earp, holding court in a Dodge City saloon, in a broadly comic segment of what is probably the most serious western ever made.

Like all makers of westerns over a long period of time, Ford had used the Indians as the enemy, although doing it with somewhat more respect than most other directors. With *Cheyenne Autumn* he appeared to be making an atonement. The plight of the Indians had finally brought out a desire to reveal their condition. Filmed in his favorite locations of Monument Valley and Moab, Utah, and with a huge cast, Ford here tells the true story of the forced migration of a thousand Cheyenne from their homeland in Wyoming to a bleak reservation in Oklahoma. The trek is miserable and many die of

As John Ford's fanciful version of Wyatt Earp.

starvation and disease. Federal aid is not forthcoming and the survivors decide, without permission, to trudge all the way back to Wyoming.

They are joined by a sympathetic Quaker teacher (Carroll Baker), whose fiancé, Captain Thomas Archer (Richard Widmark), is assigned the distasteful job of setting out after the Indians and bringing them back. Younger warriors in the group rebel and several soldiers are killed. In Dodge City a newspaper alarms people with its account of murderous savages and Wyatt Earp, along with Doc Holliday (Arthur Kennedy), is pressured into leading a posse against the Indians. However, Earp deliberately leads them in the wrong direction, and when this loud and drunken group finally see an Indian they are all for turning back. The Cheyenne undergo further miseries, until Archer brings in the humane Carl Schurz, Secretary of the Interior (Edward G.

With John Carradine and Arthur Kennedy.

With Elizabeth Allen, Chuck Roberson, Jack Williams and Ken Curtis.

Robinson), who does something about restoring peace and attending to the survivors.

The James Stewart-Dodge City segment of Ford's film is still a subject of discussion among film buffs. At the time of release some critics thought the segment was ridiculously out of kilter with the serious tone of the movie, some thought it was a brilliantly comic counterpoint, and others suspected that it was something forced upon Ford by Warner Bros. to enliven a dull picture. *Time* thought Stewart's cameo was hilarious and clearly an intentional spoof. Well-tailored and wearing a spotless panama hat, this is a Wyatt Earp totally at variance with the evidence. More cerebral critics considered the segment an anachronism stuck in the middle of *Cheyenne Autumn*, but later viewed it as a possible attempt on Ford's part to show the difference between the false concept of the West that even he himself had been party to in the movie business and the harsh truth that he was attempting to reveal in this one. The grumpy director, made the more grumpy and surly by the failure of the film, declined comment. Of the stars involved in this noble enterprise, Stewart emerged as the only entertainer, particularly in his conducting of an epic poker game. If Warners did indeed force the segment on Ford, they knew what they were doing, crassly commercial though the decision might have been.

DEAR BRIGITTE

20TH CENTURY-FOX, 1965

Produced and *Directed* by Henry Koster; *Written* by Hal Kanter, based on the novel *Erasmus with Freckles* by John Hasse; *Photographed* in color by Lucien Ballard; *Music* by George Duning; 100 minutes.

CAST:

Professor Robert Leaf, James Stewart; *Kenneth,* Fabian; *Vina,* Glynis Johns; *Pandora,* Cindy Carol; *Erasmus,* Billy Mumy; *Peregrine,* John Williams; *Dr. Volker,* Jack Kruschen; *The Captain,* Ed Wynn; *George,* Charles Robinson; *Dean Sawyer,* Howard Freeman; *Terry,* Jane Wald; *Unemployment Clerk,* Alice Pearce; *Argyle,* Jesse White; *Lt. Rink,* Gene O'Donnell; *Brigitte Bardot,* Herself.

With Glynis Johns.

For James Stewart the first half of the sixties seemed to have settled into the pattern of swinging back and forth between westerns and comedies. After his gruelling adventures with *How the West Was Won* and before setting out for *Shenandoah,* he accepted another offer from producer-director Henry Koster for what would be his final fling at light comedy— *Dear Brigitte,* the girl of the title being Brigitte Bardot. The best that can be said for this mild little amusement is that it is *nice.* It is also a waste of the talents of a gifted film actor.

Here Stewart is a tweedy, gently eccentric college professor and poet named Robert Leaf, who frowns upon the encroachment of modern technology. His is the world of arts and letters, not computers and space research. He lives with his wife Vina (Glynis Johns) and their children on a boat that looks like a small version of a Mississippi paddler. In the evenings he and the family provide their own entertainment by playing musical instruments in recital, albeit none too well. The cellist is his eight-year-old son Erasmus (Billy Mumy), who is tone-deaf and who would rather paint, except that he is color blind. However, the professor is about to learn something even more odd about his son—the boy is a mathematical genius. He can add up extraordinary

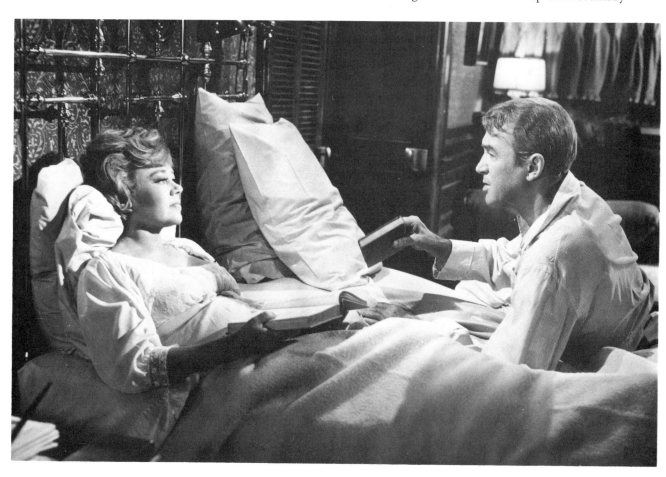

With Howard Freeman.

With Billy Mumy, Cindy Clark and Glynis Johns.   *With Pitt Herman, Glynis Johns and Billy Mumy.*

With Billy Mumy and Brigitte Bardot.

numbers in his head in a flash, even faster than a computer. His parents think it better to keep this incredible gift secret, but it soon leaks out.

Erasmus finds there is money to be made with his talent. He charges his sister Pandora (Cindy Clark) and her boyfriend Kenneth (Fabian) a fee to help with their homework. After a while it occurs to Kenneth that Erasmus can be used to handicap horses at the racetrack, to the horror of his father. More horror is on the way, in the form of a gentlemanly English con-man, Peregrine Upjohn (John Williams), who proposes that Erasmus's abilities be put to good use by having him win gambling bets that would bring in money to finance a foundation for students interested in studying humanitarian arts. The money begins to pour in but whenever Erasmus is asked what it is he would like for himself he replies that he has only one desire, and that is to meet Brigitte Bardot. He has his wish. Professor Leaf and his wonder boy visit the famous French movie star in her home near Paris and she behaves with warm

hospitality. She even gives Erasmus a puppy dog, along with a kiss.

Back home the boy continues to make money for the foundation with his accurate calls at the racetrack, but Upjohn is caught by internal revenue agents as he is about to take off with the large purse. The professor saves his neck by claiming that Upjohn is working for him and that the money is on its way to a foundation, as it is. When last seen, the chastened Upjohn is on the houseboat and struggling to play a musical instrument in recital. Life goes on in this wacky family.

Brigitte Bardot appears in a single scene in *Dear Brigitte*, as was necessary. Without the scene the film would be a lot less effective, although why an eight-year-old boy would have such a crush on a sex symbol like Bardot is a plot device open to some question. Stewart claims that he enjoyed his one day's work with the pretty French actress and that he found her very pleasant to meet and to work with. As for the film itself, it is best regarded as a Jimmy rather than a James Stewart vehicle, and one that gave him yet another opportunity to indulge in his skill with the accordion. His professor-poet-father in this outing is the kind that exists only in the mind of people assigned to concoct scripts for comedy.

221

SHENANDOAH

UNIVERSAL, 1965

Produced by Robert Arthur; *Directed* by Andrew V. McLaglen; *Written* by James Lee Barrett; *Photographed in color* by William Clothier; *Music* by Frank Skinner; 105 minutes.

CAST:

Charlie, James Stewart; *Sam,* Doug McClure; *Jacob,* Glenn Corbett; *James,* Patrick Wayne; *Jennie,* Rosemary Forsyth; *Boy,* Philip Alford; *Ann,* Katharine Ross; *Nathan,* Charles Robinson; *Dr. Witherspoon,* Paul Fix; *Paster Bjoerling,* Denver Pyle; *Colonel Fairchild,* George Kennedy; *Henry,* Tim McIntire; *John,* James McMullan; *Carter,* James Best; *Billy Packer,* Warren Oates; *Engineer,* Strother Martin; *Abernathy,* Dabbs Greer; *Jenkins,* Harry Carey, Jr.; *Mule,* Kevin Hagen; *Lt. Johnson,* Tom Simcox; *Captain Richards,* Berkeley Harris.

The kind of father played by James Stewart in his three recent comedies with Henry Koster, the gently bumbling, confused and dithery papa of *Dear Brigitte,* for example, was light years removed from the kind of father called for in *Shenandoah.* In this original screenplay by Stewart's friend James Lee Barrett, he is a leathery old Virginia farmer during the Civil War, a widower with six sons and one daughter, who refers to the war as an undertaker's business and who wants no involvement with it one way or the other. He is a hard-working, no-nonsense kind of man who is very much the dominant figure in his family. Known simply as Charlie, he is a man of firm opinion, a man who hides his warm heart under a gruff and grizzled exterior and who seldom has a cigar out of his mouth.

The war has been going on for a couple of years but, except for some distant gunfire in this remote part of Virginia, Charlie and his family are largely unaware of what it is about, and unconcerned. Although a Southerner, Charlie owns no slaves and runs his farm as a family business. When Confederate soldiers visit and try to recruit his sons he drives them away, and when Federal agents attempt to appropriate his horses Charlie and his sons use their fists to let it be known that there will be no transaction of any kind. Some of his family feel Charlie is a little too set in his resolve not to get involved in the war, but they respect his feelings and back him up.

With Philip Alford.

The war finally penetrates Charlie's isolation when his sixteen-year-old son Boy (Philip Alford) wanders off and becomes a prisoner of the Union Army, who assume him to be a rebel because he wears a Confederate cap. Boy is especially close to Charlie's heart because his mother died giving him birth. With four of his sons and his daughter Jennie (Rosemary Forsythe), Charlie goes looking for Boy, leaving his son James (Patrick Wayne) and James's wife Ann (Katharine Ross) to guard the home. Charlie turns out to be a man with some sense of military maneuvering. He sets up a blockade and burns a Union train carrying rebel prisoners, although it does not prove to have Boy aboard. Charlie and his sons give up the search but on the way back home one of them is shot and killed by a Southern sentry. His bitterness is increased when he comes home and finds that both James and Jennie have been killed by renegade soldiers. A while later, as Charlie

With Rosemary Forsyth.

With Patrick Wayne, Tim McIntire, James McMullan, Glenn Corbett and Charles Robinson.

With Paul Fix (left) and Philip Alford.

and his family attend church, Boy comes in, supporting himself on crutches but otherwise in good health.

Quite apart from the fact that the film gave Stewart one of his strongest roles in years, *Shenandoah* is of interest to Civil War buffs, with many well-staged skirmishes between the Blue and the Gray. It is also a strong antiwar statement, and one that matched much of the spirit of the times when released in the summer of 1965. The futility of war, with its power to sweep up and involve even the most innocent, was clear enough in this story of a man who loses so much of his family, although a pacifist and a supporter of no cause. But it is the performance of Stewart that is the real substance of the film and without it *Shenandoah* would be much the poorer. It is a study of a patriarch who undergoes a humbling experience that softens his arrogance. He is a different man at the end of the story than at the start, and it is a tribute to his acting skill that a scene such as his standing at his wife's grave and quietly talking to her is believeable and not mawkish.

His performance in *Shenandoah* is among the finest in his career. *Newsweek* made a good point: "What Stewart himself achieves must be a source of some discouragement as well as instruction for the young, unskilled actors working with him. He is far from young. His role of paterfamilias is more tired than his eyes. Yet Stewart compels belief with his strength and his simplicity."

THE FLIGHT OF THE PHOENIX

20TH CENTURY-FOX, 1966

Produced and *Directed* by Robert Aldrich; *Written* by Lukas Heller, based on the novel by Elleston Trevor; *Photographed in color* by Joseph Biroc; *Music* by Frank De Vol, 147 minutes.

CAST:

Frank Towns, James Stewart; *Lew Moran*, Richard Attenborough; *Captain Harris*, Peter Finch; *Heinrich Dorfman*, Hardy Kruger; *Trucker Cobbs*, Ernest Borgnine; *Crow*, Ian Banner; *Sergeant Watson*, Ronald Fraser; *Dr. Renaud*, Christian Marquand; *Standish*, Dan Duryea; *Bellamy*, George Kennedy; *Gabriele*, Gabriele Tintl; *Carlos*, Alex Montoya; *Tasso*, Peter Bravos; *Bill*, William Aldrich; *Farida*, Barrie Chase.

It is surprising in view of his own involvement with civilian and military aviation that James Stewart has not appeared in more films as a pilot. *The Spirit of St. Louis* immediately comes to mind, followed by the somewhat forgotten *Strategic Air Command* and then *The Flight of the Phoenix,* which failed to find much of an audience. In this flight, pilot Stewart is far removed from the idealistic Lindbergh and the smartly uniformed air force officer of *Strategic Air Command,* or from his own bearing as a general in the Air Force Reserve. Here, looking all his fifty-eight years, he is a somewhat grungy free-lance commercial pilot, about ready to accept any job that comes his way.

Frank Towns (Stewart) is hired to fly a battered old cargo plane to an outpost in the North African desert, carrying an assortment of oil company workers and hired experts. Among them is Towns's alcoholic navigator, Lew Moran (Richard Attenborough), a German aircraft designer, Heinrich Dorfman (Hardy Kruger), a British Army captain, Harris (Peter Finch), and his sergeant, Watson (Ronald

With Richard Attenborough and Christian Marquand.

With William Aldrich and Richard Attenborough.

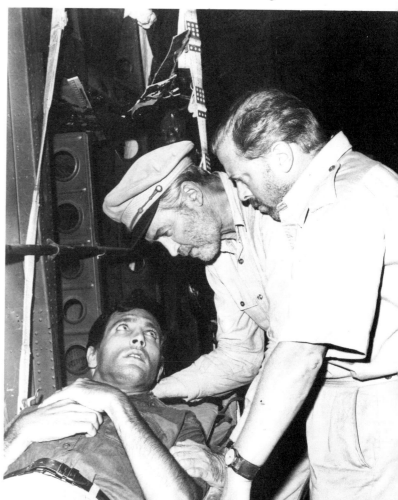

With Hardy Kruger and Richard Attenborough.

With Dan Duryea, Ian Bannen, Ronald Fraser, George Kennedy and Richard Attenborough.

Fraser), an oil driller, Trucker Cobbs (Ernest Borgnine), and a French doctor, Renaud (Christian Renaud). The tired plane crashes in the Sahara and Towns accepts responsibility, even though the fault can be pinned on his navigator. Two men are killed and others injured. They all assume that it will be only a short time before they will be missed and then rescued. This is not to be the case.

Food and drink are in short supply, and the plight of the survivors soon becomes acute. The strain begins to tell on each of the men in different

With Hardy Kruger and Richard Attenborough.

With Peter Finch and Ernest Borgnine.

ways, and reveals much about their stamina and character. Cobbs suffers a mental breakdown and wanders off to his death. The British officer and his sergeant set off for help but return to report that there is no way of tracking through the desert. It seems as if there is no hope for survival, until the German engineer comes up with a plan. He designs an aircraft which can be built from the ruins of the cargo plane. Towns thinks the idea is absurd, as do some of the others, and refuses to help. After a while it occurs to them that this is the only chance they have and they help the German with the construction, taking one of the engines and building wings on either side. The work is hard, and made the more so because of the heat of the sun and the lack of sustenance. But the plane is successfully built and it takes off—with the survivors lying on the wings and clinging to ropes.

A number of reviewers of *The Flight of the Phoenix* thought that it offered Stewart one of the most interesting roles he had played in recent years. His Frank Towns is a complicated character, a somewhat bitter old flyer who appears brusque and querulous but who has a soft side to his nature. The pity is that the film, running 147 minutes in its initial showing, is an endurance for the audience as well the men in its harrowing story. Except for a few flashbacks involving girls, it is an all-male adventure with a number of men of the kind whose company is hard to take. In this respect the film is true to life, but not one to sit through without a little shuffling of the feet. Of interest to film and aviation buffs is the fact that *Flight* bears a dedication notice to Paul Mantz, the famed film aviation stuntman and aerial supervisor. Mantz had been well employed in Hollywood for more than thirty years, but he lost his life while making this movie—flying the invented contraption called for in the script.

The film was shot in the desert country near Yuma, Arizona, a region well used by Hollywood over the years for movies about the Sahara. Stewart celebrated his fifty-eighth birthday (May 20, 1966) while on location, and in a discussion with director Robert Aldrich he admitted that every time he saw a film he had just completed he felt he should know more about acting, "So I keep on thinking about and trying to improve my characterizations." Asked about this particular one he said, "I like this man, Frank Towns, because I think as he does, that one must feel part of something, even an airplane. We cannot be ruled by machines and computers, by things which are important but things without a heart."

THE RARE BREED

UNIVERSAL, 1966

Produced by William Alland; *Directed* by Andrew V. McLaglen; *Written* by Ric Hardman; *Photographed in color* by William Clothier; *Music* by John Williams; 97 minutes.

CAST:

Sam Burnett, James Stewart; *Martha Price,* Maureen O'Hara; *Alexander Bowen,* Brian Keith; *Hilary Price,* Juliet Mills; *Jamie Bowen,* Don Galloway; *Charles Ellsworth,* David Brian; *Deke Simons,* Jack Elam; *Jeff Harter,* Ben Johnson; *Ed Mabry,* Harry Carey, Jr.; *Juan,* Perry Lopez; *Alberto,* Larry Domasin; *Taylor,* Alan Caillou; *Cattle Buyer,* Bob Gravage; *Barker,* Tex Armstrong; *Liveryman,* Ted Mapes; *Auctioneer,* Larry Blake; *Porter,* Charles Lampkin.

That the westerns of Andrew V. McLaglen should have some affinity with those of John Ford is easy to understand. His father, Victor McLaglen, was one of Ford's primary players and as a boy Andrew often watched his father working in Ford westerns. In the case of *The Rare Breed* the film has a further Fordian touch in the presence of Maureen O'Hara, who starred in five Ford movies. For James Stewart it was a welcome opportunity to work again with McLaglen, following their successful *Shenandoah,* and a chance to play the kind of westerner he had not tackled before—a slightly mangy drifter-cowpoke, not above a little cheating but, of course, a man who has a residual sense of decency. By this time in his career Stewart was leery of drifting too far from his established persona.

The title refers not to courageous men but to a line of cattle, and *The Rare Breed* has the distinction of being one of those rare westerns that actually deals with cattle as its central business. The breed in question is the Hereford, a hefty, stocky, white-faced breed bred in the British Isles and first introduced to America in 1884, which is the core of this original screenplay by Ric Hardman. According to this account an English lady named Martha Evans (O'Hara) arrives in St. Louis with her daughter, Hilary (Juliet Mills), and a prize Hereford bull called

With Maureen O'Hara and Juliet Mills.

Vindicator. Martha's cattleman husband has died on the voyage to America and it now becomes her concern to get the bull to its buyer, a flamboyant Scotsman, Alexander Bowen (Brian Keith), who lives in Dodge City. Martha's husband has maintained that the Hereford could be bred with the main line of western cattle, the longhorns. All the western cattlemen, including Sam Burnett (Stewart), look upon this notion as ridiculous.

Badly in need of a job, Sam accepts the task of delivering the bull, although he has made a side deal with another cattleman to hand the animal over to him. But the more he is exposed to the nature of the determined and spunky Englishwoman the more he realizes the goodness of her cause, and how shabby his own thinking has become. Sam decides to do the right thing, to divest himself of the crooked deal and help Martha, Hilary and Vindicator get to the Scotsman, which necessitates a goodly amount of fighting off would-be thieves and seducers. On arrival they find Bowen to be a hard-hearted man, who lives in a mixture of wealth and squalor and who treats his son Jamie (Don Galloway) with not the slightest sign of affection.

With Maureen O'Hara.

With Juliet Mills.

With Juliet Mills.

Martha has the same affect upon Bowen as upon Sam. The Scotsman comes under the spell of her honorable ways and begins to dress properly and behave more cordially. Jamie falls in love with Hilary and Bowen soon has the same feelings about Martha, while Sam goes about the business of seeing that Vindicator does the proper mating. By now Sam is completely convinced of the worth of crossing the one breed with the other. Bowen himself has doubts about the hornless Hereford being able to survive the severe western winter but he allows the bull to be turned loose on his range. In the dead of winter Sam finds the corpse of Vindicator but he also finds a longhorn cow with a Hereford calf. Vindicator has lived up to his name, and there is now a new breed in the West. Sam has also found something in which he can believe, as well as a woman he can love. The Scotsman has rediscovered his pride of ancestry and his son is bound for happiness with Hilary.

The Rare Breed may not be to the liking of lovers of conventional westerns, but for anyone with curiosity about the real job of cowboys—the caring for and raising of cattle—the film has much to offer. Little criticism can be made of the gorgeous O'Hara but the Scotsman of Brian Keith is perhaps a little too ripe. In her first American film, Juliet Mills (daughter of Sir John) is perfectly cast, and such leathery old western types as Ben Johnson, Harry Carey and Jack Elam are as authentic as the scenery through which they ride. McLaglen's direction is flecked with the Fordian sense of family and sentimentality, plus a genuine feeling for landscape, brawling, stampedes and blizzards. Stewart's Sam Burden is the work of an actor who has spent a lot of time in the saddle and who has learned a lot about westerners, about cowboys and how they move and talk. In his review in *The Hollywood Reporter*, James Powers referred to a certain scene, by way of pointing up Stewart's skill as a film actor: "The scene where Stewart finds the calf that is the offspring of the Hereford and a longhorn, with the camera entirely on Stewart's face, is one of great poignance and tenderness. It is only one shot, that of Stewart's face, but it is the crux of the picture, and Stewart once again, as he has a hundred times, shows what it means to understand acting and to make it meaningful."

With Maureen O'Hara and Brian Keith.

FIRECREEK

WARNER BROS., 1968

Produced by Philip Leacock; *Directed* by Vincent McEveety; *Written* by Calvin Clements; *Photographed in color* by William Clothier; *Music* by Alfred Newman; 104 minutes.

CAST:

Johnny Cobb, James Stewart; *Larkin*, Henry Fonda; *Evelyn*, Inger Stevens; *Earl*, Gary Lockwood; *Whittier*, Dean Jagger; *Preacher Boyles*, Ed Begley; *Mr. Pittman*, Jay C. Flippen; *Norman*, Jack Elam; *Drew*, James Best; *Meli*, Barbara Luna; *Henrietta Cobb*, Jacqueline Scott; *Leah*, Brooke Bundy; *Arthur*, J. Robert Porter; *Willard*, Morgan Woodward; *Hall*, John Qualen; *Dulcie*, Louise Latham; *Mrs. Littlejohn*, Athena Lord; *Fyte*, Harry "Slim" Duncan; *Aaron*, Kevin Tate; *Franklin*, Christopher Shea.

Apart from their episode in *On Our Merry Way*, James Stewart and Henry Fonda had to wait until 1968, thirty-two years after each of them had been in Hollywood, before someone came up with a film in which to co-star them. And whoever thought of *Firecreek* as the film to do this made a strange choice. The two old friends are here pitted against each other in a rather harsh, morose western in which Stewart is required to try to kill Fonda following a brutal fight. It was also Fonda's first film as an outright villain, both gloomy and cruel. In casting the two leading roles there was no question as to which actor would play that role. Stewart had the ability but he knew full well that the public would never accept him in that guise. Fonda, greatly respected though he was as an actor, was never taken to America's heart in the same way that Stewart had been. For Jimmy Stewart to play an absolutely rotten human being would have been a violation of public trust. Such is the power of image.

The title of the film refers to a very small town, which is peaceful until Larkin (Fonda) and his gang ride in. A couple of his young thugs, Earl (Gary Lockwood) and Drew (James Best), are soon brawling over a pretty Indian girl (Barbara Luna), and Earl is about to drown Drew in a horse trough when

With Ed Begley.

With James Best, Gary Lockwood, Henry Fonda, Jack Elam and Morgan Woodward.

With Barbara Luna.

With Ed Begley, John Qualen and Gary Lockwood.

With Henry Fonda.

Johnny Cobb (Stewart) orders them to quit. Cobb is a farmer and he is also the part-time sheriff, for which he receives a monthly wage of two dollars. Since hardly anything ever happens in the sleepy hamlet Johnny's life is mostly centered around his farm and his family. Larkin puts up at a boarding house in order to nurse a wound received in a recent robbery and he finds solace in the attentions of the daughter of the house, Evelyn (Inger Stevens), who tries to encourage him to reform. He seems to respond to this romantic interest.

During the first night a dim-witted stable boy (J. Robert Porter) hears a cry from the Indian girl and finds Drew molesting her. In the struggle he accidentally kills Drew and Larkin's men accuse him of murder. To keep the boy safe, Johnny locks him in the jail but the Larkin gang break in and lynch the boy. When Johnny returns to town to arrest Larkin and his men they jeer at him and challenge him. In the ensuing gunfight Johnny is badly wounded but he disposes of all the men except Larkin. Now face to face, Larkin approaches Johnny and raises his pistol to take aim. The shot is never fired because another one rings out and Larkin falls dead. Evelyn has shot the man with whom she has fallen in love, knowing that there can be no other way. Firecreek returns to being peaceful.

Firecreek did not find much of a following. Perhaps 1968 audiences, satiated with television horse operas, were not interested in a western as grim as this one, and they possibly expected something a little more amusing from the pairing of Stewart and Fonda. But it is a film with some merit, well crafted and acted, with splendid use of its locations in Arizona's beautiful Oak Creek Canyon and the red, rocky countryside around Sedona. Both stars, as expected, were more than capable in their roles— Stewart as a quiet, peaceful, gentle farmer pushed into violence and made furious by the bestial behavior of the unwanted visitors, and Fonda as a forelorn, cold-hearted outlaw. Both characterizations are the work of expert actors. For Stewart, now sixty, there was no need to play anything other than his age, which in this case made the plight of the farmer-sheriff all the more touching.

Whenever Fonda was reminded of *Firecreek* he would shake his head a little and refer somewhat sarcastically to its having been "somebody's bright idea" to have cast him as a villain against his old chum Stewart, and that it was not a good idea. "Any man who tries to kill Jim Stewart has to be marked as a man who's plain rotten. You can't get much worse than that."

BANDOLERO!

20TH CENTURY-FOX, 1968

Produced by Robert L. Jacks; *Directed* by Andrew V. McLaglen; *Written* by James Lee Barrett, based on a story by Stanley L. Hough; *Photographed in color* by William Clothier; *Music* by Jerry Goldsmith; 106 minutes.

CAST:

Mace Bishop, James Stewart; *Dee Bishop*, Dean Martin; *Maria Stoner*, Raquel Welch; *Sheriff Johnson*, George Kennedy; *Roscoe Bookbinder*, Andrew Prine; *Pop Chaney*, Will Geer; *Babe*, Clint Ritchie; *Muncie Carter*, Denver Pyle; *Joe Chaney*, Tom Heaton; *Angel Munoz*, Rudy Diaz; *Robbie*, Sean McClory; *Cort Hayjack*, Harry Carey, Jr.; *Jack Hawkins*, Donald Barry; *Ossie Grimes*, Guy Raymond; *Frisco*, Perry Lopez; *Stoner*, Jock Mahoney; *Bank Clerk*, Big John Hamilton; *Attendant*, Dub Taylor.

For the makers of westerns the post-Civil War era has always been an El Dorado of dramatic license, what with the migration westwards of those dispossessed by the war and the opportunities for free enterprise, especially for ex-soldiers of both sides. This was the broad canvas in which James Lee Barrett stitched his rollicking yarn *Bandelero!*, giving James Stewart one more crack at a lusty western and another chance to be a good baddie. The same might be said for Dean Martin, who made a surprising switch from crooner-comic to westerner in *Rio Bravo* (1959) and followed it up with a half-dozen other westerns, in almost all of which he played a likeable rogue given to boozing. *Bandelero!* was more of the same, this time with Martin as Stewart's younger brother. The fact that the brothers have fought on opposite sides in the war does not stop them from reuniting the family for a little larceny afterwards.

Dee Bishop (Martin) and his gang of five hold up a bank in the town of Val Verde, but Sheriff Johnson (George Kennedy) gets the better of them and the bunch find themselves in jail. They also find themselves sentenced to be hanged. On his way to join his brother and still wearing the remnants of his Union Army uniform, Mace Bishop (Stewart) comes across the hangman who is on his way to administer justice to the Bishop gang. Mace divests him of his clothes and his gear, and proceeds to Val Verde in the guise of the hangman. On the scaffold he arranges for Dee to easily overpower him and take his gun, and the gang gallop off out of town. The sheriff and some of the townspeople set out in pursuit, leaving the town unguarded. Mace takes advantage of the situation and relieves a bank of ten thousand dollars.

Dee and his group proceed to the home of a man who had been killed in the holdup for which they were arrested. They ransack the place and Dee takes a fancy to the lovely widow Maria (Raquel Welch). The sheriff and his posse arrive and engage the gang in a gunfight, which is a stand-off until Mace arrives and with his skill as a rifleman tips the scales in his brother's favor. He then joins him in making an escape to Mexico, taking Maria along. But Sheriff Johnson is a dedicated lawman and bound to bring home the stolen money. He manages to

234

The bogus hangman, with Dean Martin, Tom Heaton, Sean McGlory, Will Geer and George Kennedy.

With Dean Martin and Raquel Welch.

With Henry Fonda.

With the hangman.

overpower the gang once they get to the town of Sabina, but as he prepares to leave, bandits swoop down and attack. He is forced to give Dee, Mace and the others their guns and join in a common defense. The bandits are driven off but at heavy cost—both Dee and Mace are mortally wounded. After their death the sheriff and Maria go back to Val Verde, the sheriff with some respect for the brothers he has tracked and Maria carrying with her the memory of Dee, with whom she had fallen in love.

Bandolero! is mostly blood-and-thunder and nothing to be taken seriously. Director McLaglen, with such items as John Wayne's *McLintock*, *The Way West* and two Stewart westerns (*Shenandoah* and *The Rare Breed*) already to his credit, showed even more of his talent for brisk and noisy action with this one. The only interestingly different aspect of *Bandolero!* is the bantering but affectionate relationship between the brothers and the hesitation of the younger to let himself fall in love with the gorgeous young widow. It

With Dean Martin.

With Raquel Welch.

is the older brother who tries to persuade him that he should, in addition to giving up the life of crime, to which the younger isn't all that dedicated anyway. Without the scenes between Stewart and Martin the film would have little to offer beyond conventional western gunplay and galloping.

Stewart tells of Racquel Welch approaching him and Martin on the first day of production and wanting to discuss the motivations of her character. Martin looked puzzled and after she had walked away he asked Stewart, "What the hell's she talking about?"

Bandolero! turned out to be the last western in which Stewart rode the horse he had been riding since 1950, a sorrel (light reddish brown) stallion, part Arabian and part quarter horse. He was assigned the horse, called Pie, while he was making *Winchester '73* and liked the animal so much he tried to buy it. Its owner, a lady named Stevie Myers, would never sell it but provided Stewart with the horse whenever he needed it. Stewart claims Pie not only had unusal intelligence for a horse but also seemed to know when the cameras were on: "A ham of a horse. There was a scene in *The Far Country* in which Pie had to walk down a street at night by himself. I told him what I wanted and set him off and he did the shot in one take." In 1970, Pie was taken to Santa Fe to work with Stewart in *The Cheyenne Social Club,* but in an altitude of five thousand feet the horse labored for breath and Stewart refused to use it. Pie died a few weeks later. Henry Fonda, a painter of talent, did a painting of Pie and gave it to his friend. It still hangs in his living room.

THE CHEYENNE SOCIAL CLUB

NATIONAL GENERAL, 1970

Produced and *Directed* by Gene Kelly; *Written* by James Lee Barrett; *Photographed in color* by William Clothier; *Music* by Walter Scharf; 103 minutes.

Cast:

John O'Hanlan, James Stewart; *Harley Sullivan*, Henry Fonda; *Jenny*, Shirley Jones; *Opal Ann*, Sue Ann Langdon; *Pauline*, Elaine Devry; *Barkeep*, Robert Middleton; *Marshall Anderson*, Arch Johnson; *Willowby*, Dabbs Greer; *Carrie Virginia*, Jackie Russell; *Annie Jo*, Jackie Joseph; *Sara Jean*, Sharon De Bord; *Nathan Potter*, Richard Collier; *Charlie Bannister*, Charles Tyner; *Alice*, Jean Willes; *Corey Bannister*, Robert Wilke; *Peter Dodge*, Carl Reindel; *Dr. Foy*, J. Pat O'Malley; *Dr. Farley Carter*, Jason Wingreen; *Clay Carroll*, John Dehner.

The problem of finding a decent movie in which to co-star James Stewart and Henry Fonda was solved by Stewart himself. His friend James Lee Barrett, who had scripted several Stewart films, discussed a concept with Stewart and once the script was finished Stewart showed it to Gene Kelly. Kelly immediately agreed, provided Fonda was willing, and a company was set up with Kelly as producer-director and Barrett as executive producer. Few films have fallen into place so easily. Barrett had by now a reputation for his ability to write western characterization and dialogue, and this is apparent at the very outset of *The Cheyenne Social Club*.

Two grizzled old cowpokes, John O'Hanlan (Stewart) and Harley Sullivan (Fonda), slowly ride across a vast western landscape. Harley's drawling voice drones on and on and on…about his family and his dogs and his doings. John, a long-suffering listener, finally gets a word in edgewise. "You know where we are now, Harley?" "Not exactly." "We're in the Wyoming Territory and you've been talkin' all the way from Texas." Harley looks wounded, "Just been keepin' you company." John nods, "I appreciate it, Harley, but if you say another word the rest of the day I'm gonna kill you."

The pair are on their way to Cheyenne because John's brother has died and left him an inheritance, although he doesn't know exactly what it is. It turns out to be what the townspeople call a social club but which is in fact a nice, comfortable bordello, headed by pretty young Jenny (Shirley Jones) and a half-

With Henry Fonda.

With Shirley Jones, Henry Fonda, Elaine Devry, Jackie Russell, Sue Ann Langdon, Sharon DeBrod and Jackie Joseph.

dozen equally pretty young ladies. And it is just about the center of gravity in Cheyenne. Jenny and the girls make the new owner welcome, much to his confusion, and Harley becomes a partner in the enterprise, although all he does is enjoy the hospitality of the house. He's the kind of fellow who takes life as it comes, whereas John is somewhat more straitlaced. John thinks it might be better to change the house into a saloon, which dismays the girls, although not as much as the citizenry, who now view John with contempt.

Once he realizes that the change may make the girls destitute, John rethinks his decision. He gets into a fight in a saloon and is thrown in jail. While there he hears that Jenny has been beaten by an outlaw client, Corey Bannister (Robert J. Wilke), and to avenge her John tracks Bannister and guns him down. This brings him the respect of the townspeople, but also the enmity of the Bannister clan, who attack the club. Harley, who has been away on a trip, arrives back in time to help John win the skirmish, but they both realize they must make a drastic change because the Bannisters have many associates and the warfare is likely to be ongoing. The practical John signs over ownership of the club to Jenny, and he and Harley head out of town and over the landscape…with John presumably doomed to spend the rest of his life listening to the incessant chatter of his pal Harley.

The Cheyenne Social Club is by far the best of the Stewart-Fonda films and it would have been impossible to find a pair of actors better suited to play a pair of old friends. Whether as the grizzled old cowpokes John and Harley or as seasoned actors, they appear together in this film with the ease and naturalness that can only come from long acquaintance. It would have been nice if Stewart and Fonda had appeared together again, but they could have done worse than this as a final pairing. It is a genial if slightly raunchy western, handsomely photographed in Technicolor, not in Wyoming but near Santa Fe, New Mexico, by William Clothier, who deserves more than a mere mention. Clothier had also filmed Stewart's three previous westerns—*The Rare Breed, Firecreek* and *Bandolero!*—and the visual style and scenic splendor of all these westerns is due to his fine talent.

The moral factor in *The Cheyenne Social Club*, the activity of a brothel, might have bordered on the questionable, had it not been for the film's good humor. Only one moment in the film caused some protest, the scene where Stewart goes into the room of one of the girls (Jean Willes) and finds her wearing

239

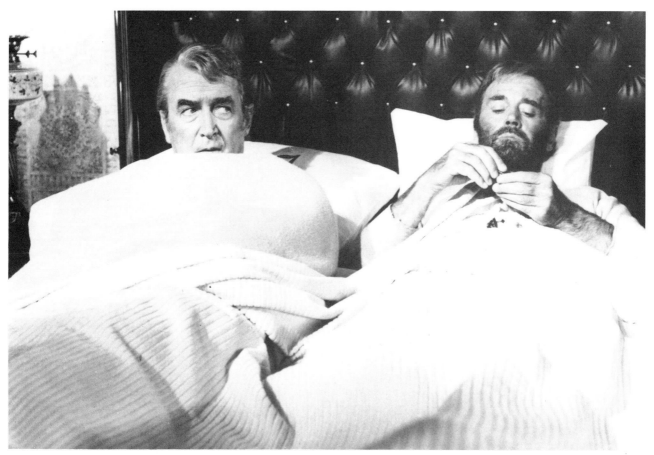

With Henry Fonda.

With Jackie Russell and Charles Tyner.

With Henry Fonda and director Gene Kelly.

a see-through negligee. With most actors this would not have been a problem, but with Stewart's almost puritanical image it caused some concern. Says Gene Kelly: "Many people didn't take to the idea of Jimmy Stewart in this setting, it was counter-image. It seemed funny at the time but looking at it later both Jimmy and I felt it should come out. But the owners,

National General, insisted it stay in, and I think that was a mistake."

The film is at its best when Stewart and Fonda are on screen together and by themselves. In this sense it is a near-perfect showcase for a couple of veteran actors who also happened to be true friends of long standing. And one piece of dialogue is also almost an inside joke. Walking along the street John refers to himself as a solid Republican and Harley affirms he is a true Democrat. This is precisely what they were in real life, but as Stewart explains, "Hank and I never, never discussed politics."

241

FOOL'S PARADE

COLUMBIA, 1971

Produced and *Directed* by Andrew V. McLaglen; *Written* by James Lee Barrett, based on the novel by David Grubb; *Photographed in color* by Harry Stradling, Jr.; *Music* by Henry Vars; 98 minutes.

CAST:

Mattie Appleyard, James Stewart; *Doc Council,* George Kennedy; *Cleo,* Anne Baxter; *Lee Cottrill,* Strother Martin; *Johnny Jesus,* Kurt Russell; *Roy K. Sizemore,* William Windom; *Steve Mystic,* Mike Kellin; *Chanty,* Kathy Cannon; *Junior Kilfong,* Morgan Paull; *Willis Hubbard,* Robert Donner; *Homer Grindstaff,* David Huddleston; *Enoch Purdy,* Dort Clark; *Sonny Boy,* James Lee Barrett; *Clara,* Kitty Jefferson Doepken; *Station Master,* Dwight McConnell.

With one very false eye.

After four westerns in a row it was obvious to James Stewart that he had fallen into the same trap as most of Hollywood's aging male stars. The unwritten law of the movie business for stars no longer at ease with young leading ladies has always been, "go West." Refusing other offers to do more westerns, Stewart decided on *Fools' Parade,* which is set in the West Virginia of the early 1930's but has many of the characteristics of a western, a fact hard to avoid in view of the director, Andrew V. MacLaglen, who had already directed Stewart in three westerns, plus others with other actors.

Fools' Parade is the story of Mattie Appleyard, a man who had just been released from jail after forty years and who has amassed during that time $25,000 in wages, working in the mines and otherwise being a model prisoner, despite the fact that he went in as a murderer. Leaving with him is a bumbling, fussy ex-bank robber, Lee Cottrill (Strother Martin), and young Johnny Jesus (Kurt Russell), who claims he never committed the rape for which he was jailed. With Mattie's money they plan to open a store and lead a respectable life. Two problems await them—one is a corrupt policeman named Doc Council (George Kennedy) and the other is Homer Grindstaff (David Huddleston), at whose bank Mattie must cash his check. Council and Grindstaff are in league to

appropriate Mattie's savings. On the train carrying them to the town in which they hope to settle down, Mattie and his friends are attacked by hired assassins, but the effort is aborted. One of the weapons Mattie uses to confuse the young assassin, Junior Kilfong (Morgan Paull), is his glass eye. Seeming to tear out his right eye, Mattie astounds and outmaneuvers the young thug.

Escaping from the train, Mattie proceeds to the houseboat of an old friend, Cleo (Anne Baxter), but she is now operating her floating home as a bordello, with sixteen-year-old Chanty (Kathy Cannon) as her only offering. Cleo would also like to get her hands on Mattie's fortune but dies when her boat is blown sky high by the dynamite Mattie has left aboard. Mattie, in his years working in the coal mines as a prisoner, has learned a great deal about explosives. The knowledge comes in useful when he visits the bank and explains that unless the money is forthcoming he will blow himself up, and the bank along with

With Strother Martin and George Kennedy.   *With Strother Martin and Kurt Russell.*

With Strother Martin.

With Strother Martin, Kurt Russell and George Kennedy.

it. He shows Grindstaff the array of dynamite sticks he has strapped around his body. The same skill with explosives brings about the death of the venal Council in his final attempt on Mattie's life.

Fools' Parade suffers from dealing with a range of not very likeable or admirable people. Mattie Appleyard, as portrayed by Stewart in a matter-of-fact, low-key sort of way, is a man to respect as a survivor but not much else. The most interesting aspects of the film are its various settings in and around Moundsville, West Virginia, and the use of the prison, the railroad yards, buildings and farm-

houses in what would seem to be late fall or early winter. With hundreds of extras dressed in appropriate clothing and driving period cars, it all looks very much like the 1930's.

The role of Mattie Appleyard required Stewart to wear, for the first time in his film career, a moustache. The one he had worn in *The Last Gangster* in 1937 had been false. It also required him to wear a contact lens over his right eye and the use of a glass eye, which caused some discomfort, being constantly put in and taken out during the filming. Unfortunately the glass eye was, for reasons that appear to make little sense, larger than a usual eye, giving Stewart a bizarre look. It is also somewhat comically offputting. However, with or without the eye, *Fools' Parade* found little favor with the critics or much of an audience, and probably had James Stewart wondering about the future of his career in films.

THE SHOOTIST

WARNER BROS., 1976

Produced by M. J. Frankovich and William Self; *Directed* by Don Siegel; *Written* by Miles Hood Swarthout and Scott Hale, based on the novel by Glendon Swarthout; *Photographed in color* by Bruce Surtees; *Music* by Elmer Bernstein; 100 minutes.

CAST:

John Bernard Books, John Wayne; *Bond Rogers*, Lauren Bacall; *Gillom Rogers*, Ron Howard; *Dr. Hostetler*, James Stewart; *Sweeney*, Richard Boone; *Pulford*, Hugh O'Brian; *Cobb*, Bill McKinley; *Marshall Thibido*, Harry Morgan; *Beckum*, John Carradine; *Serepta*, Sheree North; *Dobkins*, Richard Lenz; *Moses*, Scatman Crothers; *Burly Man*, Gregg Palmer; *Barber*, Alfred Dennis; *Streetcar Driver*, Dick Winslow; *Girl on Streetcar*, Melody Thomas; *Schoolteacher*, Kathleen O'Malley.

Even if *The Shootist* had not been John Wayne's final film it would have been a feather in his cap. Unlike the obvious shoot-'em-up westerns he had been making in recent years, this one had something to say about the changing west at the turn of the century and about a man's becoming a relic in his own lifetime. But as the film that brought his career to an end, *The Shootist* was made sadly poignant by the fact that Wayne was virtually playing his own death in public. As John Bernard Books he is an old westerner dying of cancer—as was Wayne himself. *The Shootist* is perhaps the most remarkable elegy in the history of film.

At this point in his own career James Stewart was turning down almost every film part offered him, but when offered the small but crucial role of the doctor in this one, he accepted without hesitation. He much admired Wayne and he particularly admired his courage in playing this part.

John Bernard Books arrives in Carson City, Nevada, on January 22, 1901. He is a tired old gunfighter, puzzled by the agony he is suffering in his lower back. He visits a doctor of long acquaintance, Doc Hostetler, and learns he has advanced cancer. Books wants to know how much time he has. "Two months—six weeks—less—no way to tell." Books

As Dr. Hostetler, the bearer of bad news for John Bernard Brooks.

needs somewhere to stay and the doctor steers him to the widow Rogers (Lauren Bacall), who takes in lodgers. She doesn't like him on first meeting but when he explains he is dying she becomes sympathetic and takes him in. Her teenage son Gillom (Ron Howard) is greatly impressed, having the celebrated gunman in his home, as are others, including a few men who would like to earn the acclaim from killing him. Among them is an old adversary, Sweeney (Richard Boone); a gambler, Pulford (Hugh O'Brian); and a town roughneck, Cobb (Bill McKinley).

Books goes back to see the doctor, who gives him an awful-tasting, pain-killing medicine and jokes about it being addictive. Books wants to know what is going to happen to him. Hostetler cringes when he explains that there will be increasing pain in his lower spine and groin: "If you're lucky you'll lose consciousness." And then as Books is about to leave, the doctor adds, "One more thing. I would not die the death I've just described—not if I had your

With John Wayne.

courage." Books nods and quietly leaves.

The old gunfighter moves to put his affairs in order. He sells his horse and saddle, he does his best to disillusion Gillom about the glory of being a western badman, and he wins the friendship of the widow Rogers. He also agrees to meet the three challengers in a saloon. One by one he guns them down, but getting wounded in the process. But the mortal blow is cowardly struck by the bartender, who fires a shotgun into Books's back. At this point Gillom comes into the saloon, picks up one of Books's guns and kills the bartender. Then, disgusted by what he has done, the boy slings the gun aside. With his dying breath Books looks up at the boy and faintly nods his approval. Several townspeople come into the saloon to see what has happened, among them Doc Hostetler, who looks down at Books and understands what has happened. His patient will not have to undergo any more agony.

For John Wayne buffs, *The Shootist* is a very special film. Stewart claims it is a film in which he was glad to have been involved, and about Wayne he simply says, "He was a fine man, a very fine man."

AIRPORT 77

UNIVERSAL, 1977

Produced by William Frye; *Directed* by Jerry Jameson; *Written* by Michael Schoff and David Spector, based on a story by H. A. L. Craig and Charles Kuenstle, inspired by the film *Airport* and the Arthur Hailey novel; *Photographed in color* by Philip Lathrop; *Music* by John Cacavas; 114 minutes.

CAST:

Don Gallagher, Jack Lemmon; *Karen Wallace,* Lee Grant; *Eve Clayton,* Brenda Vaccaro; *Nicholas St. Downs, III,* Joseph Cotten; *Emily Livingstone,* Olivia de Havilland; *Stan Buchek,* Darren McGavin; *Martin Wallace,* Christopher Lee; *Patroni,* George Kennedy; *Philip Stevens,* James Stewart; *Chambers,* Robert Foxworth; *Eddie,* Robert Hooks; *Banker,* Monte Markham; *Julie,* Kathleen Quinlan; *Frank Powers,* Gil Gerard; *Ralph Crawford,* James Booth; *Anne,* Monica Lewis; *Dorothy,* Maide Norman; *Lisa,* Pamela Bellwood.

Another cameo role, this one in a sure-fire winner at the box office. *Airport* in 1970 did so well that it spawned a number of adventures about the perils of commercial aviation. *Airport '77,* not to be confused with *Airport '75,* gave James Stewart the comfortable role of a vastly wealthy art collector, so wealthy that he uses his own customized 747 to transfer some of his collection from New York to his estate in Florida, along with carrying his guests in super luxury. He is a man who has everything, including the attentions of crooks who would like to get their hands on his collection and who work out an elaborate scheme to hijack the huge airliner.

In this Grand-Hotel-in-the-air-in-danger yarn the danger becomes more than the crooks had counted on. The 747 crash lands in the ocean and sinks in about fifty feet of water, while remaining intact and taking on some of the nature of a submarine, albeit one that will break up after only a few hours. The survival of the passengers becomes a race against time as the air quality diminishes and water begins to seep into the fuselage. The pilot (Jack Lemmon) manages to escape the plane and float to the surface, and get the attention of the Coast Guard. Then comes the Navy with a team of frogmen, who place air balloons around the body of the plane and gradually lift it to the surface—in the nick of time.

Airport '77 is expertly crafted hokum, at its best when dealing with the technical aspects of its story. The special effects and the naval operations are indeed impressive but the film wavers in telling the stories of too many characters, which it does with both in-flight encounters and flashbacks. For Stewart the role of the Getty-like billionaire was made the more interesting by having his rebellious daughter, Lisa (Pamela Bellwood), and her young son, along with his secretary (Brenda Vaccaro), among those trapped in the submerged plane, with grandfather anxiously awaiting the rescue while pacing the deck of a naval ship, which helps take his mind off the fact that he himself is suffering from a terminal illness. But with it all, the role of the billionaire-grandfather placed no great strains on the talents of James Stewart.

Filming the reunion scene with director Jerry Jameson (hand raised).

As millionaire-art collector Philip Stevens.

With Pamela Bellwood and Anthony Battaglia.

THE BIG SLEEP

Winkast/ITC, 1978

Produced by Elliott Kastner and Michael Winner; *Directed* by Michael Winner; *Written* by Winner, based on the novel by Raymond Chandler; *Photographed in color* by Robert Paynter; *Music* by Jerry Fielding; 99 minutes.

Cast:

Philip Marlowe, Robert Mitchum; *Charlotte Regan*, Sarah Miles; *Lash Canino*, Richard Boone; *Camilla Sternwood*, Candy Clark; *Agnes Lozelle*, Joan Collins; *Joe Brody*, Edward Fox; *Inspector Jim Carson*, John Mills; *General Guy de Brisai Sternwood*, James Stewart; *Eddie Mars*, Oliver Reed; *Vincent Norris*, Harry Andrews; *Harry Jones*, Colin Blakely; *Commander Barker*, Richard Todd; *Mona Mars*, Diana Quick; *Inspector Gregory*, James Donald; *Arthur Gwynn Geiger*, John Justin; *Karl Lundgren*, Simon Turner; *Owen Taylor*, Martin Potter; *Rusty Regan*, David Saville.

In 1975 Robert Mitchum appeared as detective Philip Marlowe in a re-make of *Farewell, My Lovely*, which, under the title *Murder My Sweet*, had been an enormous hit in the career of Dick Powell in 1944. Mitchum was a little long in the tooth for Marlowe at this point, but his performance was persuasive and the producers did an excellent job with the 1940 Los Angeles setting of the Raymond Chandler story. In 1978 Mitchum again appeared as Marlowe, this time in a remake of *The Big Sleep*, which had been an enormous hit for Humphrey Bogart in 1946. The result was a big dud, and one that featured James Stewart in a cameo role, that of General Sternwood.

The Bogart film is a classic of its kind. Apart

As General Sternwood.

With Robert Mitchum.

from a plotline that remains baffling and which is now accepted as part of its charm, Bogie's *The Big Sleep* is a movie that works on all levels, thanks to Howard Hawks's direction, the fine script and brittle dialogue, the byplay between Bogie and Lauren Bacall, the Max Steiner score, and the crisp black-and-white photography of Sid Hickox—in short, prime Warner Bros. moviemaking, circa 1946. To remake such a film invites snarls, but to remake it and place it in contemporary England and to give a well-tailored Marlowe a Mercedes convertible in which to do his sleuthing would seem incredible. But such was the decision of British producer-director-scripter Michael Winner.

The story remains much the same. Marlowe is hired by a retired general, millionaire, and invalid named Guy de Brisac Sternwood to find out why he is being blackmailed. It is all due to his two beautiful but eccentric daughters, Charlotte (Sarah Miles),

whose husband is involved in various crimes, and nymphomaniacal Camilla (Candy Clark), who is caught up with a pornographer and sundry shady characters of the London underworld. Marlowe undergoes numerous chases and several people are killed before he unravels the complexities of the plot.

Michael Winner's version of *The Big Sleep* fails on all counts, sadly so in view of the fine talents he assembled for his cast, including such British stalwarts as John Mills, Edward Fox, Oliver Reed and James Donald. For James Stewart the role of General Sternwood barely took two days of work. He has only one major scene and it is a virtual copy of the one in the Bogart version, in which Charles Waldron played Sternwood, sitting in a wheelchair, covered by a blanket, amid the plants of his heated greenhouse. It was the last role played by Waldron, who died before *The Big Sleep* was released. Fortunately Stewart's playing of the dying invalid did not have a similar effect on his own career. A footnote: Charles Waldron played Stewart's father in *Navy Blue and Gold*.

THE MAGIC OF LASSIE

LASSIE PRODUCTIONS, 1981

Produced by Bonita Granville Wrather and William Beaudine, Jr.; *Directed* by Don Chaffey; *Written* by Jean Holloway, Richard M. Sherman and Robert B. Sherman; *Photographed in color* by Michael Margulies; *Music Director:* Irwin Kostal; *Songs* by Richard M. Sherman and Robert B. Sherman; 99 minutes.

CAST:

Clovis Mitchell, James Stewart; *Gus,* Mickey Rooney; *Jamison,* Pernell Roberts; *Kelly,* Stephanie Zimbalist; *Chris,* Michael Sharrett; *Alice,* Alice Faye; *Sheriff Andrews,* Gene Evans; *Apollo,* Mike Mazurki; *Finch,* Robert Lussier; *Allan Fogerty,* Lane Davies; *Truck Driver,* William Flatley; *Officer Wilson,* James V. Reynolds

James Stewart first played a grandfather in *Airport '77,* but it was a virtual cameo role. Now he finally had the chance to wallow in the guise of a very grand sort of grandfather, a California vineyard owner named Clovis Mitchell, who looks out with pride and dignity over his rolling hills. He is so proud he even does a little singing about "That Hometown Feeling," which is one of the dozen songs that Richard M. and Robert B. Sherman supplied for *The Magic of Lassie.* Unfortunately, whereas most of their songs for *Mary Poppins* became hits, none of those for *Lassie* caught the public fancy. More unfortunately still, neither did the film.

The first Lassie film was *Lassie, Come Home,* in 1943, and it is still the best. It was followed by six other Lassie films, in addition to the television series, which started in 1954 and ran for nineteen years. The producers of the series, Jack and Bonita Granville Wrather, decided to revive the image of the beloved Collie with *The Magic of Lassie;* the title proved less than prophetic. The story takes place in the wine country of northern California, where Clovis Mitchell runs his business and also takes care of his grandchildren, Kelly (Stephanie Zimbalist) and Chris (Michael Sharrett), plus Lassie. A man named Jamison (Pernell Roberts) offers to buy the Mitchell land and when he is refused he decides instead to claim

ownership of Lassie. With faked papers he establishes ownership and takes the dog to his ranch in Colorado, from which Lassie promptly escapes. At about the same time Chris leaves home and heads for Colorado, causing Clovis to send out people to try and find him, while Jamison and his people set out to find the dog. One of the people looking for Chris is Kelly's lawyer sweetheart Allan Fogerty (Lane Davies), who also manages to prove that Jamison's claim to the dog is false. Adventures abound as boy and dog struggle along, until on Thanksgiving Day Lassie comes over the hill and down into her home amid the vineyards of Clovis Mitchell and his family. Chris, like all the others, had almost given the dog up for dead, although he shouldn't have if he had ever seen any of the other Lassie movies.

When released in the summer of 1978, *The Magic of Lassie* found itself with a G rating, a true-blue family picture of the kind for which there is always a cry but seldom a market. The critics were mild in their response, calling it contrived and sugary, and the film was soon relegated to cable television and the home video listings. Of interest to movie buffs is the appearance of Alice Faye in the small role of a waitress who sympathizes with the boy. This was the first appearance of the then sixty-six-year-old former star of movie musicals in many years and a sadly wasted one, giving her only one song. Mickey Rooney was also recruited for the film, as a wrestling manager who helps Lassie along the way and, as always with Rooney, it's a lively performance. Little can be said of the other actors, who simply perform as well as the material allows.

The only actor in *The Magic of Lassie* who emerges with any credibility is Stewart himself, whose Clovis Mitchell is a feisty, blustery oldtimer. However, after forty-three years of identity in films he had no need of anything more than his appearance sitting on a porch and gazing out over his domain in order to be impressive. The aura of authority was well set by this time. Stewart claims he took the role because it seemed like a decent movie with some moral fibre. "Look at the theatre advertisements and what have you got? You've got violence and films of an explosive nature, and films of a depressing nature. You haven't got a choice." The pity is that *The Magic of Lassie* was not good enough to make much of a case for the cause of family films.

Although this was the last theatrical film in which James Stewart has been seen to date, it was not his last work before motion picture cameras. He played the leading role in the Japanese film *Afurika Monogatari (A Tale of Africa),* shot in Kenya in late

1979 and early 1980, which has never been shown theatrically in the United States or the British Commonwealth. Re-titled *The Green Horizon* it was first seen in America on Showtime Cable in November of 1981 and it has subsequently been available as a cassette. Reviewed for *Variety* it was described as being extremely dull, "This may be the slowest moving picture this side of a Cézanne still life." It seems fair to mark it as the least successful movie in which Stewart has ever been involved and the only one that deserves to be forgotten. It apparently came about because he was visiting a game preserve in Kenya, which he and his wife had visited several times before, and "it seemed like a good idea at the time" to agree to be in a Japanese picture that was being shot on a game preserve in Kenya. In reviewing the film at its premiere in Tokyo, *Variety* noted that the famous actor, listed in the credits as "Old Man" and given not much more than a dozen lines of dialogue, seemed "ill at ease" and that the other players in the woebegone movie showed less emotional range than the animals.

Of much greater value was the telefilm Stewart made in 1982 for the Home Box Office television cable company, *Right of Way*, which was the first film made in Hollywood expressly for cable. The story of an elderly couple who decide to end their lives in suicide, the author, Richard Lees, claimed that he wrote it with Stewart and Bette Davis in mind. Both actors accepted the offer to do the picture but producer George Schaefer could not get interest from the major networks, who felt the subject matter was a little lugubrious for commercial television. HBO undertook *Right of Way* because it fitted their claim to bring different kinds of films to their customers. The reviewers thought the film admirable in intent but somewhat gloomy in content, with Stewart getting a little more praise than Davis, possibly because his is the feistier of the two characters. He is the devoted husband who plans the garage exhaust-fumes end for himself and his terminally ill wife and tells their daughter (Melinda Dillon), "Your mother and I have lived as one and we'll die as one." A worthy piece of work but not a very uplifting one.

If *The Magic of Lassie, The Green Horizon* and *Right of Way* turn out to be the final films in the career of James Stewart, there is no reason to dwell upon them as minor items. They are the work of a man who, in most other professions, would have long been in retirement. *Fools' Parade* in 1971 was his last role as a star, and what has followed since then is the exercising of muscle by an old pro who has never seen the point in complete retirement. His place in the

254

With Stephanie Zimbalist and Pernell Roberts.

With Stephanie Zimbalist, Michael Sharrett and Lassie.

With Bette Davis in the telefilm Right of Way.

Grant spoke of this man "We all love and admire—for his decency, his strength and his kindness." After speaking of his own affection for Stewart and recalling that in one scene of *The Philadelphia Story* he was so impressed with Stewart's delivery that he forgot his own cue, Grant introduced a montage of clips from Stewart films.

The montage began with a portion of the 1936 short *Important News*, with Stewart in a print shop, telling a co-worker that he likes to be known as Corn rather than Cornelius. This rare piece of virtually unknown Stewartiana was then followed by clips from his triumphs: singing "Easy to Love" to Eleanor Powell in *Born to Dance;* the scream scene with Jean Arthur in *You Can't Take It With You;* being assaulted by Marlene Dietrich in the saloon in *Destry Rides Again;* drinking with Katharine Hepburn in *The Philadelphia Story* and sounding off about the privileges of the idle rich; pointing to the Capitol dome in *Mr. Smith Goes to Washington* and telling Jean Arthur how he feels about America; introducing his Aunt Ethel to his invisible friend in *Harvey;* anxiously watching Raymond Burr tackle Grace Kelly in *Rear Window* and being able to do nothing about it; forcing himself in anger to climb the stairs of the mission tower with Kim Novak in *Vertigo;* bringing his plane in for the Paris landing in *The Spirit of St. Louis;* and saving guardian angel Clarence from drowning in *It's a Wonderful Life.*

After the montage Grant read the inscription on the base of the Oscar: "The Academy of Motion Picture Arts and Science's honorary award to James Stewart for his fifty years of memorable performances, for his high ideals both on and off the screen, with the respect and admiration of his colleagues."

Stewart thanked Cary Grant and the Board of Governors of the Academy and continued, "I'm also grateful to my fellow actors and actresses, for their help and their friendship through the years. I'm grateful to producers and writers and props and grips, make-up, wardrobe, lighting and cinemaphotographers—all of them who were with me and helped me get along so well between 'action!' and 'cut!' A part of this Oscar belongs to them. I'm especially grateful to Frank Capra and all the directors who so generously and brilliantly guided me safely through the no-man's land of my own good intentions, to more meaningful performances, for which they share abundant credit in my heart. Finally—the audience—all you wonderful folks out there. Thank you for being so kind to me over the years. You've given me a wonderful life. God bless you."

firmament of film history was well and truly fixed by the time he had reached the age of sixty and it will remain so.

Stewart's place in film history was fixed even more firmly with his being given an honorary Oscar by the Academy of Motion Pictures Arts and Sciences at the 57th Awards, held in the Dorothy Chandler Pavilion of the Los Angeles Music Center on March 25, 1985. The man called upon to present the Oscar was Cary Grant, whose rank as a fellow Hollywood legend made him the only logical choice.

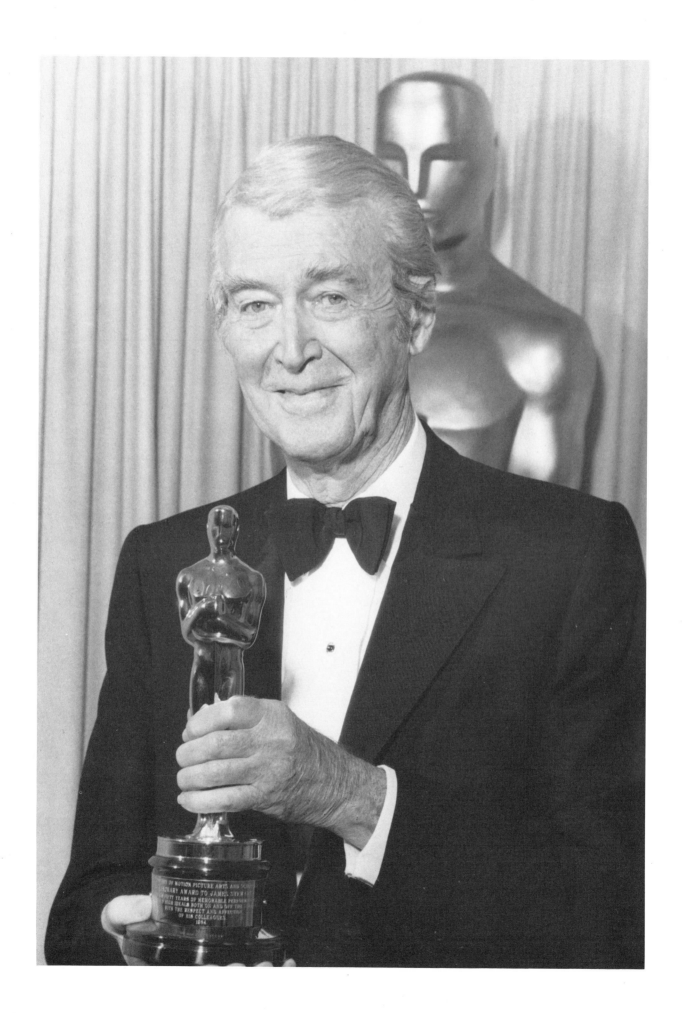